LEADERSHIP AND ISOLATION

Every organism requires an environment of friends, partly to shield it from violent changes, and partly to supply it with its wants.

You may obtain individual specimens of fine trees either in exceptional circumstances, or where human cultivation has intervened. But in nature the normal way in which trees flourish is by their association in a forest. Each tree may lose something of its individual perfection of growth, but they mutually assist each other in preserving the conditions for survival. A forest is the triumph of the organisation of mutually dependent species.

Men require of their neighbors something akin to be understood, something sufficiently different to provoke attention, and something great enough to command admiration. We must not expect, however, all the virtues. We should even be satisfied if there is something odd enough to be interesting.

— Alfred North Whitehead
Science and the Modern World

(New York: The Macmillan Company, 1925.) Reprinted by permission of the publisher.

LEADERSHIP
AND ISOLATION

A Study of Personality in Inter-Personal Relations

BY

HELEN HALL JENNINGS

Second Edition

LONGMANS, GREEN AND CO.

NEW YORK · LONDON · TORONTO

1950

LONGMANS, GREEN AND CO.
55 FIFTH AVENUE, NEW YORK 3

LONGMANS, GREEN AND CO. Ltd.
6 & 7 CLIFFORD STREET, LONDON W. I.

LONGMANS, GREEN AND CO.
215 VICTORIA STREET, TORONTO I

JENNINGS

LEADERSHIP AND ISOLATION

FIRST EDITION 1943
SECOND EDITION 1950

Printed in the United States of America

VAN REES PRESS • NEW YORK

To

MY MOTHER

WHOSE IMAGINATIVE INSIGHT,

CHEER AND SPONTANEITY

MADE A WONDERLAND FOR CHILDREN

ACKNOWLEDGMENTS

For far-reaching help in the writing of this book the author is greatly indebted to Gardner Murphy to whom in no small part is due the focus and direction this study has taken.

To Ralph B. Spence the author is indebted for illuminating criticisms which broadened immeasurably the scope of the entire study.

To Fannie French Morse, in tribute to her vision, it is here acknowledged that the strides made in developing sociometric methods under her administration culminated in the present study.

Aid in the analysis of data was generously given by Juliet O. Bell, Monema E. Kenyon, and Kathryn E. Maxfield. Among others who gave valuable advice were Robert C. Challman, Henry E. Garrett, Paul F. Lazarsfeld, and, most especially, Joan Henning Criswell and Juliet O. Bell. The drawings were made by Eleanor Kelsey.

Acknowledgments are expressed to *Sociometry*, the *American Sociological Review*, and the McGraw-Hill Book Company for kind permission to include extracts from the author's work appearing in their publications.

CONTENTS

PART THREE

THE NATURE OF EMOTIONAL AND SOCIAL EXPANSIVENESS

PART FOUR

SOCIOMETRIC DIFFERENTIATION OF GROUPS

TABLES

PREFACE TO SECOND EDITION

Since the first edition of this volume in 1943, the importance of the choice process to human personality has won a more central place in research and in life arrangements. The findings then presented have in the intervening years been confirmed in many ways by similar and different methods of study by numerous social scientists.

Work which bears directly upon the scope and value of the findings in this book has been carried out particularly by Donald E. Baier (P.R.S., A.G.O., War Department), William B. Baker (University of Saskatchewan), Merl E. Bonney (North Texas State Teachers College), Paul Deutschberger (Merrill-Palmer School), Douglas H. Fryer (New York University), Cecil A. Gibb (University of Sydney), Georges Gurvitch (University of Paris, Sorbonne), the late John G. Jenkins, Harold F. Kaufman (Mississippi State College), Charles P. Loomis (Michigan State College), Paul H. Maucorps (Centre d'Etudes Sociologiques, Paris), Hugh Murray (Monyhull Hospital, Birmington, England), Mary L. Northway (University of Toronto), Carroll L. Shartle (Ohio State University), Ralph M. Stogdill (Ohio State University), A. T. M. Wilson (Tavistock Institute of Human Relations, London), Robert H. Wherry (Ohio State University), Leslie Day Zeleny (Colorado State College of Education) and the Office of Strategic Services Assessment Staff.

This edition is not a revision—it is an expansion: Part IV presents new data and examines how the choice process operates in leisure-time; it compares these findings with those for official work and living contexts, presented in Parts I-III.

Among many associates who have encouraged and aided in the making of this second edition, I owe appreciation to Juliet O. Bell, Joan H. Criswell, Bertram Crocker, Maria Rogers, Frank A. Stewart, and Robert L. Straker.

Like all of us who work in this field, I acknowledge with gratitude the pioneering vision of J. L. Moreno.

HELEN HALL JENNINGS

Center for Human Relations Studies
New York University
New York, N.Y.

FOREWORD

Upon the appearance of Dr. J. L. Moreno's *Who Shall Survive?* in 1934, students of human nature became aware of a vital new field of research which was certain to recast the study of inter-personal relations. Dr. Moreno's basic conception was that the effective functioning of social groups, as well as the full realization of the individual personality, depends upon the spontaneity with which given individuals accept other given individuals as co-workers or co-participants in specified social activities. The economic and political planning of society will be sound only if deep roots exist in the form of genuine compatibility between the persons who are to share life together. Investigation of many types of social groups consistently showed that when once given the opportunity, people can find, through the realization of spontaneous choices, their own most effective place in group activity.

In the years since the appearance of this volume, this "sociometric" approach was effectively applied in urban and rural situations, in situations involving racial and religious tension, and in a variety of institutional situations in which the forced assignment of people to the same community made especially imperative their discovery of their own effective form and locus of participation. Sociometric assignment of the individual to the right group did much more than produce "efficient groups." It liberated the deeper forces of creativeness within the individual. As Dr. Jennings notes, "it has penetrated beneath the overt manifestations of group life to the invisible network of interrelations on which they are built." Lundberg's community studies and the Iowa in-

vestigations of the "social climates" of democracy and autoc-
racy have already demonstrated the value of sociometric
method in social research. The one thing lacking in the sociometric method appeared to many of us to be an analysis
of the *choice process*, the process within the individual which
underlies his reaching out towards some and rejection of
others.

It is, therefore, intensely gratifying to see that Dr. Helen
Jennings, the collaborator with Dr. Moreno in his pioneer
work and the initiator of many of the methods, has here presented the work of years of systematic investigation of this
choice process. The present volume represents, one may
say, the coming of age of a number of the sociometric procedures. This is by far the most sustained analysis of choice
processes yet undertaken. While the volume is concerned
with one specific population of some hundreds of individuals,
its methodological contribution goes much further. It is a
study of the foundations of the capacity to choose, the spontaneous gift of reaching out towards others, and the parallel
capacity to make oneself worthy of choice. It is moreover
not only a study of social structures but of personality
dynamics which the sociometric method here reveals.

The study shows that the individual arriving in the community possesses a certain range of outgoing response, a certain *volume*, one might almost say, of social need, which,
whether one is accepted or rejected, remains rather constant
through a long period of institutional life. This reaching
out, however, proves to be something entirely different from
the sheer tendency to make contacts initiating social relationships. The social contact range of the individual in terms of
the number of persons with whom contact is actually sought
(spontaneous greeting, etc.) is very different indeed from

the emotional range, the number of people whom one wist-
fully indicates as *desirable* team mates in one or another activity. We have then two avenues of approach to character
as it relates to social participation, the range of social contacts and the range of emotional demand.

It is the emotional demand which is most fully investigated in the present study. In terms of outgoing choices and
rejections, and in terms of choices and rejections of the given
individual by others, sociometrically secured, on two occasions eight months apart, patterns of social participation are
revealed which, properly treated, lead to a systematic study
of the qualities of leadership and followership. Likewise, the
extreme "non-leader," the "under-chosen," the person who
is far from the center of spontaneously initiated activity, is no
longer simply classified as an "isolate." The leader, treated
in earlier sociometric studies as simply the person with the
largest number of acceptances by others, is here studied in
characterological terms. By means of a prolonged and systematic study of the reputation which the individual has built
up in the eyes of peers and superiors, supplemented by specific records of what the individual has done to earn this position in the group, it is possible to define situationally the
qualities that appear wherever leadership is present. The
result is to document fully a functional conception of leadership in which, instead of defining a leader in terms of the
possession of certain static traits, one defines leadership as a
function of inter-personal relations, dependent upon the complex give-and-take between the members of the groups; it is
relative to the group processes concerned.

A clear picture emerges: the leader rebels against dominant
behavior of others; is solicitous of the welfare of less competent individuals; quick to sense group needs, and to take

steps to see that they are satisfied. And there are many "personality types" among these "over-chosen" and "under-chosen" individuals; the essential thing is the capacity to give and take, to share and participate, in the form of group living.

It thus turns out in practice that the choice structures of the community, when laid bare by sociometry, point directly to those individuals who are self-assured, dominant, effective in the group life, and towards those individuals who are so situated that they cling only with a tenuous grasp to the outer fringe of the group.

The discussion of over-chosen and under-chosen individuals is fully documented with descriptions of the appearance, speech, behavior, and reputation of several individuals of each category, so that we find by far the clearest picture yet drawn as to *why* and *how* each individual earns a specific place in the sociometric pattern. It becomes clear, for example, how one can be "dominant" yet a source of security to others; how the protection of one's own ego-needs may involve not a *violation* of, but a concomitant need to *protect* the ego needs, the status cravings, of others. For the effectiveness of these over-chosen individuals in maintaining their own position is almost inseparable from their effectiveness in supporting the needs of others within the group. The personality studies of the over- and under-chosen are, for this reader at least, the climax of the book.

Nothing could more clearly show that *field* approaches to personality study have abundantly fulfilled their promise; the individual is defined not by inherent dispositions but by the role such dispositions play in a concrete situation. Each individual brings much into the community; no one is purely a function of the group situation. But these *potentials* which are brought into the community are released, directed, actualized by a type of community living in which there is a chance for self-realization through the very fact that individuals need one another, rely on one another, achieve fullness of personality only insofar as the group structure permits. Thus it must be candidly granted that in the specific community studied some individuals failed miserably in self-realization; others, who could reach out effectively, achieved a high measure of self-realization. The successes and failures of the community are dramatically revealed. If sociometric work can maintain this degree of concreteness and realism, it has become not only a major tool of sociological analysis, but a major aid in the systematic study of personality.

GARDNER MURPHY

College of the City of New York
1943

PART ONE

THE PROBLEM OF INTER-PERSONAL CHOICE

CHAPTER I

The Significance of Choice in Human Behavior

Social relationships of choice, in which selective affinity between individual animals operates, can be observed in many species.[1,2] Man differs in this respect from lower organisms only by the greater complexity and subtlety of the choices he makes. No man lives unto himself. Each of us lives our life interacting with other persons. Particularly during the last few decades the interdependence of man has been quickened by technological advance and sharpened by his greater recognition of his needs. Today, with all men neighbors to the world, literally one kindred species, a further knowledge of the nature of choice should be useful to a broader understanding of human interaction.

Within the totality of facts that influence the individual at a given moment is an area which we might designate as the *social space* in which he finds himself. The sense of one's awareness that there are millions of individuals in the world can be as great as all mankind; even, indeed, vastly greater if we consider our indefinite sense of awareness that millions have lived before us and are to follow us. Although such an awareness is now and then present, however, it usually has

[1] "*Choice* is a term based objectively on the fact that the organism accepts or reacts positively to some things, while it rejects or reacts negatively or not at all to others. In this sense all lower organisms show choice, and at this we need not be surprised, for inorganic substances show a similar selectiveness. The distinctive thing about the choice of organisms is that it is regulatory; organisms on the whole choose those things which aid their normal life processes and reject those that do not. This is what justifies the use of the term 'choice', as contrasted with the mere selectiveness of inorganic reactions." H. S. Jennings, *Behavior of the Lower Organisms*, p. 330. 1931.

[2] H. S. Jennings, "The Beginnings of Social Behavior in Unicellular Organisms," *Science*, 92:2398:539-546, December, 1940.

little import of personal meaning. But social contact which is direct and touches our lives immediately bears for each individual particular significance. It is within this quite circumscribed area or *social space* that he lives.

An inner view of this social space would reveal it structured with all the emotional components of his experiences with others at that point in time. The influences within this social space are the particular other individuals of whom he is to a greater or less extent aware. This area is marked out to him, is meaningful in a quite specific sense, but all of it is not equally sharp in its delineations. Within it the individual is attracted and repelled in many directions and is the focus of forces of immediate concern to him. In the same way he impinges upon the social space of others.

The individual's behavior as it affects and is affected by the behavior of others sets the limits of his social space. Like all behavior, social space is also dynamic: now wide and receptive to the individual, again narrow and unreceptive, resulting in a channeling of the activities of the individual, at times according to his wishes, at times out of accord with them. The individual's happiness and effectiveness are to a degree a product of his inter-personal relationships.

The individuation process as it grows out of repressing, releasing, and augmenting forces of the social setting works upon the child to make of him an individual contributing more and more to the interaction. No individual is to be found who is not in some degree bound to others. The universe of feeling acts as a basic cohering force allowing no life to remain completely neutral, completely "objective" in respect to other lives. Even in the world of things we feel nearer to those things with which we have experience and are familiar and we also reject many more of these things. Of all living beings, man is by far the most dependent upon social relationships for his happiness and growth.

From earliest childhood, then, the educational process proceeds by offering the opportunity for development which shall include facility in entering into relationships with others and in communicating experience with others. Education is considered to fall short if the individual shows himself finally incapable of rapport with others to a degree necessary to co-ordinate the common activities of his life with others. The educational process assumes that the individual wants to and is capable of coordinating his activities with those of his fellows and that no individual will at any time in his development be entirely cut off from the social matrix of relations which have interacted to produce him. By giving some direction to the growth process, it attempts to broaden and deepen the manner and kind of his participation in the social milieu of which he must remain a part. The incapacity of the individual to cut himself off from the experiences of others, to wall himself up in an insularity of his interests and needs as distinct from those of other individuals is a primary fact in his educability.

From the beginnings of rapport with objects and others is laid the common affect which continues as a welding and assimilating medium through which we become able to communicate and feel near and understand the place of others and things in a universe which otherwise would present to us disparate, confusing phenomena, to which orientation would be impossible, much less participation in the flux of its events.

As the self grows, thought and feeling remain inseparable in the psychic make-up of the individual. The individual's behavior is more and more affected by the relationships between himself and others in the give and take of existence.

The social milieu is structured by the coordinations of functional interaction in the continuum of the self with others. The self cannot be pictured outside of such relationships. Outside of them it does not exist. The world is not comprised of millions of selves, self-directed, self-contained, self-absorbed; emotional interaction relates individuals to one another so that single action, unaffected by others, is quite impossible. We do not refer to the superficial contacts between individuals and conventionalized behavior that is largely neutral in emotional import and satisfaction to the individuals, but to the actualized adaptations which we make for the sake of the meaning of other individuals to us.[3]

The dimensions of the self may be said to reach as far as the emotional impress of the self upon others permits it to reach and to the self are extended by the same emotional process the selves of others as far as they are able to enter into the experience of the individual. The emotional milieu of the self is affected by the other selves with whom the self is in contact and the inter-personal experiences that take place between the self and others. If the self is inadequate in capacity to enter into relationships with other selves, the individual may find himself in a relatively neutral relationship to almost all the surrounding selves so that he is neither able to act upon them nor to be contacted by them, and to the extent that this is true the individual has fewer effective avenues for contributing his experience to the experience of others or to be enriched by theirs.

Each individual early begins a differentiating process in selective affinity with others. He may approach those who

---

[3] Such adaptations in our behavior may be as simple as crossing the street to speak to another, neither demanded by convention nor by necessity, but alone by the spontaneous response for each other present between the two individuals. Such behavior is not established by *chance:* not just any two individuals, but a selection by the individuals of each other due to some affinity operating between them.

respond to him or whom he wishes would respond to him; he may keep away from those whom he feels he cannot interest or who repel him.   This reaching out of the individual to other individuals may be said to be a projection of the self, a seeking for a fulfillment of a need of the individual for other persons to whom he responds, drawing him to them and causing him to want to include them in his life situation. Such a process may be considered at the base of the inter-personal organization we call society.   The structure repre-sents directly the sustaining emotional reinforcement of the different members by one another.

In the course of development, each individual comes more and more to be characterized by his inherent preferences. He gradually exerts his preferences towards people and things in ways that are to hold greater significance for him-self and others and his choices are more or less consciously made as he gains awareness and control over them.   But the important fact is that he has basic propensities that become stronger in some directions than in others.

The problem, however, appears not simply one of rela-tively stronger or relatively weaker propensities for behav-ing in given ways.   The individual is now recognized as enormously complex in his organization — not only *within* his individual organization but as an interacting organism that is not independent of the elements within his life-field and the structure these elements subjectively have for him.

We have the evidence from L. B. Murphy's intensive experimentation on sympathetic behavior that the psycho-logical structure of the field plays a direct role in determin-ing the kind of behavior which takes place in it and in the pattern this behavior will take.[4]   Every element, social and

[4] Lois Barclay Murphy, *Social Behavior and Child Personality.*   1937.

physical, within the field showed a bearing upon the form taken by sympathetic behavior and even to its presence or absence. Not how many others simply, but *what* others are in the field and their relationship to possible sympathizers and their relationship to one another. What physical space they occupy. What they bring to the situation (in the form of patterns of behavior acquired elsewhere). What behavior others are showing. And not in a quantitative sense, but in the organization existing between the various factors.

Within the life space, the psychological movements, the locomotions,[5] as Lewin puts it, appear to derive from the relation between the states of tension within the person and the valences within his environment and not alone from tensions within the person. That choice is actuated by the same principle is hardly to be questioned. There may be so little valence in the environment corresponding to the tension (referable to an arising need or unfinished purpose) within the individual that choice fails to emerge. Such may be the case in instances of true isolation where the individual appears drawn to no one and no one to him in the life space in which he is.

The individual's propensity or need to relate himself to others describes the social space which will come to be marked out to him in a meaningful way as personally significant. We see individuals seek out one another and we ourselves continually seek out others in the course of day to day living. These others who are sought out are observed to be not just *any* others but to vary according to who is initiating the contact and who are available to receive it. Likewise the degree of rapport enjoyed by the individuals may be observed to

[5] Kurt Lewin, *Principles of Topological Psychology.* 1936.

vary. Yet the individual's propensity for relating himself to others has not been explored until the present investigation and little experimental evidence has been provided on the crucially important question of how extensively individuals differ in the number and kind of relationships they seek to establish (or avoid) with others.

An exploration of individual differences in respect to emotional and social expansiveness should penetrate below the outer observable manifestations of interaction between persons to the actual bases of needs which the individual has for others; it should elicit his full expression for or against contact with those who surround him. The present investigation attempts to realize this premise.

The initial effort to bring a sociometric approach to the problem of inter-personal relations was made by Moreno and the writer in 1931.[6] The sociometric test, devised by Moreno and adapted by the writer for the study of children in a classroom situation, taps the social aspects of the individual's projections. The simplicity of the test, its lack of resemblance to a "test" in the minds of the subjects, and the fact that its results may be utilized to reorganize the functioning of the group according to the structures it uncovers, work in favor of securing the actual network of relationships existing in the population tested because of the fundamental fact that the choices in sociometric testing are always related to the life situation of the subject.

Moreno and the writer first became interested in devising techniques for exploring children's groups when it became apparent that adult institutional groups could not be made therapeutically effective as functional units on the basis of

[6] J. L. Moreno, *Who Shall Survive?* 1934. Collaborator: H. H. Jennings. (For Moreno's early work in psychodrama, see *Das Stegreiftheater*. 1923.)

attributes of individual members.[7] Such attributes, however much they might appear to "complement" or "supplement" those of another individual, did not *act* as complementary or supplementary personality factors when the individuals who seemed to possess them were placed together. In the attempt to discover what was missing it was decided to explore inter-personal phenomena generated by the interaction between individuals who were associating together. Since such a study, it was thought, would be most fruitful if it investigated the psychological organization of groups of individuals of various age levels, the pioneer work was undertaken in a public school.

Moreno ingeniously devised the use of a criterion for uncovering the inter-personal feeling of the children for one another: the criterion of studying in proximity (neighboring seats); a method of measuring group structure resulted which has not yet been surpassed in usefulness for this purpose by other methods. Consideration of the nature of this simple device reveals certain bases for its efficacy and why it is so widely adaptable to various groups.

The sociometric test allows the individual to become an agent in his own behalf, to give his personal feeling for others in the form of choices for functioning with them within the group of which he and they are members. In this regard, he acts in order to re-make the collective of which he is a part. Thus, to the subjects, the test is not a "test" at all. The wording of the test for grammar school classes, for example, was as follows:

"You are seated now according to directions your teacher has given you. The neighbor who sits beside you is not chosen by you.

[7] J. L. Moreno in collaboration with E. Stagg Whitin, assisted by H. H. Jennings: *Plan and Technique of Developing a Prison into a Socialized Community*, 1932, and *Application of the Group Method to Classification*, 1932.

You are now given the opportunity to choose the boy or girl whom you would like to have sit on either side of you. Write down whom you would like first best; then, whom you would like second best. Look around and make up your mind. Remember that next term your friends you choose now may sit beside you." [8]

First administered by Moreno and the writer to the population of Public School 181, Brooklyn, N. Y., under the condition of allowing two choices for studying with others (occupying adjoining seats), the sociometric test there disclosed that the child gains, with increase in age, increasing ability to establish mutual relationships with other individuals to whom he is drawn.[9] The concept of personality which pictures the organization of the individual as moving from the general to the specific, from the undifferentiated to the highly differentiated, was found to have a counterpart in the growth of inter-personal organization of groups of individuals compared from the kindergarten through the eighth grade. In the latter instance, too, the movement is seen to progress from a simple, loosely integrated structure to one of increasingly greater complexity, offering additional evidence on the course of maturation so long known to be characterized by this principle. Freud's theory, also, of the period of latency of sex in childhood was found to be experimentally confirmed by the age points at which cleavage between the sexes appeared in group structure:[10] starting in the fourth grade (about age nine) and lasting well up to the eighth grade classes (about age thirteen), boys choose boys and girls, girls, almost to the total exclusion of the opposite sex; then intersexual choices again begin. Racial cleavage also appeared most marked during this period[11] and the mo-

---

[8] Moreno, *op. cit.*, p. 13, in reference of footnote 6.
[9] *Ibid.*, p. 60.
[10] *Ibid.*, p. 61.
[11] *Ibid.*, p. 61.

tivations given by the children often reveal racial similarity to be considered an attractive factor in choice.[12] The same trends in results were obtained when the test of the same school was repeated about two years later, after a turnover in population of nearly 50 percent.[13] The characteristics of children's groups in classroom structure at different age levels was later further substantiated by Criswell's study of three other public schools of New York selected to have a varying percentage composition of Negro-white pupils.[14] Criswell's analysis holds special interest also as it represents the first statistical work on measuring racial cleavage and the treatment may be applied to the measurement of other kinds of cleavages.[15] Criswell found that racial cleavage occurs even in kindergarten, mainly because of the withdrawal of the white group from the Negro group; by the fifth grade mutual withdrawal of racial groups becomes consistent. Thus even radially different racial composition in the membership of the classroom does not produce a unique response on the part of one race (colored or white) towards the other but racial cleavage at whatever age levels it appears is quantitative rather than qualitative, a lessened frequency of positive responses passing between individuals of different race.[15]

As administered to the population of the New York State Training School for Girls, then numbering about 500, under the condition of allowing five choices for living in the same group, the sociometric test, thus defined, was found suffi-

[12] H. H. Jennings, *Sociometric Studies,* a supplement in J. L. Moreno's *Who Shall Survive?* pp. 374-400. 1934.

[13] Moreno, *op. cit.,* pp. 23-66.

[14] Joan Henning Criswell, "A Sociometric Study of Race Cleavage in the Classroom," *Arch. Psychol.,* p. 16, 1939, No. 235.

[15] See suggestions given by Barbara S. Burks in a review of this study, *Sociometry,* III: 105-108, January, 1940; also, Charles P. Loomis, "Ethnic Cleavages in the Southwest as Reflected in Two High Schools," *Sociometry,* VI:7-26, February, 1943. Note differences in statistical base in work of Criswell and Loomis.

ciently productive to permit an analysis of the whole community so as to further an understanding of the conduct of groups within it.[16] Under similar conditions, except for a three-choice allowance, one study of the development of structures within the *same* group, retested at 8-week intervals over a period of 2 years 7 months, was made in this community.[17] Structure could be seen not as a flat proximity of part to part but as a hierarchical interrelation of parts in which there is interdependence of one part upon another within the developing organization as a whole.[18] Yet, again, the individual's capacity to relate himself to others remained unexplored; because of the nature of the testing technique used, the focus had to be on a structural analysis only.

Sociometric and near-sociometric methods have also been utilized within a battery of other techniques in various investigations. Lippitt's[19] pioneer exploration of psychological climates is in addition important as the first experiment to equate groups by sociometric testing on the basis of inter-personal structure instead of on the basis of individual-member comparability alone. The significant findings thus carry added weight since inter-personal structure as a possible cause of differences between induced "autocratic" and "democratic" atmospheres was considered by equating the groups on this factor at the start. It is very fortunate that

[16] Moreno, *op. cit.*, pp. 197-232.

[17] H. H. Jennings, "Structure of Leadership," *Sociometry*, I:I:99-143, July, 1937.

[18] *Ibid.*, p. 122. Also treated in M. H. Krout, *Introduction to Social Psychology*, 1942.

[19] Ronald Lippitt, "An Experimental Study of Authoritarian and Democratic Group Atmospheres," in Studies in Topological and Vector Psychology I, *Univ. Iowa Stud.*, Stud. Child Wel., XVI:III:43-195, February, 1940. This study preceded the related research which appeared earlier: Kurt Lewin, Ronald Lippitt, and Ralph K. White, "Patterns of Aggressive Behavior in Experimentally Created 'Social Climates,'" *Jour. of Social Psychol.*, X:II:271-299, May, 1939, pp. 271-272. J. L. Moreno discusses aspects of this research in "Experimental Sociometry and the Experimental Method in Science," pp. 119-162, in *Current Trends in Social Psychology* (Wayne Dennis, ed.) 1948.

sociometric tests were administered periodically to the clubs in Lewin, Lippitt, and White's related work. Thus was gained the opportunity to measure the effect of social climate upon the inter-personal structure of groups.

The study of child personality at the seven-year age level by Biber, Murphy, Woodcock and Black [20] touches on certain aspects of choice. Judgments of "best" girl or boy given by the children appeared rooted in the feelings of the children towards one another rather than related to moralistic considerations. The majority judged to be "best" their particular favorite for eating or playing or both (when asked to name the "best" and "worst" boy and girl and to select individuals with whom they liked to eat or to play) and in no instance was a child nominated as "worst" and also chosen as companion by the same individual.

The first effort to relate choice-structure to various factors, made by Lundberg and Steele in a survey of a rural village, revealed that individuals will spontaneously volunteer, in response to what may appear to be a casual inquiry, dealing for the most part with other matters, information sufficient to provide considerable data on the inter-personal structure of a community. [21] The "choice" data so gathered represent replies to the question, "Who are your best friends in this community, *i.e.*, with whom do you most like to visit 'so-

[20] Barbara Biber, Lois B. Murphy, Louise P. Woodcock, Irma S. Black, *Child Life in School*, p. 218. 1942. See also the highly important work of Merl E. Bonney which deserves lengthier discussion than is feasible here, especially his "A Study of Social Status on the Second Grade Level," *J. Genet. Psychol.*, LX:271-305, June, 1942.

[21] George A. Lundberg, "Social Attraction-Patterns in a Rural Village," *Sociometry*, I:77-81, July-October, 1937, p. 79; George A. Lundberg and Mary Steele, "Social Attraction-Patterns in a Village," *Sociometry*, I:375-419, January-April, 1938, pp. 410-416; George A. Lundberg, *Social Research*, pp. 331-332. 1942. For other communities, see the interesting work of Frank Loel Sweetser (*Neighborhood Acquaintance and Association*, 1941) and Charles P. Loomis ("Social Relationships in Seven Rural Communities," *Social Research Report*, No. XVIII, U. S. Bureau of Agricultural Economics).

cially'?"   The resulting "friendship" structure shows common church membership to be a factor most clearly associated
with the groupings while family relationship and geographic
factors do not appear prominent; the groupings were correlated to some extent with socio-economic status, particularly
in the case of those showing high socio-economic status; moreover, increase in socio-economic status correlates with the
number of choices received but not with the number of choices
made.   The findings are of especial interest in relation to the
present study although the test-communities, methods, and
data of the two investigations are obviously not comparable.

   In the first intensive, long-range study of influences bearing on attitude changes in a community, Newcomb [22] finds
that the specific social relationships of the individual appear
as the factors important for prediction.   Courses of study
appear only slightly related to changes in attitude.   His results show, moreover, that attitudes representative of the
dominant trends of thought in the community are closely tied
up with the kind and direction of social relationships developed in the community and that from the relationships
thus disclosed the emergence of leadership can be predicted.
Social attitudes hence appear as an important component in
inter-personal relationships.   This study is also notable because it is the first to demonstrate that even near-sociometric
data, i.e., data given by the individual on the basis of hypothetical criteria which are not to be experienced by him and
hence "unreal" data not to be used to alter the individual's
situation, reveal crucial information about a community when
secured under circumstances which enlist the cooperation of
the population as a whole.   Newcomb used hypothetical

[22] Theodore M. Newcomb, *Personality and Social Change,* especially Chapters 8, 9, 14 and 15.   1943.

choices and "votes" to arrive at such relationships in the Bennington College community; the conditions of his investigation, however, make it appear likely that such near-sociometric data would correlate highly with sociometric data since there is overwhelmingly consistent evidence that the subjects were in this instance deeply motivated by interest in the project itself. Such cooperation, founded upon interest extrinsic to the test itself, may be difficult if not impossible to secure, except in extraordinary circumstances, and particularly when the investigation demands several retests of the same population. It would be worth while to establish for inter-personal data what degree of correlation ordinarily exists between sociometric and near-sociometric data secured from the same population.

In a study of the genetic process of group life among students, based on a recording of their social life and their development of interrelations, Price [23] considers techniques of adapting situations on the college campus so as to foster inter-personal relationships. Although this study did not employ sociometric methods, it provides an analysis of the college campus useful to the sociometric investigator.[24]

In the industrial field the importance of the worker's inter-personal situation for his productivity is no longer open to question. Roethlisberger and Dickson [25] have demonstrated that the factory situation reflects not only the immediate

[23] Louise Price, *Creative Group Work on the Campus.* 1941. For a highly informative discussion of the relation of sociometric findings to group activities in general, see Ruth Strang, *Group Activities in College and Secondary School.* 1941.

[24] Less attention has been given to group work off the campus. Factors to be considered in the application of sociometric techniques to the organizing of communities are explicitly illustrated in the original experimental work of Rose Cologne ("Experimentation with Sociometric Procedures in a Self-Help Community Center," *Sociometry,* VI:27-67, February, 1943) and discussed in the committee council work of Muriel Brown ("Some Applications of Sociometric Techniques to Community Organization," *Sociometry,* VI:94-100, February, 1943).

[25] F. J. Roethlisberger and W. J. Dickson, *Management and the Worker.* 1939.

inter-personal setting of the worker in the plant but also his home situation. Compared with such factors, the physical aspects of work become relatively unimportant. The analysis of Whitehead,[26] based on experimental findings, points conclusively to the social setting as the crucial variable, within limits of physique and skill, in work effectiveness.

The original work of Barker[27] has demonstrated that inter-personal response should be given study even as it occurs between total strangers. In the first sociometric research of its kind, Barker finds that immediate response between strangers differs significantly from chance just as Moreno and the writer[28] found true of choice made after long acquaintanceship. Moreover, Barker disclosed that such response shows the same tendency to persist noted by Criswell[29] for individuals well acquainted with one another; he noted also that shifting of choices (on later re-test) was less frequent for much chosen individuals than for least chosen. His findings further reveal that the individual's reactions to the other persons with whom he is confronted and theirs to him show no correlation on a first meeting, and only the slightest relation on a later occasion after the individuals have had a common group experience. The results of the present study, for individuals who have had a relatively long contact with one another, are closely similar (p. 53).

From its first use by Moreno and the writer, both in public school classes and at Hudson, the sociometric test has

[26] T. N. Whitehead, *Leadership in a Free Society*, p. 52, also pp. 46-47. 1937.

[27] Roger G. Barker, "The Social Interrelations of Strangers and Acquaintances," *Sociometry*, V:169-179, May, 1942, p. 179.

[28] J. L. Moreno and H. H. Jennings, "Statistics of Social Configurations," *Sociometry*, I:342-374, January-April, 1938, p. 347 ff.

[29] Joan Henning Criswell, "Social Structure Revealed in a Sociometric Retest," *Sociometry*, II:69-75, October, 1939, p. 70.

focussed upon the organization, the psychological structure of groups. Moreno has defined it as "an instrument to measure the amount of organization shown by social groups." [30] The test has proved well fitted to fulfill the task set for it. It has penetrated beneath the overt manifestations of group life to the invisible network of interrelations on which they are built. Yet the test is so constructed as not to allow a full exploration of the individual's relationships with other individuals. It explores only so far as the form of its construction permits.

The form of the sociometric test as applied up to the present has had three characteristics:

1. A specific number of choices is allowed varying according to the size of the groups tested;
2. A specific criterion for choice is used varying with the functional activity of the group (*e.g.* as above, studying in proximity);
3. Different levels of preference are designated for each choice (1st, 2nd, etc.).

The allowance of a specific number of choices assumes that the chief network of the organization of the group will be uncovered. This assumption is borne out by the evidence. Newstetter, Feldstein, and Newcomb [31] show that the organization found on the basis of a 5-choice allowance to the members of a population does not differ significantly from the organization found when choice is extended (again to a high but still specific number) as far as 7 choices. Moreno has suggested two reasons for this phenomenon. The *sociodynamic decline* of interest sets in, individuals "wear out" in

[30] *Op. cit.*, p. 432.
[31] Wilber I. Newstetter, Marc J. Feldstein, and Theodore M. Newcomb, *Group Adjustment*, p. 45. 1938.

their facility for choice, not requiring all they are allowed; and secondly, the sociodynamic *effect* of the decline is that those individuals who attract the greater proportion of the choices on a basis of a small choice allowance, continue still to profit disproportionately under the larger choice allowance, and the number of individuals unchosen under the first condition is not substantially reduced under the second condition.[32] The present research finds that the character of choice reaction implies other explanations.

Secondly, the sociometric test explores, with the use of a specific number of choices, *one collective at a time, i.e.,* it employs one criterion for choice, the function which overtly appears as that around which the activities of the group center. In consequence, while the subject chooses with reference to the given criterion, either work or play or some other activity, he may satisfy other criteria unknown to the investigator, *i.e.,* criteria not in the test instructions but which exist for him and which the test has not given him explicit opportunity to follow. For instance, the child in a school classroom may withhold the names of those he would really prefer to *study* with, and give on this criterion two names of individuals whom he wishes to be with for companionship (companionship being more important to him than studying) since the test allows him only to choose on the criterion specified. (See motivations of children for choice on criterion of "studying in proximity.")[33] Likewise groups of individuals who are living together may very well make use of

---

[32] In other words, a greater allowance of choice does not *uniformly* increase its expenditure, nor, moreover, *even out* the distribution of choices within a population; instead, the number of choices the individual requires reaches a fading out point in some cases and the persistence of the trend to leave out a number of the group remains — individuals who on a basis of 1st choices alone are centers of attraction continue to be distinguished by more choices to them.

[33] H. H. Jennings, *op. cit.,* in reference of footnote 12.

the opportunity for choice on a living-together criterion by including individuals whom they have no real desire to live with, but with whom they want to spend some leisure time, cognizant of the possibility of gaining such time if they can occupy the same residence with their choice. If not provided with the opportunity for choice on all the criteria which exist for the individual at one and the same time, research cannot justify conclusions as to the relation of criteria to choice. Precisely how the organization of groups would vary according to the differentiating factor of criteria entering into choice is therefore not known, nor to what extent individuals would differentiate among criteria. The difference in meaning of any given criterion from one individual to another or even the meaning of any criterion for certain individuals remains ambiguous without *concomitant* testing on all criteria at once.

In arriving at conclusions as to the meaning of choice it would further seem necessary to know what range of contacts exists for the individual between himself and others, brought about of his own free volition. The individual may have so wide a range of contacts with other individuals that his choices represent a true selection, or, again, his contacts may be so narrow and circumscribed (even within a large population where he is living) that his choices are not representative of such persons as he actually wants but are forced by the situation in which he is.[34]

The negative aspect of choice has been almost wholly neglected up to the time of the present investigation. Yet the individual may be assumed to be as much characterized by those he rejects as he is by those he chooses. The first com-

[34] When circumstance severs the individual from those who are his choices, he may migrate temporarily towards relationships of one or another sort with those whom previously he had hardly noticed, often towards persons available by chance. Relationships initiated by a restricted situation may fade into the background when the persons return who are fundamental choices.

munity survey of Hudson [35] occupied as it was with the positive aspect of choice, did not touch upon this problem as a part of the test itself; it explored rejections only as volunteered by individuals in interview. In investigating the negative aspect of choice, confidence established over some period of time is desirable between investigator and population. The unbroken history of sociometric procedures in the community under study made possible the inclusion of negative as well as positive inter-personal relationships in all testing of the present research. The results sustain a premise that the negative aspect of choice merits equal consideration with the positive.

The significance of a 1st choice, as compared with a 2nd choice, or of a 2nd choice as compared with a 3rd choice, etc., has in previous sociometric research been roughly approximated by considering that the subject has indicated by these distinctions respective "lower" levels of preferences for the persons chosen. It is, however, a moot question whether his choices are not corraled into these categories when he is not allowed the most complete freedom to indicate his own degrees of choices, however these may vary. Hence, in the present study, the subject is asked to assign to his choices and rejections whatever preference levels [36] they have for him.

Still more fundamentally related to the problem of intensity of choice (than preference levels) is the aforementioned contact range of the individual. A first choice drawn out of a contact range of several hundred individuals is quite likely more valid for the individual than one drawn out of a contact range of fifteen. It may be premised that even the individ-

[35] Moreno, *op. cit.*

[36] The findings on preference level are omitted in this report as it seems advisable to limit the material presented here. The problem of intensity and its role in interpersonal relations will be treated in a later report; only occasional reference is included here.

ual's freedom to reject others is related to his range of contacts.[37]   The individual's social-contact-range will be, hence, considered as defining for him his *choice base*.   This choice base will be defined as including all individuals from whom selection is possible.   Whereas the population in which the individual finds himself may consist of so and so many other individuals, this population in itself is not equally the choice base for all the individuals comprising it.   The choice base will be defined as extending *only* so far as the individual is aware of other individuals *and* has had the experience of contact with them, regardless of how wide is the field of others in which he moves.   In this sense, the social-contact-range of the individual *is* his choice base.   The problem of intensity of choice can be studied within this choice base.

Moreover, and of primary consideration, in the present research it is desired to study the individual's extent of social contacts not only in order to define the range of others from whom selection is possible but in order to discover whether the individual's *social* projection in initiating or maintaining contacts with others is related, or not, to his *emotional* projection in relating himself to others by choice or rejection.

The present research has been planned to reveal the individual psychology of choice: how individuals differ in the kind and extent of their inter-personal relationships.   In contrast to previous sociometric explorations, it is not exclusively interested in the psychological organization or structure of groups.   In consequence the sociometric test was re-oriented to this end.

---

[37] If the individual can have contact with several persons whose personality is compatible with his, he is, in a sense, *free* to reject any one of them.   If no substitute is available, he may be obliged to seek out satisfactions in what the one available person has to offer or even to find new or different satisfactions which this person *can* provide in lieu of the satisfactions he might otherwise feel uncompromisingly essential under other, richer circumstances.

The method of procedure devised for the present research allowed unlimited variations of response in order to make room for every individual to vary in whatever ways may be characteristic for him. It is aimed at disclosing the individuality of the subject's response to other subjects and the individuality of the response towards him. The full expression of the subject towards others, formulated wholly as the subject might wish to formulate it, was secured at two time points eight months apart.

The attempt is, first, to distinguish common trends in the choice process which has hitherto been unexplored — regardless of what specific individuals are shown to be the object of choice, and, second, to accompany the choice analysis with behavior data related to specific individuals, so as to further an understanding of elements underlying the expression of choice and rejection. The experiment tapped the choice process at time points sufficiently distant to admit of significant change, and, concomitantly, on all criteria of significance to the population of the community under study; in consequence, the research is in a position to determine in what directions choice differs from individual to individual, whether or not there are similarities between different individuals at the same or at different times, and whether or not there are similarities between the same individual at different times.

It is recognized that the sociometric technique here constructed, in distinction from many other methods for study of personality, must rely upon the ability of the individual to express his interrelations. This ability may vary from individual to individual. The mechanisms of identification and projection undoubtedly enter into the needs the individual seeks to fulfill through his inter-personal relationships. It is recognized also that the correspondence of overt personality

(personality as it is displayed through observable behavior) with that part of the inner dynamics of personality tapped by the choice process of attraction and repulsion is quite likely not a one-to-one relation in any case. The evidence of the present research points, however, to a considerable relationship.

Because the present investigation fulfills G. Allport's contention [38] that a study of personality should not be based on a one-layer-time-slice of the individual's behavior, but instead carried through situations in which human factors vary, at intervals sufficiently broad to allow data to be forthcoming on the persistence of certain "traits" throughout long periods, it is in a position to determine whether or not the character of choice, as first found for the individual, persists or alters.

[38] Gordon Allport, *Personality, A Psychological Interpretation.* 1937.

CHAPTER II

The Choosing Process: Its Study and Analysis

The research sets up the following propositions for the study of individual differences in structures of inter-personal relations within an individual's social space.

1. The *choice base of reference* existing for an individual is the individual's social-contact-range. The individual may be aware of many persons, but not actively aware to the extent of re-directing his behavior out of awareness of them, and thus they are *not in the field from the point of view of the subject.* Therefore the individual's social-contact-*range* is defined as: *the number of other persons within the individual's field whom he has contacted,* either through his own initiative or through continuing, however briefly, contacts initiated with him by other persons.

2. Within the raw choice base of reference is the *criteria base of reference* for positive and negative choice. Each criterion is defined as a function in a person's life situation requiring collaboration with others.

3. Choice positive or negative (rejection) exercised by an individual (or towards him) should be appraised within the context of the *full reach of positive and negative choice expression by him and towards him.*

4. The individual's structure of inter-personal relations should be compared at *different time intervals,* sufficiently distant *to indicate the presence or absence of characteristic trends.*

The method of testing used in this research was constructed in accordance with the above propositions in the following manner:

(1) by setting no limit on number of choice expressions,
(2) by allowing the individual equal freedom to express negative choice reactions of rejection,
(3) by testing concomitantly on all criteria of significance to the subject, and
(4) by asking the subject to assign to his expressions whatever preference levels they may have for him,
(5) by re-testing after an eight-month interval,
(6) by ascertaining the subject's social-contact-range.

The Experiment

The Subjects

The laboratory of the present research was the New York State Training School for Girls. For this purpose, the institution was an ideal laboratory: a closed community comprising over 400 individuals. While open communities are generally to be preferred, it would not have been possible to direct the present research with equal controls to such populations. As the field of study is a closed community, the subjects are limited in the forming of relationships to other individuals of the population and consequently the situation is uniform for all in this respect. Secondly, the advantage of so large a population is that it provides a range in personalities so great as to be stimulating to the socially most withdrawn individuals and likewise to the socially most expansive individuals.

The population consists of girls committed by the Children's Courts of the State of New York and represents a cross-section of the socially and economically under-privileged of the state's population as a whole. To be admitted, the girl must be over 12 and under 16 years of age, of normal intelligence, and appear capable of profiting from the care and training provided by the institution.[1] Psychotic cases may not be committed or retained. Thus the institution's population does not deviate too radically from the general population. In the main the precipitating cause of commitment is classified as sexual delinquency, early manifestation of precocious interest in the opposite sex. The institution is expected to provide the girl with academic and vocational training and to place her, usually by the age of 17, in a position in which she earns sufficient to be self-supporting, especially in instances where her own home is unsuitable. Vocational skills and academic success were considered insufficient equipment for the tasks facing the majority of the girls and the institution stressed an all-round development for each girl.

Validity and Consistency

The sociometric test is unlike the usual mental test in that it does not attempt to measure behavior of a certain type by eliciting related responses but employs a sample of the actual behavior studied. As such the sample is directly meaningful and need not be validated by relating it to an external criterion. Hence the mental test concept of validity as correlation with a criterion does not apply here. It may be considered, however, whether a sociometric test is valid in the sense that the behavior which it was intended to elicit actually appeared without falsification of responses on the part of the subjects.

The research examines how individuals behave in choice

---

[1] Actually the courts on occasion commit individuals who do not meet these requirements.

and rejection, under the same conditions of testing, at intervals 8 months apart. *Choice behavior*, as one kind of behavior, is valid just as any behavior is valid providing choices are made on criteria holding significance for the subjects. The question rather is one of examining *how stable* is such behavior, for the same individual, at two time points 8 months distant. Data on the individual's behavior in general, however, are given for what understanding this may offer as to the meaning of the choice behavior shown by the individual or towards him by others.

In order to secure valid data, it is evident that sociometric tests must hold "reality value" for the subjects to whom they are administered.[2] The test-population must have confidence that their expressions will be used for the group functions for which they are given. The population studied in the present research had over a period of several years come to know that they could confidently expect their expressions to be utilized in this manner.[3] Rapport with the

[2] Actually this statement is a contradiction in terms: a sociometric test is not *sociometric* unless the criterion involved exists for the subjects and the "tested" individuals believe results not only can but *will* be utilized for the criterion on which they have expressed themselves.

[3] See section on *construction and reconstruction of groups* in J. L. Moreno's *Who Shall Survive?* pp. 269-331. 1934. Also, J. L. Moreno and H. H. Jennings, "Advances in Sociometric Technique," pp. 26-40, and H. H. Jennings, "Control Study of Sociometric Assignment," pp. 54-57, both in *Sociometric Review*, 1936; this journal has been superseded by *Sociometry*. Also, H. H. Jennings, "Structure of Leadership," *Sociometry*, I:I:99-143, July, 1937, p. 101. For the present study, the utilization of test results may be briefly mentioned.

At the time of Test I, two additional cottages were added to the community. This event was felicitous for the study as it allowed the experimenter to carry out many re-assignments in constructing the new groups, while the living units in which the experimental subjects of the present study were living received by re-assignment from one another only six individuals and therefore remained comprised at the time of Test II almost exclusively of their "own" members (present at the time of Test I) and individuals newly entering the community (instead of including also many between cottage re-assignments). The new groups received 23 members from the ten cottages of Group AB. The total number of re-assignments carried out in the community as a whole on the basis of the findings of Test I was 48.

Re-assignment was based on the total picture of the individual's situation and of the situation of the individuals with whom interrelations were shown. It is to be

sociometric investigator had been maintained through such experiences. The question of the validity of the results thus rests on this "internal" evidence as well as on the general behavioral data and case studies presented.

The research endeavors to discover what changes in choice behavior take place over a period of 8 months. A re-test within a few days would have little significance because of the memory factor as well as for other reasons. In this respect, the data are different from those gathered in tests of abstract ability because it is to be expected that the results will change markedly over long periods. If correlations between occasions considerably distant were extremely high, it might be presumptive evidence even that the findings were invalid — that the test had not "caught" the flux of psychological reactions between individuals which are ever in process of development.

However, despite the fact that a reliability coefficient found for choice phenomena may carry different implications than when found for other data (as an abstract ability test's results), a résumé of findings by use of this method discloses some evidence of interest to the present research. At the same time, it should be noted that sociometric testing of the individual's total social space (as attempted in the present effort) has previously not been undertaken and that the reliability coefficients have to do with sociometric testing allowing the subject a specific number of choices and using one

---

understood, of course, that the individual need not show "poor" social adjustment in order to receive a wanted re-assignment; further, the individual might prefer to retain his present situation whether or not he appeared to have a favorable position in his group. Also, the individual's present situation might be one in which he could as readily as in other possible groups gain a "better" choice-status so that unfavorable choice-status alone does not necessarily indicate he should be transferred to a different situation. *E.g.*, Group A shows nine subjects unchosen on Test I; by the time of Test II, only five of these individuals are unchosen. (Group A represents subjects present in the *same* living unit on the occasions of both Test I and Test II.)

criterion; hence they can have no *direct* bearing on the present findings.

As previously employed, the sociometric test was found by Newstetter, Feldstein and Newcomb [4] to have an average reliability of .95 based on data given on four successive weeks with a five-choice allowance on one criterion (tent-mates in summer camps). Zeleny [5] found, at the college level using also five choices and one criterion (membership in a discussion group), reliability coefficients ranging from .93 to .95 on re-administering such a sociometric test on successive days. These coefficients just quoted are based on the extent to which the subject is chosen by others on one occasion and on another occasion (sometimes on several occasions); they thus relate to the *choice-position* the individual *receives from others*. Such evidence is an important indication that the "choice-status" of the individual does not rapidly change.

The more stringent comparison which the present study makes, by use of unlimited choice and a much longer re-test interval, also reveals that even under these conditions, there is a fairly high correlation (see p. 57) between the individual's choice-status on different occasions when he remains in the same community. Thus the evidence indicates that the test-population do not differ in respect to choice behavior, *so far as this is reflected in choice-status*, from the college students tested by Zeleny nor from the boys in summer camps studied by Newstetter, Feldstein, and Newcomb. If, in contrast, some population should some day be found to show very fluctuating, "undependable" choice behavior *towards one another*, this would not be evidence necessarily that the

[4] Wilber I. Newstetter, Marc J. Feldstein, and Theodore M. Newcomb, *Group Adjustment*, p. 35. 1938.

[5] Leslie Day Zeleny, "Sociometry of Morale," *Amer. Sociol. Review*, IV:VI:799-808, Dec., 1939, p. 804.

test results were unreliable; they might be authentically reporting the changes which they were experiencing towards one another.[6]

A comparison of the *individual's consistency with himself* on separate occasions (his extent of expenditure of choice) could not be made in previous research as the extent to which the subject could choose others was allotted in advance. By allowing the subject unlimited expression of choice and rejection the present research focusses upon the individual's consistency in expansiveness or rejection: his extent of choice, positive and negative, for others at two points in time eight months apart. Only one effort was made to ascertain by *immediate re-test* the consistency of choice behavior under these conditions. A re-test of one housing unit was made after a 4-day interval; this gave a reliability coefficient of .96 for positive choice and .93 for rejection, based on the gross number of reactions given by the individual *towards others* on the two occasions. The findings as a whole in the present research lead to the conclusion that the high reliability coefficient obtained by the method of immediate re-test is indicative only of the slowness with which individuals change in their extent of choice and rejection of one another. The consistency of the individual's reactions, as revealed by the method constructed here, can be estimated only by review of the total findings. The validity of the findings can be ascertained by review of the behavior data and case studies.

---

[6] The concepts of validity and reliability do not have the same application here as in the field of intelligence testing. The test here is not intended as an indirect measure of other behavior. It is a sample of the actual behavior studied and as such is in itself directly meaningful and need not be validated by relating it to an external criterion. It also need not be consistent from one application to another, since it is not required to be related to a supposedly unchanging criterion (*e.g.* as intelligence is supposedly related to an unchanging criterion in the nervous system). The present research, however, reveals the individual's behavior in choice to show considerable stability.

Experimental Approach Used

In planning the present research the motivating of the subjects to give valid information was of primary importance. Because of the background of understanding for the testing which had been built up over the course of five years in this institution, this population could not simply be asked to give the data. The members of the population were used to being considered collaborators in planning their own assignments. Group discussions always preceded any course of sociometric procedure affecting the whole group. The experimenter had spent many hours with the girls in discussions leading to one or another plan of testing and related work. Out of the discussions many of the girls' suggestions had been utilized. It was therefore decided to hold group discussions in each cottage or other living unit, each discussion to be so guided by the experimenter as to *encourage the subjects to collaborate in the plan of research and to volunteer to give the information.* This approach was followed and the subjects rightfully could feel that the method used was their plan since they were instrumental, through their reception and discussion of the original plan, in shaping the final form.

The Test Instructions

Preceded by a general, informal discussion to establish rapport, during which a plan was agreed upon (by subjects and experimenter), the following rules were observed:

1. Each individual chose or rejected as few or as many persons as he wished on four criteria: "living"; and/or "working"; and/or "recreation or leisure"; and/or "studying."
2. Both positive choices (for inclusion in a grouping) and negative choices (rejections against inclusion in a grouping) were expressed separately for each criterion. Thus each individual

could choose or reject the *same* person on different criteria, or, choose or reject him for one criterion and not name him at all on any other criterion.

3. In addition each individual was privileged to use any other function which occurred to him as needed for choosing or rejecting other persons if he felt in particular instances that the four criteria were not appropriate. This "undetermined" criterion was to be named by the subject who employed it.

4. The subject assigned to his expressions whatever preference levels he wished.

5. Conversation was ruled out.

The following protocol material [7] illustrates the simplicity and directness of the approach used:

"You will notice that your paper is divided into 8 squares or boxes. In the first 'Yes' box, marked 'live with,' write the names of whatever girls there are anywhere on the campus or in your own house whom you would prefer to live with. In the 'No' box of 'live with,' write the names of whatever girls there are anywhere on the campus or in your own house whom you would prefer not to live with. Do the same for the 'work with' boxes. Then those you would prefer not to work with, place in the 'No' box for work. Next, do your 'recreation or leisure' and then, your 'study or school' boxes, having in mind the same instructions. . . The 'No' boxes should contain only the names of those, *if any,* whom you definitely *don't* want in your group for the particular functions or function, which it happens to be. The 'Yes' boxes should contain only the names of those, *if any,* whom you definitely *do* want in your group for the particular functions or function, which it happens to be. . . Do the boxes in any other order than that suggested if you prefer."

The second technique used, which also was preceded by a discussion leading to its "definition," was a social contact listing or "test." The verbatim directions were as follows:

---

[7] The complete protocol material appears in H. H. Jennings, "A Sociometric Study of Emotional and Social Expansiveness" in Roger G. Barker, Jacob S. Kounin, and Herbert F. Wright (edrs.), *Child Behavior and Development.* 1943.

"We will now turn to the other points we discussed: How many contacts each of us has throughout the campus and the number of times we have used our contacts. You remember we agreed that a contact was 'Another person you take the trouble to speak to, not including persons who may have spoken to you and to whom you therefore *had* to reply; the persons whom you had to reply to are contacts only if at another time you again spoke to them when you didn't have to.'

"In the widest column on your paper list all your contacts as we have defined them. Do not include any girls living in your cottage, as of course it is understood that they are contacts. But *do* include the names you have written on the paper you have just handed in. We shall need to check certain things for these names. Notice that to the right of the widest column are 4 narrow columns, headed 1-2, 3-5, 6-10, and 11-or-more. These columns we can let indicate the number of times you have spoken to the person. (Experimenter explained how headings were arrived at by having done experiment herself.) You will find it is fairly easy to recall which heading is just about right.

"You will notice also that there is a column marked 'X' to the left of the widest column. You may put an 'X' in the column with this heading next to any names in your list of contacts which represent persons you would like to talk to many more times. If it doesn't make any difference to you whether you ever get a chance to talk again to some of your contacts, do not put anything in the 'X' column opposite their names. Thus, your paper will tell exactly which persons each of you would like to have further opportunity to contact. Remember you are to put an 'X' only beside the names of persons whom you care very much about knowing better. If there are no such persons, other than the ones you have chosen, you will have 'X' only beside their names."

Dates and Spacing of Tests

The first tests were given during the last week of December, 1937. The test-population included all individuals (443) comprising the population of the New York State Training School for Girls as of January 1, 1938. The period of Christmas vacation was selected for the testing because during this period academic school and most vocational assignments were suspended. Thus less than usual opportunity existed for discussion to take place between tested and untested individuals before all had been tested. Re-tests were given during the first week of September, 1938. The re-test-population included all individuals (457) comprising the population of the community as of September 3, 1938.

The spacing of the re-testing at an interval eight months distant from the original testing was selected (1) because it was considered sufficient to allow the presence or absence of characteristic trends to be shown in the individual's structure of inter-personal relations through a comparison of the data of both tests, and (2) because it was desired for the purpose of the research that the majority of the members comprising the population at the time of the first test be present for the re-test.

The methods used in the first testing were duplicated in the second except for one omission. In the re-testing, the social contact "range" or listing was not taken. Its repetition did not appear necessary to the present study, the results on its initial use being sufficient for the purpose. The period used for the re-testing was selected, in addition to the reasons stated above, because it came just prior to the opening of academic school and the starting of new vocational assignments, incurring new contacts that might disproportionately have affected the choice process.

Subjects of the Research

The analysis will be concerned with a portion of the subjects living in the School, even though the entire population present at either time were the subjects of the testing on both occasions, as the primary purpose of the study is to compare the individuals who were present on both occasions.

The population at the time of Test I comprised 443 individuals, of whom 320 were white and 123 Negro girls. To increase uniformity of conditions, only white girls living in cottage units are the subjects of the analysis, thus making the living-together groups similar. White girls living in other than regular cottage units (as hospital or farm units) are excluded also because their opportunities for contact with other individuals varied greatly from those of the population in general.

The white girls living the regular cottage life of the community at the time of Test I numbered 236 and were housed in ten cottages.[8] Eight months later, of the 236, there remained 133 individuals living in the *same* cottage units as formerly. The analysis is primarily concerned with the 133 individuals who were present for both test and re-test, and occupied on both occasions the same housing unit. This group of 133 will be designated as A_I when reference is made to data from its first test, and as A_{II} when reference is made to data from its re-test. Complete data on choice and rejection are presented for A_I and A_{II}.

For the purpose of examining the positive choice process as it operates in a larger group, the positive choice data on the 236 white subjects are also presented.[9] This group of 236 subjects will be designated as Group AB.

The population as a totality enters into the analysis, it

---

[8] These cottage units housed from 20 to 28 individuals, each provided with a room of her own. Thus the criterion of *living-together* indicates common housing and does not involve sharing the same room. Of the ten cottages, two were comprised of 20 individuals and one each was comprised of 21, 22, 23, 24, 25, 26, 27, and 28 individuals.

[9] As these data confirm the findings on positive choice on the 133 subjects (who form part of the 236), it was not considered necessary to analyze the data on rejection for the 236 subjects, and their positive choices only are therefore included.

should be recalled, as the expression of choice and rejection by the subjects may involve any member of the whole population and the subjects may be chosen or rejected by any member of the whole population as well as by one another.

To examine the choice process under conditions which were uniform for all subjects, the data used in the analysis include all choices and rejections given either on the criterion of living or on the criterion of working. This analysis is presented in Chapters I to XI inclusive. These data, then, represent choices and rejections for or against association with others in a "formal" collective, that is, a collective grouping which has official and visible existence in the community, as a housing unit or a vocational unit, and might develop many common objectives which could become formalized in codes for doing things as a group out of common considerations as well as the obvious sharing by members with some regularity of their time and mutual obligations. The importance of the two criteria applies to each member of the community. No individual lived apart from a group of other individuals and likewise no individual worked at a vocation in which a number of other individuals were not also occupied.[10]

All subjects could use leisure time to associate freely and little or much, and with many or few other individuals, according to their inclinations. The results of the analysis of choices and rejections for or against such association in leisure time is presented in Chapter XII. The sociometric structure of formal grouping and of leisure grouping are considered together in Chapter XIII and also in Chapter XII.

[10] On the other hand, all the subjects did not have academic studies in common with others; the results on this criterion are omitted as not comparable from one individual to another. For leisure-time context, see pp. 229-232.

PART TWO

EMOTIONAL AND SOCIAL EXPANSIVENESS

CHAPTER III

Character of the Choice Process

Every community is structured by attraction and rejection growing out of the population's intimate association with one another. Within this problem, many questions can be explored. Does negative reaction surpass, equal, or fall below reaction of positive choice? Is either positive choice or negative choice (rejection) a narrowly channeled and not widely spread phenomenon? What is the nature and extent of mutual attractions and rejections? Is there any relation between the amount of positive choice and the amount of negative choice exercised in a community?

A study of individual differences in respect to positive and negative choice must first examine into the many-sided picture of the relationships which may exist between one or another aspect of choice expression and any other aspect its expression may take. The significance of such *individual* differences as are found may then be seen against the background of the character of the choice process in its general operation.

Method of Treatment of the Problem

In the present research, the extent to which the individual chooses others is a measure of his *emotional expansiveness* towards others; the extent to which he rejects others is a measure of his *rejection* of others. It must be immediately obvious that the line of demarcation here taken to mark off the number of individuals towards whom the individual reacts by positive choice or by negative choice does not rigidly divide off those towards whom his reaction has come to have emotional components to some degree, from those towards whom such reaction is non-existent. The problem is clearly not this simple. It is doubtful if two persons can meet without some emotional reaction, however slight, taking place between them. But in most passing contacts, the reaction is a matter of so little concern to either individual (quite aside from its slightness) that he may be hardly aware of any reaction. The line of demarcation between choice or rejection and non-reaction on a choice or rejection basis divides off those whom the individual has a positive emotional reaction of choice for including in his situation or a negative emotional reaction of rejection for excluding from his situation, from those towards whom he has neither reaction, when the possibility is open to him to express preferences which may be used to maintain or alter his personal situation in respect to being associated with others.

The persons who are chosen or rejected are selected for choice or rejection by the individual out of the range of contacts he has established with others. Since many of the persons in the individual's social-contact-range may not become either chosen or rejected by him, and yet the individual is socially expansive towards them as shown by his continuing to maintain contact with them, it is convenient and appropriate to designate the extent of his social-contact-range as a measure of his *social expansiveness*. The extent of all contacts, initiated or continued upon the initiative of the individual, can thus be differentiated from the number of contacts towards whom the individual comes to be emotionally drawn to the extent of choosing or repelled to the extent of rejecting. Social expansiveness and emotional expansiveness can then be studied as two distinct phenomena in inter-personal relations, two phenomena which may or may not show correspondence in their expression.

The measure defined in this research as the individual's social-contact-range should not be confused with the measure defined in previous research as the individual's "acquaintance volume." The *social-contact-range*, it should be noted, is the *range* of contacts an individual *has himself established or maintains between himself and other persons*; it is explored for the first time in the present report. In previous research, a listing of *the number of persons an individual has spoken to* has been taken to define his *acquaintance volume*.[1,2] The two measures are essentially different. An individual's acquaintance volume is more inclusive and will always exceed his social-contact-range since the former is not limited to persons towards whom the individual shows social initiative in contacting and maintaining contact with, but instead contains also persons towards whom the individual may show no initiative or interest and who have come to be "acquaintances" through *their* initiative towards the individual, obliging him to speak to them when he may not have done so of his own accord. Consequently, the individual's acquaintance volume cannot be used as a measure of the individual's social expansiveness. It is, however, a useful measure for other purposes. (See references given in footnotes 1 and 2.) The acquaintance volume is also an index easier to obtain than the social-contact-range, especially as, for the accurate securing of the latter, it is practically necessary to secure also the *extent* to which each contacted person has been contacted. (The latter analysis will not be included here but the full instructions to the subject are included as these are necessary

[1] J. L. Moreno, *Who Shall Survive?* p. 138. 1934.
[2] H. H. Jennings, "Structure of Leadership," *Sociometry*, I:I:99-143, July, 1937, p. 130.

to an understanding of the nature of the problem. See pp. 33-34.)

In reporting the findings of this research, the term "social expansiveness" will always be used to designate the social-contact-range of the subject, but "expansiveness" will frequently be used, for brevity, instead of the term "emotional expansiveness" in referring to the number of individuals chosen by the subject.

Under the conditions of the testing, the number of choices and rejections given by a subject is not necessarily the number of individuals chosen or rejected by this subject. The subject may choose or reject the same individual on more than one criterion or on one criterion only. Likewise the number of choices or rejections focussed upon the subject may or may not correspond with the number of individuals by whom the subject is chosen or rejected. The results, differentiated according to criteria, are given in Chapters XI-XIV [3] in order to simplify the presentation of the major problems undertaken by the study.

The *method of the analysis* is a comparison of the number of different individuals reacted to positively (chosen) or negatively (rejected) by the subjects, with the number of different individuals reacting positively or negatively to the subjects, and with the number of different individuals who reciprocate the subjects' choice or rejection. The results of this analysis are given in Tables I, II, and III.

[3] See below, pages 218-323. For the present purpose, it should be mentioned that there is almost always an overlap between the individuals reacted to by the subject from one criterion to another and at the same time almost invariably a differentiation between the individuals reacted to by the subject from one criterion to another. "Studying" produced fewest reactions, and "recreation-leisure," the next smallest number. The latter criterion showed most overlap with the criterion of "living." The "undetermined" criterion was only occasionally employed, chiefly for functions of special interest, *e.g., singing.* The vast majority of both positive and negative choices occurred on the criteria of "living" and "working," the former being the most productive of all criteria used.

The analysis is next directed towards the relation of the above results to the subject's social-contact-range. The latter results are given in Table IV.

Product-Moment coefficients of correlation (with critical ratios of $Zr/\sigma z$) between different aspects of the above findings are given in Table V.

It will be recalled that the expression of choice and rejection by any subject may involve any member of the whole population, which numbered 443 individuals at the time of Test I and 457 at the time of Test II, and that the subject may be chosen or rejected by any member of the whole population other than himself. It should also be noted that for purposes of comparison of the results on Test I with the results on Test II, the main analysis is concerned with the group of 133 subjects present for both tests and to be designated as Group A_I and Group A_{II} respectively as reference is made to their results on Test I and Test II. Also it will be recalled that additional data given by analysis of the results on positive choice for a larger group of 236 subjects is to be designated as AB, of whom A_I formed a part.

RESULTS

Length of Residence and Positive Choice

The positive expression of choice by Group AB shows a median of 7.60 individuals chosen by the subject; for Group A_I the median number is 7.52. Both AB and A_I as a group had been in the community for a considerable period by the time of Test I: the median length of stay of AB was 14.3 months; of A_I, 11.7 months; the range in both instances extended from 1 month (15 days or over) to over 3 years. Increase in length of time individuals are together does not

TABLE I. CHOICES AND REJECTIONS
TEST I AND TEST II
Criteria: Living; Working

The choices and rejections are taken from the total population: 443, Test I; 457, Test II

Number of persons	Chosen by the subject Test I	Chosen by the subject II	Rejected by the subject I	Rejected by the subject II	Choosing the subject I	Choosing the subject II	Rejecting the subject I	Rejecting the subject II	Reciprocating choice by subject I	Reciprocating choice by subject II	Reciprocating rejection by subject I	Reciprocating rejection by subject II
24	1					1						
23						1						
22						2						
21												
20					1	1	1					
19					1	3	1					
18		1			3	3		1				
17		1			3	7		1				
16	1	3			3	3	1	1	1			
15	1	4			5	6	1	1				
14	2	2			2	7		1				
13	2	5		2	4	3	3	2				
12	8	10	1	3	5	9	2	2				
11	7	6	2	2	4	11	2	3				
10	11	10	6		7	5		3		1		
9	9	18	9	6	5	9	5	5	2	1		
8	25	19			13	9	3	5	1	8		

TABLE I. CHOICES AND REJECTIONS (*Continued*)

TEST I AND TEST II

Criteria: Living; Working

The choices and rejections are taken from the total population: 443, Test I; 457, Test II

Number of persons	Chosen by the subject		Rejected by the subject		Choosing the subject		Rejecting the subject		Reciprocating choice by subject		Reciprocating rejection by subject	
	Test I	II	I	II	I	II	I	II	I	II	I	II
7	21	12	9	6	8	5	8	6	2	6	1	
6	19	12	10	18	14	8	4	3	6	13		3
5	13	14	22	20	10	10	7	15	7	16	2	1
4	8	6	25	28	12	8	13	10	13	13	1	3
3	4	9	19	19	5	9	14	17	23	16	5	9
2	1	1	16	14	9	2	17	19	24	26	14	18
1			8	6	10	6	26	20	33	21	27	35
0			6	9	9	5	25	18	21	12	83	64
N.	133	133	133	133	133	133	133	133	133	133	133	133
Median	7.52	8.16	4.20	4.16	6.32	9.00	2.41	3.06	2.02	2.97	0.30	0.57
Mean	7.86	8.39	4.41	4.29	7.21	9.40	3.71	4.23	2.47	3.43	0.68	1.00
S.D.	2.99	3.45	2.43	2.39	5.14	5.62	4.06	3.99	2.25	2.40	1.17	1.33
r	.37		.27		.65		.66		.12		.33	
All reactions	1045	1116	587	571	959	1250	493	562	328	456	91	133
D/σD	1.65		.50		5.48		1.86		3.69		3.20	

TABLE II. SUM OF CHOICES AND REJECTIONS
TEST I AND TEST II
Criteria: Living; Working

Number of persons	Chosen or rejected or both by the subject		Choosing or rejecting the subject, or both	
	Test I	II	I	II
28			1	
27			1	1
26		1		2
25		1		2
24	1	1		
23	1	1		1
22		3		3
21	1	1	1	2
20	1	4	4	3
19	5	3	6	6
18	1	4	7	7
17	10	5	1	11
16	11	6	9	7
15	7	10	6	9
14	11	19	4	14
13	14	11	5	4
12	9	8	10	18
11	10	13	12	12
10	14	4	5	6
9	12	12	14	3
8	16	7	11	7
7	4	9	7	4
6	1	4	10	4
5	1	2	3	2
4	2	2	6	4
3	1	1	4	
2		1	3	
1			2	1
0			1	
N.	133	133	133	133
Median	12.11	12.82	10.54	13.61
Mean	12.27	12.68	10.92	13.62
S.D.	3.92	4.69	5.39	5.00
r		.29		.45
All reactions	1632	1687	1452	1812
D/σD		.91		5.87

TABLE III.   DIFFERENCE BETWEEN CHOICES AND BETWEEN
REJECTIONS (Test II minus Test I)

		Chosen by subject	Rejected by subject	Choosing subject	Rejecting subject
	16			1	
	15				
	14			1	
	13				
	12			1	
	11			1	
	10	2		1	
	9	1		6	1
	8	2		9	2
	7	5	1	2	4
	6	4	2	6	5
Number of persons	5	2	1	11	4
	4	9	6	8	7
	3	14	8	10	12
	2	9	15	16	12
	1	16	20	13	15
	0	13	25	15	22
	−1	13	15	9	12
	−2	20	20	8	17
	−3	10	6	5	6
	−4	5	8	2	7
	−5	4	4	1	1
	−6	2	1	3	3
	−7	1	1	1	2
	−8			1	1
	−9				
	−10				
	−11			1	
	−12				
	−13	1		1	
N.		133	133	133	133
Median		0.31	−0.04	1.91	0.30
Mean		0.53	−0.12	2.19	0.52
S.D.		3.66	2.53	4.57	3.33

show for the test-population any correlation with the number
of individuals for whom they express positive choice ($r =$
.06 for A_I and also, for A_{II}). If finer units of a few days
up to 4 weeks were to be studied (and all the individuals
were new to one another) it might be that extent of choice

TABLE IV. SOCIAL-CONTACT-RANGE: CONTACTS INITIATED OR MAINTAINED BY SUBJECT (exclusive of own housing unit membership)

181–190	2	
171–180		
161–170		
151–160	1	
141–150		
131–140	5	2
121–130	1	1
119–120	3	
101–110	9	6
91–100	3	1
81– 90	14	8
71– 80	14	10
61– 70	19	12
51– 60	29	12
41– 50	38	24
31– 40	21	11
21– 30	34	19
11– 20	29	21
0– 10	14	6
N.	236	133
Median	45.8	44.5
Mean	50.5	47.7
S.D.	32.9	28.9

(left axis label: Number of persons)

TABLE V. CORRELATIONS ON CHOICE AND REJECTION

	Test	N.	r	Zr/σz
Number chosen by subject and number choosing him:	I	236	.20	3.12
Same:	I	133	.30	3.44
Same:	II	133	.12	1.34
Number chosen by subject and number reciprocating him:	I	236	.51	8.66
Same:	I	133	.32	3.68
Same:	II	133	.43	5.11
Number choosing subject and number reciprocating him:	I	222*	.59	9.68
Same:	I	124*	.70	9.64
Same:	II	129*	.67	9.01
Number rejected by subject and number rejecting him:	I	133	.001	
Same:	II	133	.01	
Number rejected by subject and number mutually rejecting him:	I	127†	.20	2.25
Same:	II	124†	.20	2.25
Number rejecting subject and number mutually rejecting him:	I	108†	.73	9.29
Same:	II	115†	.62	8.06
Number chosen by subject and number rejected by subject:	I	133	.03	
Same:	II	133	.26	2.96
Number choosing subject and number rejecting him:	I	133	—.33	3.81
Same:	II	133	—.50	6.10
Number chosen by subject on Test I and number chosen by him on Test II:		133	.37	4.32

TABLE V. CORRELATIONS ON CHOICE AND REJECTION
(*Continued*)

	Test	N.	r	Zr/σz
Number choosing subject on Test I and number choosing him on Test II:		133	.65	8.61
Number rejected by subject on Test I and number rejected by him on Test II:		133	.27	3.08
Number rejecting subject on Test I and number rejecting him on Test II:		133	.66	8.81
Number reciprocating choice by subject on Test I and number reciprocating choice by him on Test II:		133	.12	1.34
Number reciprocating rejection (mutual rejection) by subject on Test I and number reciprocating rejection by him on Test II:		133	.33	3.81
Number chosen by subject and subject's contact range:	I	236	.18	2.80
(the latter taken at the time of Test I only) Same:	I	133	.22	2.48
Same:	II	133	.06	
Number choosing subject and subject's contact range:	I	236	.40	6.52
Same:	I	133	.29	3.32
Same:	II	133	.09	
Number reciprocating choice by subject and subject's contact range:	I	236	.22	3.44
Same:	I	133	.22	2.48
Number rejected by subject and subject's contact range:	I	133	.16	1.78
Number rejecting subject and subject's contact range:	I	133	.004	
Number reciprocating rejection by subject (mutual rejection) and subject's contact range:	I	133	.02	
Sum of number chosen and number rejected by subject and sum of number choosing and number rejecting him:	I	133	.21	2.37
Same:	II	133	.09	
Sum of number chosen and number rejected by subject on Test I and the similar sum on Test II:		133	.29	3.32
Sum of number choosing and number rejecting subject on Test I and the similar sum on Test II:		133	.45	5.39
Sum of number chosen and number rejected by subject on Test I and subject's contact range at time of Test I:		133	.26	2.96
Sum of number chosen and number rejected by subject on Test II and subject's contact range at time of Test I:		133	—.005	
Sum of number choosing and number rejecting subject on Test I and subject's contact range at time of Test I:		133	.27	3.08
Sum of number choosing and number rejecting subject on Test II and subject's contact range at time of Test I:		133	.06	

* In calculation of the coefficient of correlation (Product-Moment), the unchosen individuals are omitted as they could not have reciprocations if they received no choices.

† In calculation of the coefficient of correlation, the individuals who do not reject are omitted as they could not have reciprocated rejections. Likewise, in the correlation of number rejecting the subject with number mutually rejecting him, the unrejected individuals are omitted so as not to bolster the correlation.

NOTE: The critical ratio of Zr/σz at 2.58 (or above) indicates significance at the .01 level of chance; the ratio at 1.96 indicates significance at the .05 level of chance. (Clear discussion of this ratio is given in J. P. Guilford, Psychometric Methods, p. 548, 1936, and R. A. Fisher, *Statistical Methods for Research Workers,* 4th ed., 1932; for Product-Moment *r's,* see Henry E. Garrett, *Statistics in Psychology and Education,* 2nd ed., 1937.)

would be found to be related to length of time individuals are in contact with one another. There are only a few such subjects in the present study. Thirteen individuals in Group A$_I$ had been in the community from 15 days up to 3 months. Four of these subjects who were respectively 15, 16, 16, and 17 days resident, chose respectively 5, 3, 10, and 6 individuals. Six subjects who were 2 months resident chose from 6 to 11, and three subjects who were 3 months in the community chose from 5 to 10 individuals. The number of individuals chosen by the subjects as a whole is equally varied; inspection of the subjects' use of choice at any level of length of stay shows the median to fall at practically the same point as that of test-population A$_I$ (or of AB) as a whole. Thus there is no evidence that length of time individuals are together will either increase or decrease the extent of their positive choice for one another. It appears that on the average individuals early in their stay in a community show an extent of positive emotional expansiveness which does not increase appreciably no matter how long they remain together. The subject who is relatively more or relatively less expansive towards others will react to them more or less independently of the length of time he is in association with them as far as this population goes. (For extent of reaction to the subject in relation to length of residence, see Chapter VII.)

Positive Choice by and towards Subject

The positive expansiveness of others towards the subject, as measured by the number of individuals choosing the subject, shows for AB a slight correlation with the positive expansiveness of the subject towards others, as measured by the number of individuals he chooses. The r is .20 and is significant at the point .01 level of chance. The correlation is somewhat higher and similarly significant for A_I, the r being .30; but for A_{II} the correlation is not significantly different from zero, the r being .12. Thus the small relationship between the individual's positive expression of choice for others and that of others for him tends to disappear by the time of Test II. It should be noted that the greater average length of stay is that of A_{II}, next, of AB, and least, that of A_I. On the other hand, the extent to which the individual's choice of others is reciprocated by them correlates at both periods fairly highly with the extent of his choice for others: $r = .51$ for AB, .32 for A_I and .43 for A_{II}. Further, the extent to which the individual's choice of others is reciprocated correlates still more highly with the extent to which he is chosen by others: $r = .59$ for AB, .70 for A_I and .67 for A_{II}.

Thus whereas there is shown only a slight relationship between the positive expansiveness of the subject and the positive expansiveness of others to him (a relationship which is not maintained after the length of time in the same community has been extended), the degree to which the subject's choice of others is reciprocated by them is appreciably related, not only to the degree of his expansiveness but also to the degree of others' expansiveness towards him. The subject who is relatively more expansive than others appears as a subject who more likely than not is expansive towards some of those who respond to him or better able than other subjects to gain reciprocation from those to whom he responds. And the subject to whom the population shows itself to be relatively more expansive is a subject who chooses in the direction of those who are drawn to him; or that the facility to form mutual relationships of choice is one attribute of the individual towards whom others show relatively greater emotional expansiveness as expressed in choice for him. The subject who chooses relatively many or who is chosen by relatively many is hardly ever an individual who is not himself drawn to some of the persons who are drawn to him. While the individual cannot have a reciprocated response without himself making a response, it is notable that the sheer number of responses of attraction to others (as well as the sheer number of others' responses of attraction to the individual) contributes positively to the likelihood of reciprocation. The equally significant finding, of course, is that sheer quantity of expansiveness on the part of the individual for others *does not* assure a similar response towards the individual; and, conversely, sheer quantity of expansiveness expressed by others towards the individual does not assure from such individual a like response in expansiveness.

Rejection by and towards Subject

The negative aspect of choice shows similar findings. There is no correlation found between the extent to which the subject rejects others and the extent to which he himself is rejected by others. For A, $r = .00$ on both Test I and Test II. On the other hand, the correlation is significant, at the .05 level of chance, between the extent to which the subject rejects others and the extent of mutual rejections between himself and others. For both A_I and A_{II}, $r = .20$ (critical ratio 2.25). The extent to which the subject is rejected by others and the extent to which he is mutually rejected by them correlates as highly as expression of positive choice by others for the subject and its reciprocated expression. For A_I $r = .73$; for A_{II}, .62. Thus the subject who is rejected to a relatively great extent appears as a subject who rejects more likely than not some of the individuals who are rejecting him; or the facility to form mutual relationships of rejection between himself and others appears as an attribute of the individual towards whom others show relatively greater rejection.   The individual who is much rejected is not likely to be an individual who does not return rejection to some of the very persons who are rejecting him.   The sheer number of responses of rejection he arouses from others appears to contribute positively to the likelihood of his reciprocating them with rejection.

Relation between Positive Choice and Rejection

The extent of the positive expansiveness of the subject towards others shows no correlation with the extent of his rejection of others on Test I: $r = .03$ for A_I.   But a slight positive correlation which is significant at the .01 level of chance appears on Test II: $r = .26$ for A_{II} (critical ratio, 2.96).   Hence, the number of individuals the subject rejects and the number he chooses are correlated to a small degree by the time of Test II.   On the other hand, the number of individuals who reject the subject and the number who choose him is inversely related for A_I, with r at —.33, and still more highly inversely related for A_{II}, with r at —.50.   Thus the likelihood appears that the greater the extent of positive expansiveness towards the individual the smaller is the extent to which he is rejected.

Total Reactions as a Sum

While the positive choice expression of the individual does not, as reported above, show a correlation until Test II with his negative choice expression of rejection, the total expression of the individual as a *sum* of both his positive and negative choice expressions on Test I shows a positive correlation of .29 with his total expression on Test II, and is significant at the .01 level. In view of this finding it is of further interest that the sum of the number of individuals choosing or rejecting the subject on Test I and on Test II correlate at .45.

Positive and Negative Reactions, Singly

The significance of the correlations between total reaction by the subject and towards the subject becomes further apparent by inspection of the consistency of his positive or negative reaction and the consistency of the positive or negative reaction to him by others. Between Test I and Test II the positive expression of the subject for others correlates at .37; between Test I and Test II the negative expression of rejection of others by the subject correlates at .27, and both coefficients are above the .01 level of significance. The individual subject is thus shown to maintain to some extent his relative position in respect to other subjects in the expression of choice and in the expression of rejection. It is notable, too, that the critical ratio of the difference between the correlated means on the two tests are for positive choice by the subject, 1.65 and for negative choice by the subject, .50 (see Table I). Hence the mean change or typical change in either expression from Test I to Test II is non-significant. While the individual subject in his expression shows increase and decrease on Test II in a manner that is not highly consistent with his expression on Test I (consequently resulting in low r's), the average change in performance of the individuals as a group from Test I to Test II is insignificantly different from zero. The individual differences in the amount of change (see Table III) show the median and mean of their frequency distribution to fall at zero both for positive choice and for negative choice.

The positive expression of choice *for* the subject on Test I and Test II correlate at .65; the negative expression of rejection for the subject on Test I and Test II correlate at .66. In both instances the individual subject who elicits relatively more or relatively less reaction, whether positive or negative, appears to continue to elicit relatively the same amount. There is evident some agreement (some consensus) from one time to a later time. Whatever has initially brought about his position in respect to others continues to manifest itself in this or other forms definitely acceptable or inacceptable to others as shown by the consistency of their reaction to him. But whereas the subjects as a group do not show significant change from Test I to Test II, eight months later, either by increase or decrease, in the extent of the number of individuals they choose or in the extent of the number they reject, there is found a significant change in the number of individuals who choose them from Test I to Test II (C. R. = 5.48) and no significant change in the number of individuals who reject them from Test I to Test II (C. R. = 1.86). Thus, whether or not a significant change takes place in the gross amount of reaction to the test-group of subjects, the subject is found to maintain to a high degree the relative position accorded him by the general population from one time to a time eight months later.

Implications of Consistencies

The findings up to this point suggest a conclusion that the individual has a characteristic value in respect to the amount of positive and negative reaction he arouses from other indi-

viduals. This individual characteristic may be called his
stimulus-value.[4] On the other hand, the extent of his own
capacity to exercise choice and rejection is not limitless or
randomly variable: it shows a definable range, a range that
may be called his *emotional repertoire* (for responding by
choice or rejection) in expansiveness to others, an attribute
that may be seen as a relatively permanent attribute.

The findings also suggest a hypothesis as to the nature of
choice. The individual is found not to react by positive
choice only: almost universally he reacts by both choosing
and rejecting. Nor is he reacted to by positive choice only:
he is both chosen and rejected, also scarcely without exception. And the longer the period of inter-personal experience
he spends with others, the more particularized and definite
appears the picture of choice and rejection as a single process
in which a separating out of positive choice from negative
choice distorts the total process. Positive choice as it is expressed by the individual or as it is focussed upon him by
others and rejection as it is expressed by the individual or as
it is focussed upon him by others may be viewed not as two
separate and distinct aspects of *a* choice process, but as forming *one* choice process in which the negative and positive aspects of choice bear particular relationships to each other —
a single process in which the positive and negative aspects of
choice do not operate independently of each other but within
which rejection is a partial aspect and positive choice likewise
but a partial aspect.

Proportion of Positive to Negative Choice

The gross number of positive choices expressed by the sub-

---

[4] Whereas the term *stimulus-value* is hardly the most apt expression that could be
desired to carry the meaning intended here, it appears more fitting than the term
valence since the latter as Lewin employs it carries connotations not under consideration here.

ject in Group A for different individuals on Test I is 1045 and on Test II, 1116. The gross number of rejections expressed by the subject for different individuals on Test I is 587 and on Test II, 571. Thus on both occasions tested, the positive expression for participating with others is practically twice as great as the expression of rejection.

The number of individuals reciprocating the subject's choice to them is 328 on Test I and 456 on Test II. Thus 31 percent of the individuals chosen on Test I and 41 percent of the individuals chosen on Test II reciprocate the subject's positive choice. The number of individuals mutually rejecting the subject who has rejected them is 91 on Test I and 133 on Test II, or 16 percent on Test I and 23 percent on Test II. The increase of 10 percent in positive reciprocation is accompanied by an increase of 7 percent in negative reciprocation. The evidence further supports the finding that positive and negative responses have a concomitant development. The number of structures of mutual positive choice are three times as frequent on Test I as the number of structures of mutual rejection (328::91) and the positive aspect of mutuality continues to exceed in volume the negative aspect of mutuality (456::133) as the latter increases after contact of longer duration among the members of the test-population.

Mutuality: Positive and Negative

The mean increase from Test I to Test II of both positive reciprocation and negative reciprocation is a significant increase in both instances (C. R. = 3.69 and 3.20 respectively). The number of individuals who on Test I and on Test II reciprocate rejection by the subject correlates at .33 but the number of individuals who reciprocate positive choice

by the subject shows an insignificant correlation, the r being
.12. The insignificant correlation in the latter instance is
found to be a favorable fact in the choice process rather than
the contrary because it does not reflect a lack of "better" performance: it reflects irregularly better performance in general. The individual's increase in capacity to form positive
mutual relationships shows a sharp rise unpredictably greater
than the past performance for some individuals: the 21 subjects who on Test I had no reciprocated choices on Test II
show a range from zero to 8 in number of individuals reciprocating them, with only 6 receiving no mutual responses.
Of the 21 subjects, four are reciprocated by 1, four by 2,
three by 3, one by 4, one by 5, one by 6, and one by 8, with
only six chosen by no one whom they have chosen. The increase is equally irregular for the 33 subjects who on Test I
were mutually chosen by only 1 individual: on Test II, two
of them are mutually chosen by no one, nine by 1, nine by 2,
two by 3, two by 4, five by 5, two by 6, one by 7, and one by
10. On the other hand, subjects who on Test I were reciprocally chosen by from 8 to 15 show a decrease; they are
mutually chosen on Test II by from 6 to 8, a retrenchment
that may reflect a withdrawal on their own part from the demands made upon them by others, causing them not to choose
others to the same extent as formerly so that there are in consequence fewer reciprocal choices between themselves and
others.

It also appears that positive reciprocation between himself
and others is difficult for the individual to develop and he
shows himself slow in achieving his full capacity in this respect. But when he begins to meet with success in the direction of mutually positive relations, he seems to have a rapid

rather than gradual success, quickly gaining within a comparatively short time reciprocation by a relatively large number of persons. It is understandable that, at the start of an individual's stay in a community, the initial reciprocation he gets would be slow to come about. It appears abundantly evident from this research that structure in general does not suddenly alter radically in the test-community; it is more marked by stability than by flux — even in spite of the fact that relatively many new members are entering and "old" members are leaving the population. The individual enters a community the members of which have their emotional expansiveness already channeled to a large extent. Since the capacity for emotional expansiveness on the part of any individual appears from the findings to be not limitless but generally to range within a relatively definable repertoire of expression in choice for others, the individual's task is frequently that of rechanneling choice *away from persons* who are receiving it from the person or persons he wants to be attracted to him.

In contrast to positive mutual reactions, the mutual rejections correlate significantly between Test I and Test II since the rise in reciprocated rejection is more regular and gradual. The individual does not "jump" from 1 or 2 mutual rejections to so unpredictably larger a number, as is the case in positive mutual structures once the subject begins to achieve them. Also the "retrenchment" in number of individuals chosen by the much chosen subject is not found in respect to number of individuals rejected for the very much rejected subject: his performance is in the opposite direction, rejecting more rather than less on Test II. Where there is decline in number of reciprocated rejections from Test I to Test II, this likewise is in general a gradual decline.

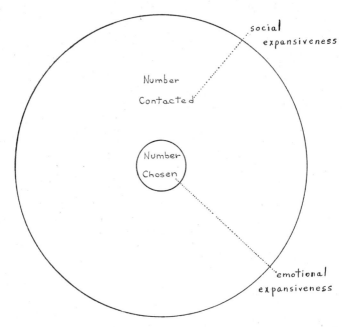

Fig. 1. Proportional Representation of the Average Individual's Social-Contact-Range and Positive Choice Expression. The individual contacts several times as many persons as he shows himself to be emotionally related to by choice.

Social Expansiveness

The field of other individuals out of which the subject chooses and rejects, although it was for each the entire population of the community, varied greatly from subject to subject according to the initiative he displayed in contacting and maintaining contacts with others who may have contacted him. The actual reference-base-for-choice (or rejection) can thus be considered the social-contact-range of the individual. The number of individuals the subject is in contact with at the time of Test I shows a median of 45.8 individuals for AB and 44.5 for A. Thus social expansiveness, as defined by the number of individuals in the social-contact-range is on the average about six times as many as the subject chooses (see Fig. 1), about ten times as many as he rejects, and about four times as many as he reacts to on a basis of either positive or negative choice.

The extent of the subject's social-contact-range shows a correlation of .34 for Group A with the subject's length of stay in the community and is significant at the .01 level of chance.   Thus while the subject's emotional expansiveness was found to bear no relation to his length of stay in the community, his social expansiveness shows a positive relationship to the length of his residence.

The subject's contact-range shows a slight relationship to the number of individuals chosen by the subject in AB: $r = .18$ and is significant at the .01 level. A similarly slight relationship is shown for A_I: $r = .22$, just less than significant at the .01 level ($Zr/\sigma z = 2.48$). There is also found a correlation of .22 for both groups of subjects between social-contact-range and number of individuals reciprocating positive choice by the subject. The highest correlation appears, however, for both groups between contact-range and number of individuals expressing positive choice for the subject: $r = .40$ for AB and .29 for A_I. There is found no correlation differing significantly from zero between the subject's contact-range and either number of individuals rejected by him or rejecting him or for number mutually rejecting the subject. (See Table V.) But the sum of individuals reacted to by the subject, by choice or rejection, and the sum of individuals reacting positively or negatively to the subject correlate with the subject's contact-range at .26 and .27 respectively.

Thus there is indicated a very low but positive correlation

between the individual's social expansiveness and the extent to which he shows emotional expansiveness in choice of others or the extent to which emotional expansiveness is expressed in choice for him; there is indicated, too, a somewhat higher relation between the individual's social expansiveness and the extent others reciprocate him in choice. But his rejection of others or others' rejection of him appears unrelated to his social expansiveness in contacting others. The sum of other individuals to whom he reacts or who react to him positively or negatively, the total impress he makes upon others or others make upon him, is significantly related although to only a very small degree to his social expansiveness.

The social expansiveness of the subject as found on Test I shows no correlation whatever with either choice or rejection or both, by or towards the subject on Test II. Thus the individual's social expansiveness at one time shows no relation to emotional expansiveness measured at a later time.

The individual's contact-range, when considered only for those subjects present from 1 to 9 months, shows a gradual progressive average increase up to this period of residence, after which length of time the correlation to be noted between contact range and further increase in length of stay in the community is much smaller and hardly significant. In view of the fact that in exercise of positive choice towards others the individual shows no such gradual increase but instead, so far as the present findings indicate, is drawn to choose others to as great an extent from the beginning of his stay in a community as he is to choose later after he has been resident for a comparatively much longer period, it may be concluded that social expansiveness differs essentially from emotional expansiveness as each is defined in this research. Whatever enters into the subject's spontaneously choosing others operates, it appears, from the start of his contact with others to as large an extent as it does later when the individual's range of contacts has provided him with a larger field for choice.   It may be conjectured that social expansiveness is an expression more peripheral to the needs of the individual than emotional expansiveness.

CHAPTER IV

Spread and Focus of Choice and Rejection

The choice process has been found to structure the community in essentially the same way on the two occasions examined. From this finding it need not follow that every "section" within the population shows like choice behavior. It might be surmised that within so large a population there might be located a section or two within which the choice process might be found to vary from its characteristic manner of operation throughout the community. The "test" of whether or not this is true might be made by examining the choice behavior of the "over-chosen" as compared with the "under-chosen." Then, a number of questions may be directed at the problem.

Does the choice process show a different manner of operation among the "over-chosen" compared with the general population or compared with the "under-chosen" of the community? Does the extent of emotional expansiveness shown by the "over-chosen" equal, surpass or fall below the extent of emotional expansiveness shown by the "under-chosen" of the population? Does either "group" differ from each other and from the general population in extent of *social* expansiveness? For the purpose of such analysis, what subjects may be considered as chosen to an exceptionally great extent and what subjects may be considered as chosen to an exceptionally small extent by the population of the community?

Emotional Expansiveness: Over-chosen and Under-chosen

Whatever points, in the range of number of individuals choosing the subject, are taken to mark off, for the purpose of analysis, subjects who are chosen by many others and subjects who are chosen by very few others, the selection is necessarily arbitrary. However, inspection of the range shows that if an upper and a lower point falling respectively at 1 S.D. above the mean and 1 S.D. below the mean in number of individuals choosing the subject are taken to mark off the two groups, a sufficiently large number of subjects are secured to make possible a comparison of the group of subjects who are chosen by relatively many individuals with the group of subjects who are chosen by relatively few. The subjects who comprise the former may be considered "over-chosen" to the extent thus defined and the subjects who comprise the latter, "under-chosen," to the extent thus defined, by comparison with the subjects as a whole.

The number of subjects who are over-chosen (by this definition) is approximately the same as the number of subjects who are under-chosen (by this definition): 16 percent and 19 percent respectively in Group AB (N = 236).[1] In AB the over-chosen subjects, numbering 37, show a range in number of individuals choosing them from 15 to 44, while the under-chosen subjects, numbering 45, are chosen by no one or by 1 or 2 individuals. Likewise in Group A1 (N = 133), in which 17 percent are over-chosen (22/133), the number by whom they are chosen extends from 13 to 21 other individuals, but the under-chosen who constitute 14 percent (19/133) are either chosen by no one or by 1 other

---

[1] The frequency distribution for AB is given in a previously published report; see H. H. Jennings, "Quantitative Aspects of Tele Relationships in a Community," *Sociometry*, II:IV:93-100, Oct., 1939, p. 94.

individual; and in Group A_{II} in which 16 percent are over-chosen (22/133) the number by whom they are chosen extends from 16 to 24 individuals, while the under-chosen who comprise 17 percent (22/133) are chosen by from zero to 3 individuals.

Within the total test-population there is found a slight positive correlation ($r = .30$ for A_I; $r = .20$ for AB; see Table V, p. 50) between the extent of positive expansiveness towards the subject and the subject's positive expansiveness towards others on Test I but after eight months of further participation together in the community, the correlation drops to insignificance ($r = .12$, A_{II}). It need not follow that there is no correlation between the extent of expansiveness accorded the over-chosen and their extent of expansiveness towards the population. Nor need it follow that no correlation exists between the extent to which lack of expansiveness is accorded the under-chosen and their extent of expansiveness towards the population. Since both the under-chosen and the over-chosen cover relatively but a small portion of the range for positive choice to the subject of the test-population as a whole, there might be some relationship in both instances in spite of the findings for the total test-population. However, there is found no significant correlation for either the under-chosen or the over-chosen in either AB or A_I or A_{II}. (See Table VI.) Moreover, at whatever level the extent of choice by and to the subject is examined, this is found to be true. *E.g.:* six subjects among the over-chosen in AB are chosen by from 25 to 44 individuals; they themselves choose from 5 to 10 individuals: one, 5; one, 6; two, 8; and two, 10. In this group the most expansive subject chooses 24 and is chosen by only 18; and one subject chooses and is chosen by the same number,

16 persons. In A_{II}, the 21 over-chosen subjects choose from 5 to 15 individuals and are chosen by from 16 to 24; within the range of their choice for others, 8 are below, 9 above and 4 at the mean of the distribution for A_{II} as a whole. Similarly, the under-chosen show a lack of proportionate use of choice in accordance with the extent to which they are under-chosen. Of the 45 under-chosen of AB, 14 are unchosen, 17 are chosen by one, 14 by two; yet the unchosen choose from 4 to 15 individuals, the one-choice receivers choose from 2 to 10 persons, and the two-choice receivers choose from 2 to 13 others, while in each instance the distribution of number chosen by the subject is about equally unrelated to the degree to which they are themselves under-chosen. Even when inspection is made of the 9 subjects who are three-choice receivers among the under-chosen of A_{II}, four are found to have chosen from 2 to 5 persons, and five, to have chosen from 9 to 16 persons.

Thus the extent of exceptional emotional expansiveness expressed for the subject does not apparently result in his expressing proportionately exceptional emotional expansiveness towards the population in which he is over-chosen. Likewise the extent of meagerness of emotional expansiveness expressed for the subject does not apparently accompany an expression by him which is in turn proportionately meager towards the population in which he is under-chosen. Individuals generally do not evidently depart to any appreciable extent from the expression of their emotional expansiveness according to the manner in which the situation in which they are is structured in respect to them. On the contrary, the individual's capacity for emotional expansiveness appears as a relatively constant characteristic which is not so elastic that he can readily extend or reduce its expression according as others "want" or "don't want" him, are receptive to him or inexpansive to him. The range of the *individual's* choice, the fluctuation he shows in number chosen at different times, is apparently *stable within his repertoire of expression.* Whether the structure of the situation in which he finds himself invites choice from him or rebuffs choice by him, he appears impelled to find an outlet in expression for others which is determined more by his own need for and response to others than by theirs for him.

Nevertheless, although no correlation is found between the extent of expansiveness of either the over-chosen subject

TABLE VI. CORRELATIONS ON CHOICE AND CONTACT-RANGE: OVER-CHOSEN AND UNDER-CHOSEN

	r	Zr/σz
Number choosing the subject 1 S.D. above the mean in Group AB (N. 236) and number chosen by the subject, Test I; N. 37 (16%).	.001	
Same for Group A_I (N. 133), Test I; N. = 22 (17%).	.17	.75
Same for Group A_II (N. 133), Test II; N. = 21 (16%).	.24	1.02
Number choosing the subject 1 S.D. below the mean in Group AB (N. 236) and number chosen by the subject, Test I; N. = 45 (19%).	.00	
Same for Group A (N. 133); Test I; N = 19 (14%).	.00	
Same for Group A (N. 133); Test II; N. = 22 (17%).	.00	
Number choosing the subject 1 S.D. above the mean in Group AB (N. 236) and the subject's contact range, Test I; N. = 37 (16%).	.63	4.36
Number choosing the subject 1 S.D. above the mean in Group A_I (N. 133) and the subject's contact range, Test I; N. = 22 (17%).	.36	1.64
Number choosing the subject 1 S.D. above the mean or lower to include down to 9 choices received Group A_I (N. 133) and the subject's contact range, Test I; N. = 43 (32%).	.13	.87
Number outside own housing group choosing the subject 1 S.D. above the mean in Group AB (N. 236) and the subject's contact range, Test I; N. = 35 (15%).	.59	3.77
Number choosing the subject 1 S.D. below the mean in Group AB (N. 236) and the subject's contact range, Test I; N. = 45 (19%).	—.01	
Number choosing the subject 1 S.D. below the mean in Group A_I (N. 133) and the subject's contact range, Test I; N. = 19 (14%).	.01	

or the under-chosen subject and the extent of expansiveness towards them, both the over-chosen *as a group* and the under-chosen *as a group* do appear to show certain differences as compared with each other and as compared with the test-population as a whole in respect to emotional expansiveness.

The under-chosen show a mean of 6.58 individuals chosen by the subject in AB; 6.89 by the subject in A_I, and 8.27 by the subject in A_{II}. The over-chosen show a mean of 8.73 individuals chosen by the subject in AB; 9.59 in A_I; and 8.48 in A_{II}. Thus both the under-chosen and the over-chosen differ from the subjects as a whole: the mean for AB in number chosen by the subject is 7.78, for A_I, 7.86, for A_{II}, 8.39. The under-chosen as a group show a smaller performance on the average in positive expansiveness to others than the test-population as a whole on Test I and the over-chosen as a group, a somewhat greater performance on the average. Yet, both under-chosen and over-chosen on Test II approach approximately the same mean as the test-population when there is an insignificant rise for the subjects as a whole $(D/\sigma D = 1.65)$. It thus appears that neither the under-chosen nor the over-chosen as a group, although they differ from each other and from the population as a whole in emotional expansiveness towards others at the time of Test I, maintains a difference in emotional expansiveness from that of the test-population generally by the time of Test II, eight months later. The base from which the subject may choose or be chosen does not affect the result as it is practically limitless, 442 for A_I and 456 for A_{II}, the total population less the one individual chooser.

An explanation of the findings appears when inquiry is directed into whether the under-chosen and the over-chosen on Test II are the same subjects who respectively comprised the under- and over-chosen on Test I. Then psychological as well as practical implications are seen to underlie the results. The over-chosen may be considered first.

The mean number by whom the individual of the general population is chosen rises from 7.21 in A_I to 9.4 persons in A_{II}, and the standard deviation also shows an increase, from 5.14 in A_I to 5.62 in A_{II}, so that ranking among the over-chosen does not register an equal absolute measure of the extent to which the subject is chosen on both occasions: it registers instead an equal *relative* standing in respect to the standing of the subjects as a whole.   To be among the over-chosen in A_I requires being chosen by 13 or more and in A_{II}, being chosen by 16 or more individuals.   There might be a completely different group of subjects over-chosen at one time and over-chosen at the later time.   Actually, however, there is found great over-lap.   Of the 21 subjects in A_{II} who meet the requirement of being chosen by 16 or more persons, 11 ranked among the over-chosen in A_I, 4 others were within two or one choice of this rank, and all but 2 of the 21 were at or much above the mean of the population in number of individuals choosing them.   Thus for the over-chosen of A_{II} as a group, the situation of being chosen to an exceptional degree is not new.

When members of a population spontaneously show much regard for an individual over a period of some duration, the need for that individual to seek others may become less and less a necessity and result rather in a relative withdrawal in the extent to which he expends affect towards others.   At the same time, it appears that his relative withdrawal in *extent* of emotional expansiveness to many is accompanied by a more *intensive* expenditure of affect towards a fewer number.   (See Chapter IX.)   The decrease in extent of positive choice for others on the part of the over-chosen will be subsequently discussed as it is reflected in shifts in the patterns of their relationships.   (See Chapter V.)

The under-chosen in some respects show the reverse of this reaction. In distinction from the group of over-chosen, the group of under-chosen show an increase in emotional expansiveness from A_I to A_{II}. To be among the under-chosen of A_I requires being chosen by no one or by one person, and this registers an equal *relative* standing only in respect to the population as a whole since to be among the under-chosen of A_{II} requires being chosen by no one, by one, two or three persons. (See above.) Of the 22 under-chosen in A_{II}, 12 are among the under-chosen in A_I, 5 are chosen by two, and all with but one exception are below the mean of A_I. There are 5 subjects chosen by no one in A_{II}; these five unchosen subjects were also among the unchosen in A_I. The individuals who are under-chosen in A_{II} thus appear in the main as chronic occupants of the lower end of the range in attractiveness to others, as measured by the number who express positive choice for them. Yet they as a group are at the mean of the general population of A_{II} in extent of positive choice for others, showing a mean of 8.27 compared with a mean of 8.39 for A_{II} as a whole. In fact, the 11 least chosen among them (5 unchosen and 6 chosen by one) average 8.64 persons chosen, or slightly above the mean of A_{II}. Their positive choice range is also practically as wide as that for the general population, a number of them placing almost at the top of the range, others placing at the lower extreme, and the remainder at the mean. See Table VII. Furthermore, the 17 subjects who in A_I were among the under-chosen or else chosen by only two persons and are found among the under-chosen of A_{II} show a mean of 7.41 in positive choice for others on Test I; hence their performance differs little from the mean of A_I as a whole (*i.e.*, 7.86). It therefore appears that the fact of their being "chronically under-chosen" cannot be referred to an essential lack in extent of positive expansiveness on their own part towards others who in turn respond little to them.

In this connection, it is noted that among the under-chosen in A_I are 7 subjects who in A_{II} become chosen to an average or somewhat below average extent; 5 of these subjects show an average of 5.20 individuals chosen on Test I and an average of 8.60 individuals chosen on Test II. (The other two subjects exceed the mean somewhat on both occasions.) There appears a more dynamic interplay between the under-chosen subject and his situation in at least five of the instances in which the situation is to alter favorably than between the under-chosen subject and his situation in the 17 instances in which the subject does not move to a more favorably structured situation. In the first case, the subjects appear to "withhold" their full expression towards others, as though they were sensitive to the lack in reception meeting their attraction to others; in the latter case, the subjects show no such "reaction" to their situation. Nor does examination of the 17 individuals' repertoire of choice expression at one time and at a later time reveal them to differ in this respect from the individuals of the general population. Like them, the 17 vary in the main between $+3$ and -2 in the number they choose on Test II compared with Test I (see Table III, p. 49) with a few scattering above and below this range of change. (This finding in a sense is to be expected since they are as variable as the general population in the range of their choice expression, but it need not necessarily follow.) They show themselves "normal" both in quantitative output of positive expansiveness towards others and in repertoire of extent to which they as individuals are drawn to others at one time and at a later time.

Social Expansiveness: Over-chosen and Under-chosen

Within the test-population as a totality, the extent of the subject's social expansiveness as measured by the number of individuals with whom he initiates or maintains contact shows a slight correlation with his positive emotional expansiveness, just high enough to be significant ($r = .18$, AB; $r = .22$, A_I). It may or may not follow that the under-chosen and the over-chosen show a similarly slight relationship between these two variables. However, no significantly higher or lower relationship between emotional expansiveness and social expansiveness appears, in this instance, to distinguish the under-chosen from the over-chosen or either from the general population; in fact, as both the under- and the over-chosen are so few in number, even the low significant correlation for the subjects as a whole does not appear. (For r's and critical ratios, see Table VI.) It will be recalled that both the under-chosen and the over-chosen are found to scatter throughout the range of positive expression of choice for others.

On the other hand, the extent of the subject's social expansiveness correlates to a more considerable degree with emotional expansiveness towards him ($r = .40$, AB; $r = .29$, A_I). It may or may not follow that the over-chosen and the under-chosen contribute to the degree of this correlation.

The extent of positive choice to the over-chosen subjects of AB correlates with the subjects' social contact range at .63, an r exceeding that found for the test-population as a whole. The over-chosen of A_I show, however, a correlation not high enough to indicate significance: $r = .36$, C. R. = 1.64. (See Table VI, p. 70.) The under-chosen of both AB and of A_I show no relationship whatever ($r = .00$). It will be recalled that the over-chosen of AB were chosen by from 15 to 44 individuals; the over-chosen of A_I, by from 13 to 21 individuals. Thus the correlation between the subject's social contact range and the extent to which he is chosen appears high only for the subjects who are *most* chosen by the population. The over-chosen of AB comprise 16 percent of AB; the over-chosen of A_I comprise 17 percent of A_I. A higher correlation is found between social contact range and extent of choice to the subject if only the subjects who comprise the upper half (or less) in either group are considered, *i.e.*, the most chosen 8 percent (or less). But examining a larger percent of subjects extending downward in the range of choice to include subjects who are chosen by 9 or more individuals shows no significant correlation (*e.g.*, in A_I, r then $= .13$).

A further finding is notable. The over-chosen are subjects who are chosen to the extent of 1 S.D. above the mean of the population. Thus the extent of choice to them is measured by the number of persons choosing them from the entire population. If, on the other hand, the over-chosen are considered as comprised only of the subjects who are chosen by others *outside their own living unit* to the extent of 1 S.D. above the mean of the population, the correlation is found to be .59 for AB. Thus it appears not only that the most highly chosen subjects show a considerable correlation between the extent of emotional expansiveness towards them and the extent of their own social expansiveness, but that this correlation is equally high and significant under the condition of excluding those choices to them coming from individuals within their own housing unit. The reason lies in the fact that the subjects in general in this community who are highly chosen *within* their own housing unit are also highly chosen by the membership of the community as a whole. There are also subjects who show a large social-contact-range and yet the population is very sparse in expression of positive choice for them. The subjects who are singled out by the population for choice to an exceptional degree more likely than not are individuals whose social expansiveness *is* correlated to the degree to which they are singled out.

As a group, moreover, the over-chosen somewhat exceed the mean of the population in social expansiveness: they show a mean social contact range of 56.44 for AB and 54.88 for A_I, compared with the test-population's mean of 50.5 for AB and 47.7 for A_I. The under-chosen as a group fall below the mean of the subjects as a whole: they show a mean social contact range of 25.38 for AB and 26.02 for A_I. This finding suggests that there may be a slight tendency for individuals who are more or less excluded from choice by others to be individuals who themselves show decidedly less than average social initiative in contacting and maintaining contacts with others; and, on the other hand, for individuals who are greatly "over" chosen by others to be individuals who themselves show more than average social initiative in contacting and maintaining contacts with others. It may equally well also suggest the interpretation that in the one case social initiative is encouraged by the "warmth" of reception of the individual and in the other, discouraged by the lack of such warmth. In any event, the social expansiveness of the over-chosen subjects generally appears to have a basis different from that which appears for that of the population generally or for the few individuals among the under-chosen who show an almost equal social contact range. (See chap. IX.) The finding that it has so apparently different a basis is, in a sense, not surprising since the over-chosen find exceptional emotional expansiveness meeting their exceptional social expansiveness, and this is true for no other group in the population.

Well-chosen and Isolated or Near-isolated

The spread and focus of choice resulting in a section within the population which is over-chosen and another section which is under-chosen (whatever points are arbitrarily taken to mark off either) may be studied from another standpoint: How do the over-chosen and the under-chosen react to each other, between them what relations exist, and how do they react to the population as a whole which has thus reacted to them?

For such an analysis, subjects who are extremely little chosen are studied as they react to and are reacted to by those who are well-chosen. In the two groups, at one end are taken subjects who are isolated from choice (unchosen) or chosen by only one person, and at the other extreme, subjects who are chosen well above average, *i.e.*, at least by twelve or more persons. A sharp psychological contrast in choice-status is thus provided even though the well-chosen are not all chosen to the same extent as the over-chosen, *i.e.*, by sixteen or more on Test II. The well-chosen group, as defined, of course includes the over-chosen and, in addition, provides a wider base for the analysis than the over-chosen alone would present. (The comparison for the latter group singly may be made by inspection of the total data given in Table VIII.) For the analysis, the data on choice and rejection as given on Test II are examined; using A_{II} (in preference to A_I) omits the inclusion of individuals among the "isolated or near-isolated" or among the "well-chosen" whose presence in either section of the population may be a transitory stage in their relation to others or of others to them. Each section on A_{II} has become constituted in large part of those who "belong" in the respective section. For convenience of later reference (in chap. IX), fictionized names for the subjects are included in Tables VII and VIII in which the data are presented.

The term "isolated" (and the term "near-isolated"), as employed, connotes the status *given* by the membership of the community as a whole to the individuals whom they do not choose; it in no sense indicates that the unchosen (or little chosen) are isolated of their own accord for if this were the case, they would not express choice for others. All the evidence of the present research suggests the contrary conclusion: the interpretation that such individuals as are "isolated" or "near-isolated" in the community under study neither desire this status in respect to their peers, or become reconciled and in time inured to it. Likewise, the term "well-chosen" connotes the status given by the population's membership to certain of its members. It in no sense should be taken to indicate that these individuals are fully aware of their status in respect to others, nor even that they necessarily "are happy" because of this status. There are many "varieties" of well-chosen and many "varieties" of isolates. (See case studies, Chapter IX.)

The "isolated" (totally unchosen, 5) and "near-isolated" (chosen by only one individual, 6) comprise 11 subjects in A_{II}. The five isolated on Test II were also isolated on Test I. Of the six near-isolated, two were also chosen by only 1 individual on Test I (Alice, Ruth); two had been chosen on Test I by 2 individuals (Eva, Amelia); one had been chosen by 4 individuals (Martha); and one had been

TABLE VII. SPREAD AND FOCUS OF CHOICE AND REJECTION BETWEEN ISOLATED OR NEAR-ISOLATED AND BETWEEN ISOLATED OR NEAR-ISOLATED AND WELL-CHOSEN (with the total number chosen or rejected by or choosing or rejecting the isolated or near-isolated)

TEST II

"Well-chosen" denotes chosen by 12 or more. "Isolated" or "Near-isolated" chosen by 1 or none.

S = subject
N. = 11

Total	No. of individuals				No. of isolated or near-isolated				No. of well-chosen			
	chosen by S.	choosing S.	rejected by S.	rejecting S.	chosen by S.	choosing S.	rejected by S.	rejecting S.	chosen by S.	choosing S.	rejected by S.	rejecting S.
Anna	8	1	4	3	—	—	—	—	4	—	1	4
Alice	6	1	7	15	—	—	—	—	5	1	—	4
Margo	8	—	3	16	—	—	—	1	2	—	—	4
Vera	9	—	4	18	—	—	1	—	4	—	—	4
Mary	16	—	6	12	—	—	—	—	6	—	—	1
Martha	8	1	6	13	—	—	—	—	3	—	1	3
Ruth	10	1	2	7	—	—	—	—	1	—	—	1
Jessie	9	—	4	17	—	—	—	—	2	—	—	6
Amelia	15	1	11	—	—	—	—	—	6	—	4	—
Ida	3	—	2	11	—	—	—	—	1	—	—	1
Eva	3	1	3	3	—	—	—	—	2	—	—	—
Totals	95	6	52	115	0	0	1	1	36	1	6	25

TABLE VIII. SPREAD AND FOCUS OF CHOICE AND REJECTION BETWEEN WELL-CHOSEN AND BETWEEN WELL-CHOSEN AND ISOLATED OR NEAR-ISOLATED (with the total number chosen or rejected by or choosing and rejecting the well-chosen)

TEST II

"Well-chosen" denotes chosen by 12 or more. "Isolated" or "Near-isolated" chosen by 1 or none.

S = subject
N. = 46

	Total	No. of individuals				No. of well-chosen				No. of isolated or near-isolated			
		chosen by S.	choosing S.	rejected by S.	rejecting S.	chosen by S.	choosing S.	rejected by S.	rejecting S.	chosen by S.	choosing S.	rejected by S.	rejecting S.
Vivian		9	12	6	10	—	2	3	4	—	1	1	2
Gladys		13	12	5	2	6	3	1	1	—	1	—	—
Magdeline		15	14	5	11	5	3	1	1	—	1	—	1
Bertha		8	15	4	—	3	3	1	—	—	1	—	—
Elizabeth		10	19	5	7	3	3	1	1	—	1	—	—
Agnes		4	12	3	3	3	6	—	1	—	—	1	—
Jacqueline		10	22	5	—	3	4	—	—	—	1	1	—
Helen		6	19	—	3	3	5	1	1	—	1	—	—
Annette		12	14	5	1	5	3	1	—	—	—	1	—
Beta		9	14	5	2	5	2	1	1	—	1	—	—
Catherine		15	22	7	1	4	7	1	—	—	1	1	—
Marie		7	17	2	1	5	5	—	1	1	1	—	—
Mabel		9	17	5	—	4	4	—	—	—	—	2	—

TABLE VIII. SPREAD AND FOCUS OF CHOICE AND REJECTION BETWEEN WELL-CHOSEN AND BETWEEN WELL-CHOSEN AND ISOLATED OR NEAR-ISOLATED (with the total number chosen or rejected by or choosing and rejecting the well-chosen) — (*Continued*)

TEST II

"Well-chosen" denotes chosen by 12 or more. "Isolated" or "Near-isolated" chosen by 1 or none.

S = subject

N. = 46

Subject	No. of individuals				No. of well-chosen				No. of isolated or near-isolated			
	chosen by S.	choosing S.	rejected by S.	rejecting S.	chosen by S.	choosing S.	rejected by S.	rejecting S.	chosen by S.	choosing S.	rejected by S.	rejecting S.
Lucille	8	17	8	—	3	4	—	—	—	2	2	—
Marjorie	11	17	6	2	4	4	—	—	—	1	2	—
Barbara	5	14	4	2	1	4	—	—	—	1	1	1
Olga	12	19	4	2	4	6	—	—	—	1	1	—
Jean	7	24	4	2	3	2	—	—	—	1	1	1
Becky	8	23	3	4	2	3	—	—	—	2	—	—
Natalie	5	16	4	4	2	4	—	1	—	1	—	—
Mildred	10	15	4	—	2	1	1	—	—	1	—	—
Virginia	8	15	6	3	2	3	1	1	—	1	—	—
Isabelle	9	12	6	2	7	3	1	—	—	1	1	—
Josephine	17	15	3	—	4	1	1	—	—	—	—	—
Henriette	10	12	6	—	4	4	—	—	—	1	—	—
Cornelia	12	15	10	2	4	3	1	—	—	1	1	—

TABLE VIII. SPREAD AND FOCUS OF CHOICE AND REJECTION BETWEEN WELL-CHOSEN AND BETWEEN WELL-CHOSEN AND ISOLATED OR NEAR-ISOLATED (with the total number chosen or rejected by or choosing and rejecting the well-chosen)—(*Continued*)

TEST II

Total	No. of individuals				No. of well-chosen				No. of isolated or near-isolated			
"Well-chosen" denotes chosen by 12 or more. "Isolated" or "Near-isolated" chosen by 1 or none. S = subject N. = 46	chosen by S.	choosing S.	rejected by S.	rejecting S.	chosen by S.	choosing S.	rejected by S	rejecting S.	chosen by S.	choosing S.	rejected by S.	rejecting S.
Eleanor	16	12	—	1	3	—	—	—	—	—	—	—
Lois	8	20	9	5	2	4	—	1	—	—	—	—
Dora	6	18	3	—	2	3	—	—	—	1	—	—
Grace	8	12	7	7	2	2	—	—	—	—	—	—
Clara	13	16	6	—	1	1	—	—	—	—	1	—
Augustine	5	15	4	4	—	1	—	—	—	—	—	—
Olive	13	12	3	9	1	2	—	1	—	1	1	—
Beatrice	6	16	3	1	5	4	—	1	—	1	1	—
Minna	9	18	5	2	5	1	—	1	—	—	1	—
Martha	5	13	4	1	5	4	1	—	—	—	1	—
Betty	13	13	8	5	5	4	1	—	—	1	1	—

TABLE VIII. SPREAD AND FOCUS OF CHOICE AND REJECTION BETWEEN WELL-CHOSEN AND BE-TWEEN WELL-CHOSEN AND ISOLATED OR NEAR-ISOLATED (with the total number chosen or rejected by or choosing and rejecting the well-chosen)—(Continued)

TEST II

"Well-chosen" denotes chosen by 12 or more. "Isolated" or "Near-isolated" chosen by 1 or none.

S = subject
N. = 46

Total	No. of individuals				No. of well-chosen				No. of isolated or near-isolated			
Subject	chosen by S.	choosing S.	rejected by S.	rejecting S.	chosen by S.	choosing S.	rejected by S.	rejecting S.	chosen by S.	choosing S.	rejected by S.	rejecting S.
Cecilia	5	17	3	1	3	2	—	—	—	1	1	—
Edith	6	17	7	3	3	7	1	—	—	1	1	—
Sally	7	14	4	5	6	2	—	1	—	—	—	—
Gertrude	9	18	—	—	3	2	—	—	—	2	—	—
Jane	11	14	4	—	3	5	—	—	—	1	—	—
Elsa	15	14	6	5	3	2	1	—	—	1	—	1
Thelma	8	17	—	—	3	4	—	—	—	2	1	—
Sarah	4	12	1	—	2	4	—	—	—	2	—	—
Lillian	7	13	1	2	2	3	—	1	1	1	—	—
Totals	423	724	202	116	148	148	18	18	1	36	25	6

isolated on Test I (Anna). The "well-chosen" comprise 46 subjects in A_{II}. All but 9 of the 46 were above the mean of A_I, none were among the under-chosen of A_I, and 25 were chosen by 12 or more also on Test I. Thus the well-chosen, like the isolated or near-isolated, show from Test I to Test II a tendency to stay within the same area of the distribution of positive choice expression by the population. The population as a whole has consistently maintained its attraction to the members who are a well-chosen group on re-test and likewise has maintained its lack of attraction to the members who are an isolated or near-isolated group on the re-test. Therefore the reaction of these subjects to the "press" of others towards them may be considered a more or less characteristic reaction for them.

The great disparity between the positive emotional expansiveness of the population towards the well-chosen and towards the isolated or near-isolated is found to be accentuated by the vastly greater extent to which they reject the latter as compared with the extent to which they focus rejection upon the well-chosen. The 46 well-chosen are given 724 positive choices by individuals to 116 rejections; or 86 percent positive to 14 percent negative expressions. The 11 isolated or near-isolated are given 6 positive choices to 115 rejections by the membership, or 5 percent positive to 95 percent negative reactions. Under these circumstances, it is a surprising finding that the proportion of positive to negative reactions given *by* both groups shows no difference. The well-chosen show 68 percent positive to 32 percent negative reactions (423 positive, 202 negative); the isolated or near-isolated show 65 percent positive to 35 percent negative reactions (95 positive, 52 negative). The finding further supports the evidence given earlier (see p. 58) that the individual's own reaction to the total structure of others' reactions to him in the situation in which he finds himself is usually but little affected by the nature of the structure, but determined by his own repertoire of reaction to others and that this reaction is an expression of needs which are, so to speak, so "central" to his personality that he must strive to fulfill them whether or not the possibility of fulfilling them is at hand or not.

The isolated or near-isolated may, of course, not be completely aware of or have any definite sense of how the situation is structured in respect to them. But it can hardly be supposed that they are totally unmindful that they are not, as compared with others, "wanted" by others. That this is so is evidenced by the fact that they expend 37 percent of their choices to the well-chosen (36/95) who are the only group within the membership of the population which as a group cannot be observed to "betray" their feeling in the behavior they show to them. (See Chaps. VIII and IX.) They also expend 11 percent (6/52) of their rejections to the well-chosen. The implication of this finding is clear when it is recalled that the well-chosen comprise only 10 percent of the whole population (46/457). The disproportionately great attraction that the well-chosen constitute for the isolated or near-isolated must be sought in the whole behavior picture of both groups singly and also in relation to each other. (Chaps. VIII and IX.) The isolated or near-isolated are found likely to turn in choice to the well-chosen because of the reception they receive elsewhere, and also *naturally* to turn to them because of the greater satisfaction coming to them from contact with the well-chosen. The well-chosen do not, nevertheless, choose them. Instead they express for them 12 percent of all their rejections towards the population (25/202). But it is notable that this percent is no higher than that which the isolated or near-isolated express for the well-chosen. It is evidence of *active* contact between them, as well as a registering of what may be considered a natural reaction on the part of both to each other as a group. (See Chaps. VIII and IX.) The isolated or near-isolated as a group fail by a large margin to fall within the liberal tolerance of the well-chosen, and the latter show themselves skilled in daily disguising this fact.

The one choice made by a well-chosen individual to a near-isolated individual results in a mutually positive structure. But of the 36 choices of isolated or near-isolated for well-chosen subjects, 12 or 33 percent result in rejection by the well-chosen, or incongruous mutual structures of positive and negative choice. There is only one such incongruous mutual structure among the 46 well-chosen subjects. On the other hand, there is one mutual rejection between a near-isolated and a well-chosen, but among the well-chosen among themselves there are 6 mutually negative structures, or 33 percent (6/18) of their rejections for each other. Again, whereas the well-chosen, who comprise 10 percent of the total population (46/457), expend 35 percent (148/423) of their positive choices among each other, 64 percent (94/148) of their choices for each other result in mutually positive expressions. In only one instance is there any reaction whatever between isolated and near-isolated among themselves, and then it is one lone rejection. Thus neither positively nor negatively do they respond to each other. The well-chosen, on the other hand, not only show much active response to each other but also a high incidence of mutual response, positive to positive, and rejection to rejection.

It is in point to examine choice to the well-chosen in the perspective of how *much* wanted they are, as well as how widely they are wanted, in the community under study, by inspection of the choices expressed for them. In one respect, a *first* choice can be assumed to have for each chooser the same strength relative to other choices: it registers the subject's expression for the person chosen as *most* wanted on the criterion of the choosing. The population gives to the 46 well-chosen subjects 724 choices; 220 of these choices, or 30 percent, are expressed as a first choice. The well-chosen are thus chosen as first choice by an average of 4.78 persons. (Duplication of choice on more than one criterion is not included in the analysis.) Further, the over-chosen among the well-chosen (hence the more highly chosen among them) show an average of 5.62 persons choosing them on a first choice basis. Thus the well-chosen are distinguished from the least-chosen not only by number of choices received but also by the strength which is expressed in the choices received.[2]

Between the interval of Test I and Test II, 66 individuals entered the community as newcomers and were placed in the housing units of the subjects of this report. On Test II, the well-chosen 10 percent are found to have 45 mutually positive choices with the newcomers and to have received 59 percent of the choices which the latter express for the subjects of A_{II} (128/217). It thus appears that the well-chosen are also above average in facility to draw positive response from individuals who are relatively new to them as

[2] In general, intensity of choice appears related to the extent to which the individual feels he can communicate to the chosen person his problems and "innermost" thoughts and have them fully understood; see Chapter IX.

associates, that the well-chosen as a group apparently do not "retire" into old relationships exclusively, avoiding further effort in other directions, and that they are exceptional in spreading their choice-interest at various levels of the structure as well as throughout the level in which they themselves are.

Résumé

It appears that whereas the very much chosen and the very little chosen members of the population, both on Test I and on Test II, show no correlation between their respective expression of positive expansiveness and the extent of expansiveness shown towards them, thus resembling the findings for the general membership (see pp. 68-69), they nevertheless *as groups* differ from the general population and from each other at the time of Test I, the under-chosen showing a smaller performance on the average in emotional expansiveness towards others and the over-chosen a somewhat greater performance on the average. This difference, however, is not maintained at the time of Test II, eight months later.

Moreover, the social expansiveness of the individuals who are the most highly chosen members of the population shows a very much greater correlation with the extent to which they are chosen than is found for the general membership (in which the correlation is slight); the social expansiveness of the least chosen members, however, shows no relationship to the extent to which they are chosen.

Neither well-chosen subjects nor isolated or near-isolated subjects *as individuals* are found to differ from each other or from the population at large in the extent of their choice behavior towards others: their emotional expansiveness in choice for others as well as the extent to which they reject others appears determined not by the total structure of others' reactions to them but by the individual's own repertoire of reaction to others.

CHAPTER V

The Patterning of Interrelations

Is it sufficient to have a general knowledge of the choice process? Is not a particularized analysis of the constellation the choice process forms around one individual, as compared with that around other individuals, able to yield a more readily comprehensible comparison of the individual's characteristic differences *as a whole*?

As the individuals who are the carriers of the choice process stand in particular relation to one another, should not the question be: *in what ways* do they differ from one another in the *total structure* of their positive and negative choice relationships? Can the individual's constellation [1] of relationships be meaningfully compared as a unit with that of other members of the population so as to arrive at individual differences in total structure around each individual? In such a comparison, is there any "patterning" in the sense that the individual's rank in performance in one aspect of interrelations has a certain relation to his rank in performance in other aspects of his interrelations? Is there any tendency for the individual's rank in performance in one or several aspects of his relationships to others to be associated with a like (or an inverse) rank in all or some of the other aspects of his relationships?

How persistent are such patterns as are found? From one time to another eight months later, does the pattern shown

[1] The term *constellation* is used in Chapter V instead of the term *social atom* in order to simply the presentation of the data. See glossary, p. 324, for terms as experimentally defined in this research. Terms which have previously been employed by Moreno and the writer follow, whenever possible, previously used wording. (For examples of social atoms, see Sociograms 1-7, pp. 104-111.)

by the individual remain constant or does it alter? If it alters, does the change it registers occur in every possible way that it might occur or does it show changes "typical" for the kind of pattern it had on the first occasion — shifting only in given ways?

Up to this point, the analysis has been directed at various aspects of interrelations, each aspect considered *singly*. Further, the analysis studied the relation of each aspect singly to each other aspect, again, singly. Such a dissecting is, of course, artificial from a structural point of view. While it helps to throw light on the manner of operation of the choice process, it cannot lead to an understanding of individual differences in constellations formed by the choice process around the individual, and the interrelations between all aspects of emotional expansiveness, from the individual and towards him, taken as one unit, in the center of which is the individual. Such an attack is, however, important for the study of the problem of individual differences. By such an examination it becomes possible to view as one whole the individual's matrix of relationships in which he is actually functioning, and to compare it as one unit with the matrix formed around other individuals of which they are the active foci.

It thus appears necessary to examine as one total the positive and negative choice expressions by and towards the individual, together with the mutual expression between the individual and others. For this purpose, the positive expression of the subject for others, *i.e.*, the number of individuals chosen by him for inclusion in his life situation, may be called his performance in emotional expansiveness towards others. Likewise the positive expression by others for the subject, *i.e.*, the number of individuals choosing him for inclusion in their life situations, may be called the subject's performance in emotional expansiveness "achieved from" others. The positive reactions by the subject which are reciprocated by positive reactions from the individuals chosen may be called the subject's performance in positive reciprocation. The decision to include the measure of reciprocal reaction as an important performance (just as important as gross reaction by or towards the subject) rests on the finding reported previously (see Table V, p. 50) that such performance is significantly related to several aspects of interrelations. The negative reactions by and towards the subject and reciprocated rejections may likewise be considered as three further performances in which the subject may be compared with other subjects. Each performance of the subject may then be studied as it ranks in respect to the respective performance of the other subjects, with the mean being taken as dividing subjects who have a plus (+) score in a given performance from subjects who have a minus (—) score in the respective performance. The analysis aims to make readily visualizable (in a manner not possible unless the total constellation is studied) the nature of individual differences in all six aspects of the choice process examined in this research. Neither a + score nor a — score should be taken as indicating respectively a "creditable" or a "discreditable" performance; the study is exclusively concerned with how the individual's constellation of interrelations *varies from the mean of the group* on both occasions tested. (There will, of course, be subjects who barely place within a + score or who barely place within a — score on either occasion tested; consequently in comparison of the pattern of the individual on both Test I and Test II, a certain percentage of shifts in pattern is thus accounted for.)

In the present analysis, it is convenient to describe the scores on positive emotional expansiveness in a given order: first, the expression of the subject towards others (number chosen by him); second, the expression of others towards the subject (number choosing him); and third, the reciprocal expressions between the subject and others (number reciprocating the subject's choice to them). Thus, the subject who has a — score in each of the above performances ranks below the respective average performance of the test-population. It is further convenient to follow the same order in describing the scores on negative reaction. Then, the total six performances may be called for brevity, the choice-and-rejection pattern of the individual.

The presenting of the findings is simplified by referring to the first three performances (positive choice) as the individual's *choice pattern*; and the latter three performances (negative choice), as his *rejection pattern*. Either the choice pattern or the rejection pattern, considered separately, gives a partial picture of the structure of the individual's total constellation, given by his choice-rejection pattern as a unit.

The analysis is concerned exclusively with the patterns found for Group A, the 133 subjects who were present for both Test I and Test II.

The individual may vary from average in a plus or minus direction in three scores on positive expansiveness; hence, there are 8 possible choice patterns: $- - -$, $+ + +$, $+ - +$, $- + -$, $- - +$, $+ + -$, $+ - -$, and $- + +$. He may likewise vary in the same number of ways on rejection scores; hence, there are 8 possible rejection patterns.

The choice process has been found to be characterized by significant correlations between one or another aspect of emotional expansiveness or of rejection.   (See Table V, pp. 50-51.) The choice patterns and the rejection patterns consequently cannot have a chance frequency. The implications for the structure of the individual's constellation of choice and rejection interrelations are strikingly evident, however, only by inspection of the extent to which individuals are found to have particular patterns and the persistence or the fluctuation these patterns show.   In the analysis of Test I, the means for positive choice on AB are taken as the basis for comparison.

The largest group of the subjects on Test I is found to have a — — — pattern of positive choice, thus ranking below the mean of the test-population in number chosen, number chosen by, and number reciprocally choosing them.   These persons comprise 31 percent of the subjects. The second largest group of subjects, 24 percent, have a + — — choice pattern, being above the mean in number chosen but below in the other two expressions.   It will be noted that since many more than half of the members of the group place below the mean of the total group in number by whom they are chosen (69%) and in number by whom they are reciprocated (60%), patterns showing a — score in these two performances occur much more frequently than patterns having a + score in such performances. However, in the instance of the score for number chosen by the subject, half of the subjects place above (51%) and half below (49%) the mean of the total group.   Hence the positive choice patterns of — — — and + — — would be expected to be the most frequent patterns of positive choice.   (See Table IX.)

The + + + choice pattern is found for only 16 percent of the subjects, and each of the five other choice patterns is shown by 10 percent or fewer subjects. On Test II, the

TABLE IX. CHOICE-AND-REJECTION PATTERNS

TEST I

Positive Choice Pattern

Rejection Pattern	1 (− −)	2 (+ +)	3 (+ −)	4 (− +)	5 (− +)	6 (+ +)	7 (+ −)	8 (− +)	Total	Percent
1 (− −)	13	4	3	2	3	2	8	6	41	31
2 (+ +)	5	3	3	0	0	0	7	0	18	13
3 (+ −)	1	5	1	0	0	0	1	0	8	6
4 (− +)	3	3	0	0	1	0	0	2	9	7
5 (+ −)	3	1	0	0	0	0	0	1	5	4
6 (− +)	2	0	0	1	0	0	1	1	5	4
7 (− −)	4	5	3	0	3	2	8	3	28	21
8 (+ +)	10	1	1	0	1	0	5	1	19	14
Total	41	22	11	3	8	4	30	14	133	
Percent	31	16	8	2	6	3	24	10		100

TABLE IX. CHOICE-AND-REJECTION PATTERNS (*Continued*)

TEST II

Positive Choice Pattern

Rejection Pattern		1 − − −	2 + + +	3 + − +	4 − + −	5 − − +	6 + + −	7 + − −	8 − + +	Total	Percent
1	− − −	7	7	1	11	1	0	2	5	34	26
2	+ + +	5	4	2	0	2	0	3	2	18	13
3	+ − +	4	4	2	0	2	0	2	2	16	12
4	− + −	3	1	0	2	0	0	1	0	7	5
5	− − +	5	3	1	1	0	0	1	3	14	11
6	+ + −	1	1	1	0	0	0	0	0	3	2
7	+ − −	4	6	0	0	0	2	5	3	20	15
8	− + +	6	2	1	2	1	0	8	1	21	16
Total		35	28	8	16	6	2	22	16	133	
Percent		26	21	6	12	5	1	17	12		100

LEGEND: The 3 scores in each pattern refer respectively to the extent of: subject's reaction to others, others' reaction to the subject, and mutual reaction; + and − indicate whether the performance is above or below the mean of the population. See p. 94. For convenience the patterns are numbered.

same three patterns characterize the majority of the subjects and the same five patterns are relatively infrequent. The number of subjects in the − − − choice pattern has decreased to 26 percent, the number having a + − − pattern has decreased to 17 percent, and the + + + pattern shows an increased incidence, having 21 percent of the subjects. The rarest pattern on both occasions is that of + + −, shown by 3 percent of the subjects on Test I and by 1 percent on Test II; thus only very seldom does the individual rank above the average score in emotional expansiveness in choice for others and in choice from others and place below the average of others in reciprocation of choice from them. Also very rarely is the reverse situation found: only 6 percent on Test I and 5 percent on Test II show a − − + choice pattern, registering an above average score in reciprocation but a below average score in emotional expansiveness towards others and from others. Logically, of course, the + + − and the − − + patterns should be very rare since there is greater chance probability of reciprocation if the individual chooses many and also less chance probability of reciprocation if he chooses few and is chosen by few.

Thus certain choice patterns on both occasions are relatively frequent and certain other patterns on both occasions 8 months apart are relatively infrequent, for the same subjects; but the absolute incidence of a given pattern fluctuates from one time to another time.

The rejection patterns show findings remarkably similar to the results for the choice patterns. The same three patterns most frequent for positive choice are also most frequent for rejection, and in nearly the same order of frequency: on Test I: − − −, 31 percent; + − −, 21 percent; + + +,

13 percent. In difference from the positive choice pattern, however, the rejection pattern of − + + is more frequent, being shown by 14 percent of the subjects on Test I. With this exception, the least frequent positive choice patterns are also the least frequent rejection patterns on Test I. As in the case of choice patterns also, the rejection patterns which were found for the majority of the subjects on Test I are also found for the majority of the subjects on Test II. The rarest pattern on both tests is that of + + −, registering a below average performance in mutual rejection and above average scores in rejection given and received from others. This pattern shows the same infrequency for positive choice. The reverse of this pattern, − − +, however, increases from 4 to 11 percent for rejection, whereas it shows about an equally small percent for positive choice, from Test I to Test II.

It thus appears that the incidence of patterns at one time and at a later time in the same community is a relatively constant factor in the structure of attractions and in the structure of rejections which characterize it.

Yet, while the incidence of certain patterns may be relatively constant, the findings further show that the individuals occupying particular patterns at one time may or may not be the same individuals who occupy them at the later time. The subjects who remain in the same choice pattern on Test I and on Test II number 53, or 40 percent; the subjects who remain in the same rejection pattern on Test I and Test II number 46, or 35 percent. Thus the majority of the original occupants of a specific pattern have shifted to another pattern by the time of Test II, and the change is about equally great for both choice and rejection.

TABLE X. POSITIVE CHOICE PATTERNS

TEST I AND TEST II

Positive Choice Pattern on Test II

Positive Choice Pattern on Test I	1 (- - -)	2 (+ + +)	3 (+ - +)	4 (- + -)	5 (- - +)	6 (+ + -)	7 (+ - -)	8 (- + +)	Total shifting	Total Test I
1 (- - -)	19	5	4	5	1		3	4	22	41
2 (+ + +)	3	11		3				5	11	22
3 (+ - +)	3	1	2	2	2		1		9	11
4 (- + -)	1	1		0				1	3	3
5 (- - +)	1	2		3	0			2	8	8
6 (+ + -)		1				2		1	2	4
7 (+ - -)	7	4	1	1	1		16		14	30
8 (- + +)	1	3	1	2	2		2	3	11	14
Total shifts from Test I to II:	16	17	6	16	6	0	6	13	80	
Total remaining in same pattern:	19	11	2	0	0	2	16	3	53	
Total Test II:	35	28	8	16	6	2	22	16	133	133

LEGEND: The 3 scores in each pattern refer respectively to the extent of: the subjects' reaction to others, others' reaction to the subject, and mutual reaction; + and − indicate whether the performance is above or below the mean of the population. See p. 94. For convenience the patterns are numbered.

TABLE XI. REJECTION PATTERNS

TEST I AND TEST II

Rejection Pattern on Test II

Rejection Pattern on Test I	1 (− − −)	2 (+ + +)	3 (+ − +)	4 (− + −)	5 (− − +)	6 (+ + −)	7 (+ − −)	8 (− + +)	Total shifting	Total Test I
1 (− − −)	14	5	5	2	4		6	5	27	41
2 (+ + +)	5	7	1		1	1	1	2	11	18
3 (+ − +)	1		3		2		2		5	8
4 (− + −)	1			3	1		1	3	6	9
5 (− − +)	1		1		2	1			3	5
6 (+ + −)	1	1	1			0	1	1	5	5
7 (+ − −)	8	5	3	1	1	1	8	1	20	28
8 (− + +)	3		2	1	3		1	9	10	19
Total shifts from Test I to II:	20	11	13	4	12	3	12	12	87	
Total remaining in same pattern:	14	7	3	3	2	0	8	9	46	
Total Test II:	34	18	16	7	14	3	20	21	133	133

LEGEND: The 3 scores in each pattern refer respectively to the extent of: the subject's reaction to others, others' reaction to the subject, and mutual reaction; + and − indicate whether the performance is above or below the mean of the population. See p. 94. For convenience the patterns are numbered.

The choice patterns which show the greatest frequencies on Test I are retained by a relatively greater proportion of the same individuals on Test II than in the case of the infrequent patterns. (See Table X.) The rejection patterns show the same results, the more frequently occupied patterns on Test I retaining a relatively greater proportion of the original occupants on Test II. (See Table XI.) Certain patterns are occupied on Test II entirely by different individuals than on Test I: positive choice patterns $- + -$ and $- - +$. It may be that such patterns register transitory stages in interrelations, and that at a still later time all the individuals having these two patterns would be found to have shifted to another pattern. On the other hand, when a pattern which is very rarely found retains some of its occupants, it may be an indication that the pattern is peculiarly typical for the individuals retaining it. This appears to be the case for the two subjects who have a positive choice pattern of $+ + -$ on both tests. On the other hand, apparent lack of fitness for the individual's interrelation adjustments and a shifting which is "logical" may be reflected in the change of fourteen individuals from the choice pattern of $+ - -$ to other patterns, 7 of which changes may be considered to register more "satisfaction" to the individual (patterns 2, 3, 4, 5), and the other 7, to register a withdrawal to a $- - -$ pattern. On the other hand, the five shifts from a $+ + +$ choice pattern to a $- + +$ appear understandable as a "voluntary" withdrawal on the part of the individual in expression of emotional expansiveness towards others, as he is well intrenched in their positive choice for him. Again, individuals who have shown on Test I a pattern which reflects a "desirable" situation in interrelations with others do not appear invariably to be able to retain it. Three individuals move from a $+ + +$ choice pattern on Test I to a — — — choice pattern on Test II. The shifting, in general, however, reflects further growth in achieving positive relationships of choice with others. Twenty-two individuals move from a — — — pattern on Test I. The "irreconcilableness" of the individual to the kind of situation in which he may be in respect to those about him is also notable. Sixteen individuals who have a + — — positive choice pattern on Test I retain this pattern on Test II; they continue to express above average expansiveness towards others despite the under average expression found for them and the less than average reciprocation meeting their choice for others. Their repertoire of expansiveness does not alter accordingly.

The rejection patterns are not readily understandable apart from their respective positive choice patterns and must be considered with them.

As any one of the 8 possible choice patterns may be combined with any one of the 8 possible rejection patterns, there are 64 technically possible choice-rejection patterns. Since, of course, the number of subjects studied in this analysis is only 133, it would not, even by chance, be possible for all the patterns to show some occupants. Nevertheless, it is of interest how relatively few patterns are found for the test-group. The results reflect the fact that the choice process operates in particular ways. In the test-population only 52 choice-rejection patterns appear: 12 do not occur in either Test I or Test II. There are 8 other patterns which are occupied on Test I only and 12 which are occupied only on Test II. Of the 64 choice-rejection patterns, only 10 are shown on Test I by 5 or more individuals; only 10 also are shown on Test II by five or more individuals; and 7 of the 10 are the same patterns. (See Sociograms 1-7.)

LEGEND TO SOCIOGRAMS 1-7

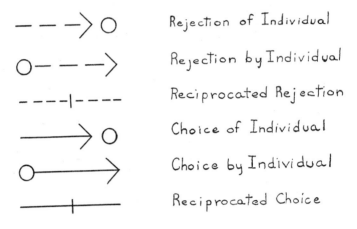

Rejection of Individual

Rejection by Individual

Reciprocated Rejection

Choice of Individual

Choice by Individual

Reciprocated Choice

The sociograms which follow illustrate the seven Choice-Rejection-Patterns most commonly found in the community of the study. In each instance, the sociogram presents an *extreme* example of the pattern in question as it is found in the social atom of a particular member of the community. Extreme examples were preferred for illustration so as to make the patterns readily distinguishable. For volume of positive and negative inter-personal reaction, the social atoms in Sociograms 1-7 may be compared with the average individual's social atom, as illustrated in Figure 2, p. 113.

Legend. The pattern represents the rank of the individual in respect to whether it is above $(+)$ or below $(-)$ the mean of the population in six performances: the first three relate to positive choice; the second three, to negative choice. The three scores $(+$ or $-)$ refer respectively to the extent of: the subject's reaction to others, others' reaction to the subject, and mutual reaction.

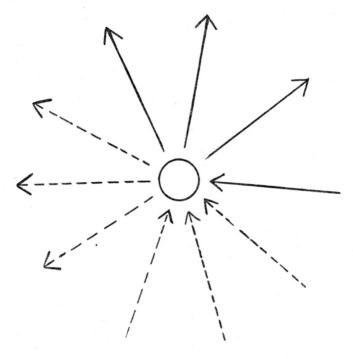

Sociogram 1

A Social Atom illustrating:

Choice-Rejection-Pattern — — — — — —

Shown by Eva; see Table VII and p. 118.

It is to be noted that this pattern is most frequent for individuals in isolated-or-near-isolated positions of choice-status. See Table XII

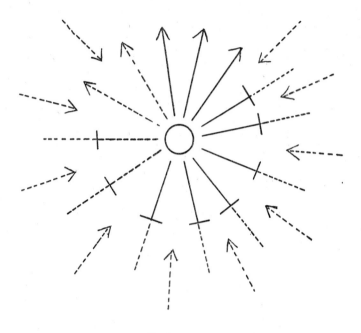

Sociogram 2

A Social Atom illustrating:

Choice-Rejection-Pattern + — — — + +

Shown by Vera; see Table VII and pp. 179-184.

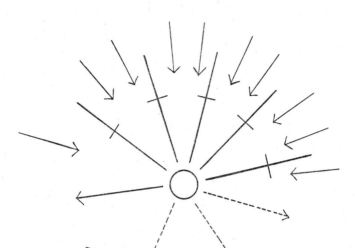

Sociogram 3
A Social Atom illustrating:
Choice-Rejection-Pattern — + + — — —
Shown by Beatrice; see Table VIII.

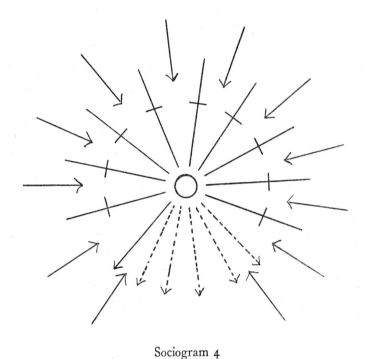

Sociogram 4

A Social Atom illustrating:

Choice-Rejection-Pattern + + + + − −

Shown by Jacqueline; see Table VIII and pp. 189-195.

It is to be noted that this pattern is most frequent for individuals in leader-positions of choice-status. See Table XIII.

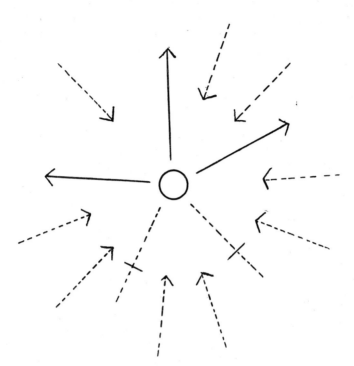

Sociogram 5
A Social Atom illustrating:
Choice-Rejection-Pattern — — —   — + +
Shown by Ida; see Table VII.

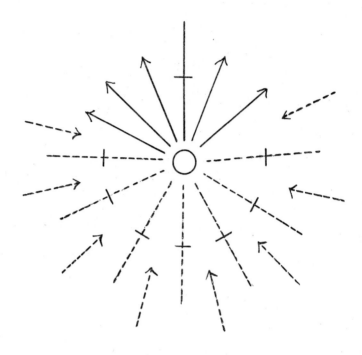

Sociogram 6

A Social Atom illustrating:

Choice-Rejection-Pattern — — —   + + +

Shown by Alice; see Table VII and p. 194.

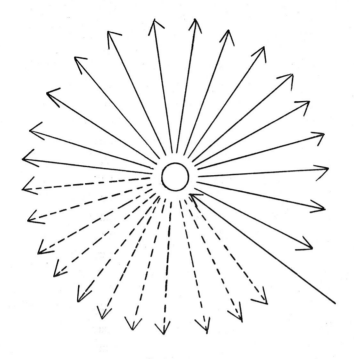

Sociogram 7
A Social Atom illustrating:
Choice-Rejection-Pattern $+ - -$ $+ - -$
Shown by Amelia; see Table VII and pp. 166-169.

The most frequent choice-rejection pattern on Test I consists of − − − − − −, registering an under average score in each of the six aspects of interrelations. On Test II, the pattern of − + − − − − is most frequent. The subjects who have a choice pattern registering a completer integration of their constellation of interrelations with the constellations of other individuals, than the pattern of − + − − − − indicates, show much more frequently than otherwise a + score in rejection of others. Conversely, individuals who show choice patterns having a − score in positive reciprocation frequently show rejection patterns also having a − score in negative reciprocation. Such individuals neither choose nor reject in the direction of like reaction centered on them. Only three of the sixteen subjects who on Test II have a choice pattern of − + − have a rejection pattern with a + score for mutuality; the three subjects who on Test I have a − + − choice pattern each have a − score in mutuality of rejection. On the other hand, a rejection pattern of + + +, registering the individual's performance as above the average of others in the extent to which he rejects others or is rejected by them and in the number of mutual rejections between himself and others, is found about equally often to have either a choice pattern of + + + or one of − − −.

A few individuals show on Test I choice-rejection patterns which no subjects show on Test II. In the light of the results on the choice process as it was found to operate at the two periods eight months apart, the eight choice-rejection patterns which have disappeared are patterns which cannot remain at the second period in view of the character of operation of the choice process. The correlations between various aspects of the choice process from the period of Test I to that of Test II preclude individuals retaining such patterns. Five of the choice-rejection patterns which were thus "destined" to disappear are: $+ - + + - - -$; $- - - + + - - -$; $+ + - - - - - -$; $- + + - + -$; $- + + + + -$. *E.g.* the inverse correlation found on Test I between the extent to which the subject is chosen and the

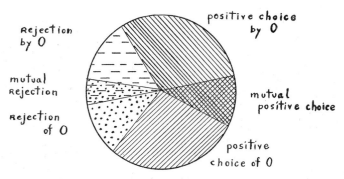

positive choice
by O

Rejection
by O

mutual
Rejection

Rejection
of O

mutual
positive choice

positive
choice of O

Fig. 2. Proportional Representation of Inter-Personal Positive Choice and Rejection for Official Grouping in the Average Individual's Social Atom

extent to which he is rejected becomes more accentuated on Test II, thus making the latter two mentioned patterns less possible of occurrence. On the other hand, twelve choice-rejection patterns not shown by any subject on Test I are found on Test II. (See Table IX.) Their appearance on the second occasion registers the more definite and particularized relationship that comes to mark positive choice and rejection *as a single process* the longer the period of inter-personal experience the individual has with others; at the earlier period this relationship was likewise significant but less marked. (See Chapter III.)

The picture of choice-rejection patterns for the subjects as a whole is very complex and ramified. Individual differences in pattern are very great. The shifts from one pattern to another from one time to another further complicate the

study of individual differences.   The patterns shown by the
individuals who are exceptionally well-chosen and by the
exceptionally under-chosen present, however, a very much
less complicated picture of interrelations.

For the purpose of examining patterns typical for the
individuals towards whom the population as a whole shows
unusual expansiveness in positive choice and towards whom
they show unusually little expansiveness in positive choice,
the subjects who respectively rank 1 S.D. above or below the
mean may be compared, without regard to whether or not
the position occurs on Test I or Test II or is shown by the
same individual on both occasions.   The position of 1 S.D.
above the mean of the population may be referred to as a
"leader-position" and that 1 S.D. below the mean of the
population, as an "isolated or near-isolated" position, as the
individuals occupying the respective positions are found in
the one instance to be recognized and given "leadership" by
the members of the community and in the other, to be hardly
at all recognized even as participants by the population as a
whole.   (See Chapter IX and footnote p. 119.)

There are 43 leader-positions and 41 isolated-or-near-
isolated positions, as defined, found on Test I and Test II,
counted together.   The number occurring on Test I and
Test II is in both instances approximately equal.

Individuals in an isolated-or-near-isolated position could
technically place in four possible choice patterns: — — —,
+ — +, — — +, or + — —.   They are found, however,
only in two of these patterns: 54 percent show a positive
choice pattern of — — — and 46 percent, a positive choice
pattern of + — —.   (See Table XII.)   They could technically place in any of the eight rejection patterns.   Thirty
percent show a — + + rejection pattern and 30 percent

also a — — — rejection pattern, with the next most frequent
pattern of rejection being + + +. Their choice-rejection
patterns are in order of frequencies: — — — — — — (9);
+ — — + + + (7); and + — — — — + + (7). Thus
only three choice-rejection patterns are found in 56 percent
of the instances (23/41).

Individuals in a leader-position could technically place in
four possible choice patterns: + + +, — + —, + + —,
or — + +. They are found, however, in 49 percent of the
instances to have a + + + pattern, in 35 percent to have a
— + + pattern, and only rarely in either of the other two
patterns. (See Table XIII.) Thus at the time an individual
has a leader-position he very likely will place above average
in mutual positive choice with other individuals. In marked
difference from the isolated-or-near-isolated, the individuals
in leader-positions show a + — — — rejection pattern in 40
percent of the instances, a pattern shown only in 2 percent
of the instances by the former group. Thus in 40 percent
of the instances, the individual in a leader-position in the
test-community is above average in the number of persons
he rejects while at the same time he is rejected by others to
a smaller extent than the average member of the population
and likewise has fewer than the average number of mutual
rejection structures between himself and others in his constellation of interrelations. Furthermore, if all the patterns
containing above average expression of rejection by the individual towards others are added together (rejection patterns
#2, #3, #6 and #7 in Table XIII), it appears that 56 percent
of the individuals in leader-positions, as contrasted with 23
percent of the individuals in isolated-or-near-isolated positions, are above average in the number of persons they reject.
Thus above average rejection of others is found more often

TABLE XII. CHOICE-REJECTION PATTERNS SHOWN BY 41 ISOLATED-OR-NEAR-ISOLATED-POSITIONS *

TEST I AND TEST II

Positive Choice Pattern

Rejection Pattern		1 - - -	2 + + +	3 + - +	4 - + -	5 - - +	6 + + -	7 + - -	8 - + +	Total	Percent
1	- - -	9						3		12	30
2	+ - +							7		7	17
3	+ + -							1		1	2
4	- + +	4								4	10
5	- - +	3								3	7
6	+ - -	1								1	2
7	+ - +							1		1	2
8	- + +	5						7		12	30
Total		22						19		41	
Percent		54						46			100

* Ranking 1 S.D. below the mean in choices received: Test I and Test II. Each pattern represents the rank of the individual who shows an "isolated-or-near-isolated-position," as compared with the mean of the test-population (above the mean being indicated by + and below, by —), in three performances: the first + or − in a given pattern represents the individual's expression towards others; the second, the expression of others towards him; and the third, the reciprocal expression between the individual and others. See p. 114. For convenience the patterns are numbered.

TABLE XIII. CHOICE-REJECTION PATTERNS SHOWN BY 43 LEADER-POSITIONS *

TEST I AND TEST II

Positive Choice Pattern

Rejection Pattern	1 - - -	2 + + +	3 + - +	4 - + -	5 - - +	6 + + -	7 + - -	8 - + +	Total	Percent
1		4		3				6	13	30
2		1						1	2	5
3		4							4	9
4		1						1	2	5
5		2						2	4	9
6				1					1	2
7		9				3		5	17	40
8									0	0
Total		21		4		3		15	43	
Percent		49		9		7		35		100

* Ranking 1 S.D. above the mean in choices received: Test I and Test II. Each pattern represents the rank of the individual who shows a "leader-position," as compared with the mean of the test-population (above the mean being indicated by + and below, by —), in three performances: the first + or — in a given pattern represents the individual's expression towards others; the second, the expression of others towards him; and the third, the reciprocal expression between the individual and others. See p. 115.

to characterize the interrelation pattern of individuals in the test-population who are very highly chosen.

The — + + rejection pattern found frequently for the isolated-or-near-isolated is totally absent for the individuals in leader-positions. The two groups, however, equally often show the — — — rejection pattern (30 percent for either group). The most frequent choice-rejection pattern for the individual in a leader-position is + + + + — —, as compared with the most frequent pattern of — — — — — — found for the individual towards whom the population shows little or no positive choice.

It thus appears that individual differences in pattern within their respective total constellations of interrelations mark the individuals who as a group are shown to be relatively highly chosen members of the population or isolated-or-nearly-unchosen members of the population. Certain of the individual differences are consistently prevalent in their respective patterns. Yet, on the other hand, in still further aspects either group may resemble or differ from the other in its pattern of interrelations. In the latter instances, the aspects of the choice process are apparently not crucially related to the position the individual is accorded by those in contact with him.

The constellation of personal interrelations of choice and rejection around the individual in the general population shows more frequently certain patterns than other patterns. The patterns reflect the total impress of others upon the individual and the total impress he in turn makes upon others. The individual differences in structure of constellations of interrelations are seen to be very much more complex than the view permitted by study of the character of the choice process in its general operation, apart from the individuals themselves from whom choice and rejection emanate and upon whom the choice and rejection of others impinge.

The patterns reflect various conditions that characterize the individual's interaction with other persons at a particular point in time; they register an *active* state, the dynamic interplay of the individual-personality within the total field in which he is but one of many participants.[2]

[2] Among other evidence that high choice-status is closely related to leadership in the community under study, the following may be cited. Elections to a House Council were held in the fall (prior to Test I). The individual receiving the highest number of votes in a given house automatically became a member of the Community Council. The election was held under the supervision of the Club Director and the ballots were closed. Four members were elected to the Council in each house. For the purpose of comparing membership in the Councils with rank in positive choice received from others, only data for the two members in each living unit receiving the highest and second highest number of votes are used.

This comparison reveals that of the 20 such Council members (two from each of the ten housing units of this study) 18 or 90 percent are among the over-chosen (*i.e.* rank 1 S. D. above the mean). The two Council members who do not so rank place just below this point. When allowance is made for the difference between being chosen from a community wide base and being elected from the limited house popula-'ion, it is evident that there is practically a one-to-one relationship between being elected to represent the house body in matters concerning the group and being chosen by community members on the sociometric criteria of living and/or working with them.

Approximately three months intervened between this election and the time of Test I. During this period, it would have been possible for elected Council members to lose their standing with their respective house population, had members been elected who were found incapable of representing and acting in behalf of the group to the satisfaction of their "electorate."

CHAPTER VI

THE INTERNAL STRUCTURE OF THE INDIVIDUAL'S SOCIAL ATOM

The individual's constellation of interrelations, when studied by comparison with the constellations of other individuals, has been revealed to be patterned by the choice process in various ways. This analysis has shown not only differences between individuals in interrelation patterns but also similarities. These differences and similarities, however, relate solely to the individual's *performance considered in terms of the average performance of the group*. The question may be raised whether a study of inter-personal relations should not also consider the individual *in terms of the relation* of his *own* choices and rejections to the choices and rejections of *others towards him*. Then, the problem of individual differences immediately suggests several inquiries:

Should not the extent of expansiveness shown towards the individual be considered in terms of the extent to which he is himself expansive towards others? How greatly do individuals differ in what they "want" as compared with what they "receive" in choice? Does the extent of the individual's emotional expansiveness for others usually equal, exceed, or fall below the extent of emotional expansiveness others show for him? Are any individuals found whose constellation of interrelations is characterized by a perfect coordination of their choice expression for others — who are reciprocated by all the persons to whom they are attracted to the extent of choice? What ratio of reciprocation is achieved by the average individual?

Further, does the ratio of reciprocation which characterizes the individual's constellation at one time show any
significant degree of relation to the ratio of reciprocation that
marks his constellation at a later time? Similarly, does the
ratio between expansiveness expressed by and towards the
individual on one occasion show a significant correlation to
that found on a second occasion?

Up to this point, individual differences have been described within the test-population as a whole between one
individual and another in various aspects of the choice process
taken singly and also in all of the six main aspects of the
choice process taken as a unit; in both instances, the individual's rank as compared with the population as a whole
has been determined. The analysis in terms of the group
has revealed very extensive individual differences. Further,
these differences show certain consistencies from one time to
another eight months later. The nature of the differences
within a given individual's constellation hold equally important implications.

In the analysis in terms of the individual, the comparison,
within a constellation, between the extent of choice expressed
by the subject for others and the extent of choice expressed
by others for the individual may be termed the ratio of
balance in expansiveness or more briefly the Inter-Choice
Ratio. If the number chosen by the individual exceeds the
number choosing him, the ratio will vary from 1.00 in a
minus direction reflecting the degree of excess of the individual's expansiveness compared with the expansiveness of
others for him. If the number chosen equals the number
choosing him, the ratio of balance is consequently 1.00, registering complete correlation between the extent of his ex-

pansiveness towards others and that of others for him. If he is chosen by more individuals than he himself chooses, his ratio of balance will vary in the plus direction, registering the proportion of excess in expansiveness for him compared with his expansiveness for others. The persons chosen by the individual and those choosing him may be entirely different persons, the comparison being simply that of the inter-choice exchange—the extent of positive reaction by and towards the individual. There might be wide differences in the number chosen by the members of the population and wide differences also in the number choosing the members of the population, yet there need not be wide differences in the ratios of inter-choice balance *within* the single individual's constellation. Wide differences would appear only if there were proportionately great discrepancy between the number chosen by the individual and the number choosing the individual.

The test-population shows on Test I a median ratio of inter-choice balance of .84. (See Table XIV.) The largest ratio is 3.79. Four subjects show a ratio of 3.00 or over and five, of 2.00-2.99. While the "desirability" of the individual as an associate may be twice or three times as great as the desirability of others to the individual, the ratio is not found to be many times as great. Also, the number of individuals who are the foci of choice from 2 or 3 times as many persons as they themselves choose is a relatively small number. On the other hand, extremely small ratios are more frequent: 37 subjects are chosen only to the extent of half as many persons as they themselves choose.

Eight months later, the test-population shows a median of 1.27 on Test II. On Test II, also, the number of subjects who show a ratio of less than .50 has decreased from 37 to 26; the number who have a ratio of 2.00 to 3.00 has

TABLE XIV. INTER-CHOICE RATIO OF BALANCE: NUMBER CHOOSING THE SUBJECT/NUMBER CHOSEN BY THE SUBJECT

	Test I	Test II
3.70–3.79	1	
3.60–3.69		1
3.50–3.59		
3.40–3.49		2
3.30–3.39		1
3.20–3.29	1	1
3.10–3.19		1
3.00–3.09	2	5
2.90–2.99		
2.80–2.89	1	3
2.70–2.79		1
2.60–2.69		2
2.50–2.59	1	1
2.40–2.49		1
2.30–2.39		
2.20–2.29		2
2.10–2.19	1	1
2.00–2.09	2	4
1.90–1.99	1	1
1.80–1.89	4	7
1.70–1.79	2	
1.60–1.69	6	3
1.50–1.59	9	8
1.40–1.49	2	2
1.30–1.39	5	7
1.20–1.29	5	10
1.10–1.19	9	5
1.00–1.09*	8	5
.90– .99	1	5
.80– .89	10	7
.70– .79	14	12
.60– .69	5	4
.50– .59	6	5
.40– .49	10	8
.30– .39	6	4
.20– .29	5	3
.10– .19	7	5
.01– .09		1
0 **	9	5
N.	133	133
Median	.84	1.27
Mean	.99	1.29
S.D.	.71	.89
r		.46
Z_r/σ_z		5.53
$D/\sigma D$		2.47

* 7 on Test I and 5 on Test II have a ratio of 1.00.

** Note that ratios at zero, representing unchosen individuals (see Table I), are separately listed.

increased from 5 to 15; and the number having a ratio
of 3.00 or over has increased from 4 to 11. The mean
Inter-Choice Ratio increases between the two tests from .99
to 1.29, and is a significant rise (C.R. = 2.47). The correlation between the individual's ratio on the two occasions
8 months apart is .46 and is significant at the .01 level.

It thus appears that individual differences in ratio of expansiveness within the individual's constellation of interrelations increase significantly from one time to a later time and
the ratio he shows on one occasion correlates to a significant
extent with the ratio he shows on the second occasion.

Within the individual's constellation of interrelations, the
comparison between the extent of choice expressed by the
subject for others and the extent of choice they in turn reciprocate for him may be termed his *Positive Reciprocation
Ratio*. The individual cannot be reciprocated by more persons than he chooses so that the range of ratios of reciprocation can extend only from 0 to 1.00.

The findings on the ratio of reciprocation resemble in
several respects the findings on the ratio of balance of expansiveness. In both instances, the number of individuals having high ratios is markedly fewer than the number having low
ratios. (See Table XV.) Likewise the Positive Reciprocation Ratio on Test I and on Test II correlate at about the
same point as the ratio of expansiveness on Test I and Test
II: r = .42 and is similarly significant. But in other respects
the two ratios differ. The ratio of reciprocation shows a
median of .28 for Test I and .42 for Test II. Whereas 50
percent of the subjects are reciprocated by less than 30 percent of their choices on the first test and by little more than
40 percent of their choices on the second test, only 20 percent
of the subjects on Test I (26/133) and only 11 percent

(14/133) on Test II have so low an Inter-Choice Ratio of balance as .30. Thus it appears that a greater number of individuals show a closer proportion between the extent of their own positive reactions and the extent of positive reac-

TABLE XV. POSITIVE RECIPROCATION RATIO: NUMBER RECIPROCATING THE SUBJECT/NUMBER CHOSEN BY THE SUBJECT

	Test I	Test II
1.00	2	7
.90– .99	1	
.80– .89	4	5
.70– .79	2	12
.60– .69	8	15
.50– .59	20	18
.40– .49	8	13
.30– .39	16	18
.20– .29	27	15
.10– .19	21	17
.01– .09	3	1
0 *	21	12
N.	133	133
Median	.28	.42
Mean	.33	.45
S.D.	.24	.27
r		.42
Zr/σz		4.97
D/σD		1.71

* Note that ratios at zero, representing individuals having no reciprocated choices (see Table I), are separately listed.

tions expressed towards them than is the number of individuals who in their ratio of reciprocation show a similar proportion. Moreover, in contrast to the Inter-Choice Ratio which shows a significant rise in mean from Test I to Test II, the Reciprocation Ratio does not show an increase between the mean on Test I and Test II (C.R. = 1.71) which is significant at the .01 level.

From one time to another 8 months later, the individual's constellation retains a significant but low consistency in its ratio of reciprocation and in its ratio of balance in positive reactions. Thus the structural proportions within an individual's constellation as it undergoes changes from time to time alter as a whole in a manner that is significantly related to the proportions of its structure at a previous time. Just as the repertoire of the individual in choice expression for others does not vary in limitless ways, the whole constellation of his interrelations of positive reactions between others and himself evidently does not vary in random or limitless ways.

The meaning to the individual of the proportions of reciprocation and of positive reaction found to characterize his constellation of personal interrelations is a problem of immense complexity. In a strict sense, it might be argued that any response to the individual from others, short of all the response he wishes from any of them, is less than a satisfactory achievement in personal interrelations. The evidence, however, precludes the possibility of setting up a premise that the requirement for "satisfactory adjustment" must be so stringent as to be defined as positive response to the subject from all individuals towards whom he responds positively. Such a definition would be invalid in the light of findings on the psychology of choice for the chooser and for the chosen. (See Chapters VIII and IX.)

One of the simpler differences in "choice-meaning" may be briefly mentioned at this point. It is a difference which is not equally frequent in the choices given by the individuals but varies with the "location" of the individual in the structure of the population as a whole and with other factors. (See Chapter IX.)

Depending upon the satisfaction accruing to the individual

from his personal interrelations with others and depending also upon his degree of dependence upon these satisfactions, his choices for others may be described as those which are essential to him and those which are desirable but non-essential. For certain individuals, all of their choices are "essential" (*e.g.* see Vera's motivations, pp. 182-183; for others, widely different implications are implicit between their various choices; see Doris, pp. 191-194.) When the individual wants strongly to be appreciated, respected, and, to some extent, held in affectionate regard by certain of his fellows, mutual responses to his choices for such of his fellows *are* essential to him. No individual, it may be conjectured, is totally immune from the need in this sense of response from *some* of his fellows. But there are other expressions of the individual which appear as not merely less essential, in terms of the subject's attraction to others, but actually non-essential (*e.g.* see Doris for Alice, p. 194). They are non-essential in that, although they are a free, spontaneous expression of his response and he is authentically attracted also to these individuals, it is of practically no moment to him whether such of his fellows return his response or not. His satisfaction is *in his own feeling for them.* He "enjoys" them, their "speech," their "ways," or, again, he may simply watch with approval their manner of life. He would like "to have them around." Their behavior and their "values," often contrasting with his own, he may consider appealing. But this "distant" approval and affection he bestows does not honor its receivers by asking like or "deeper" return. The bestower is on one plane and they, from the former's point of view, on one much lower. He sees no avenue of "essential" communication between himself and them. He is "older," or "wiser," or "more complex" to his notion (or the reverse), and his way of life and his values he considers beyond or outside of their comprehension. He expects nothing (mutual) of these persons and he does not see them as able to aid him in his problems or as offering the *possibility* of a true exchange. The giving, if any, is from his side; even if it were possible for it to be less one-sided, his attitude prevents such a development.

Then there are other non-essential choices which are a genuine burden to the chooser, but a burden freely assumed. He is an active giver to the chosen, perhaps through sympathy because of their relative lack of general competence and through actual desire to be of help to them, as doing so requires so little exertion on his part. But in this case, too, wherever the choice is non-essential to the chooser, its recipient is not raised, in the mind of the chooser, to the level of co-participation with him. (See motivations of choice, pp. 191-195.)

Nevertheless, although such choices, in the sense described, appear non-essential to the individual expressing them it should not be implied that no "value" resides in such choices. There is a peculiar value in such choices for the structure of the community as a whole and for the structure of any group in which they occur, quite aside from the fact that they naturally contribute to the constellation of interrelations of the persons who are their foci. The contribution of so-called "non-essential" choice consists in its addition to the sum total of the "psychological milieu" produced by the prevalence of positive reactions in general between the members of a population who are living in common participation together.

CHAPTER VII

Choice and Choice-status as Affected by High Opportunity for Contacts and Other Factors

The choice-status the membership as a whole gives to one or another member might conceivably be related to the individual's age, intelligence, or length of residence, since the differences in these factors are wide in the population of the community under study. Similarly, the individual's emotional expansiveness towards the membership or the extent to which he reciprocates their expansiveness towards him might also possibly be related to such factors as age, intelligence, or length of residence. The problem suggests further questions: do individuals who occupy leader-positions, average positions, or isolated-or-near-isolated positions differ as groups from each other and from the general population in age, intelligence, or length of residence? Are the individual differences found in the pattern of the individual's total constellation of interrelations attributable to one or more of such factors?

Moreover, does exceptional opportunity to contact and know the members of a community make for a greater degree of social expansiveness on the part of the individual? In turn, are the individual differences in extent of positive choice expressed by others for the individual attributable to a wider opportunity he may have to know and be known by others?

Choice and rejection have been found not to be randomly produced; instead the findings demonstrate positive and negative choice to be but two aspects of a single choice process — a choice process in which the positive and the negative aspects are related significantly in particularized ways, as spread throughout the community and focussed upon its membership. It can therefore be assumed that factors must underlie the inter-personal reactions of individuals tending to relate them positively or negatively. Within the total field in which choice and rejection were explored, the most readily examinable factors are the membership's differences in age, intelligence, length of residence, and opportunity for contact with one another. Such factors are admittedly but isolated abstractions from the total field, but as they lend themselves to quantitative measurement their analysis will precede the qualitative material on the membership's composition (Chapter IX).

The community's population as a whole had generally an equal opportunity to meet and to contact one another. The members of each housing unit of the test-population participated as groups equally in the common activities of the community. As in other communities, however, certain individuals because of their functional role have a much greater opportunity to contact and know the membership generally.

The differentiating factor in extent of opportunity for contacts in the test-population is produced by three vocations in which the students met and might talk more or less at length with a wide sampling of the population until eventually such students could have been in contact with all the members of the population. In general the program of each individual of the population comprised one half day of academic school and one half day of vocational "work" with the recreational and special electives given in late afternoon or early evening. The vocations were known as work since practice as well as study of the vocation was required; the practicing was as thorough as facilities allowed. Only three vocations, however, brought the student unusually extensive contacts and no other part of the program differentiated in this respect one member of the test-population from another in social opportunity. The three vocations were: salesmanship, beauty culture, and telephone operating.

The salesmanship practice was provided by a merchandising center known as the store, in which school currency, in the form of an allowance to each individual, was the medium of exchange for buying all necessities. "Luxury" merchandise was also purchasable by the students with money earned or received from home. The store in consequence was patronized by the entire population. The beauty culture shop was also patronized by the entire population. The students of the third vocation giving unusual opportunity for contacts practiced telephone operating and switchboard work in the administration building in an office at which the members of the population had frequent occasion to call. The academic requirements generally were higher for enrollment than in other vocations offered. The subjects were free to select any vocation desired but knew that a longer course of preparation was needed for the three mentioned. At the time of Test I, there were 33 subjects in Group AB (N = 236) practicing salesmanship, beauty culture or telephone operating in the community. In the analysis, they will be termed "high opportunity" subjects since they are over-privileged as compared with the average subject in respect to the extent of social contacts they might readily make with others. The findings on the population as a whole may be compared with the findings for high opportunity subjects as a group. The analysis of high opportunity subjects is based on Group AB as the number of such subjects is greater in AB than in A.

The individual differences in chronological age in the test-population of Group A range from under 12 or over 18 years, with the median at 16. The individual differences in intelligence quotient range from 60 to 118, with the median at 84.[1] In length of residence the membership of Group A varies from 15 days to over 3 years, with the median at 1 year, 1.2 months. Thus the range in each of the three factors is sufficiently wide to permit an examination of individual differences. (The analysis may be based on either AB or A, but as the comparison on re-test can be made only of Group A, the findings are reported only for Group A.)

On both Test I and Test II, chronological age and intelligence quotient each show a zero relationship to each of the three aspects of positive choice: the individual's expansiveness towards others, the expansiveness of others towards the individual, and the extent of reciprocation of positive choice between the individual and others. Length of residence also shows no correlation with the extent of the individual's expansiveness towards others on either Test I or Test II. The factor of length of residence, however, while also showing no correlation with the extent of expansiveness expressed towards the individual by others on Test I or with the extent of reciprocation of his choice for others on Test I, shows a slight inverse correlation, approaching significance, on Test II: $r = -.17$ (C.R. $= 1.91$) and $= -.20$ (C.R. $= 2.25$) respectively between length of residence and number choosing the subject and between length of residence and number reciprocating the subject. (See Table XVI.) The finding is partially on Test II the reflection of the tendency (previously mentioned, pp. 71-72) for chronically over-chosen individ-

---

[1] IQ's are based on the Stanford-Binet Test (old form).

uals to retrench somewhat in their expenditure of choice for others, thus diminishing the number of *possible reciprocal* choices others may form with them. However, the trend towards a significant but small inverse correlation is mainly produced on both Test I and Test II by the extremely low

TABLE XVI. CORRELATIONS ON CHRONOLOGICAL AGE, IQ, AND LENGTH OF RESIDENCE

Group A (N. 133)

	Test	r	Zr/σz
Chronological age and number chosen by subject:	I	.11	
Same:	II	—.07	
Chronological age and number choosing subject:	I	.15	1.68
Same:	II	.02	
Chronological age and number reciprocating subject:	I	.08	
Same:	II	.03	
IQ and number chosen by subject:	II	—.05	
IQ and number choosing subject:	II	.04	
IQ and number reciprocating subject:	II	.10	
IQ and subject's social-contact-range:	I	.34	3.93
Length of residence and social-contact-range:	I	.34	3.93
Length of residence and number chosen by subject:	I	.06	
Same:	II	.06	
Length of residence and number choosing subject:	I	.05	
Same:	II	—.17	1.91
Length of residence and number reciprocating subject:	I	.01	
Same:	II	—.20	2.25

scores of the five individuals who have been longest in the community; the prolonged stay of all five of the individuals was due to their greatly under-average progress in vocational and other training. The correlations in both cases are likewise at zero if the performances of the five subjects are excluded. It is to be noted that their scores on emotional expansiveness towards others do not likewise produce an inverse correlation; this result is characteristic of the individual's repertoire of expansiveness for others (see p. 70).

Thus individual differences in positive choice in none of its three aspects can be attributed to individual differences in intelligence,[2] chronological age or length of residence of the membership in the community studied. Likewise the constellation of positive interrelations around the individual shows no apparent and consistent tendency to differ in pattern according to the intelligence level, age, or length of residence of the individual. The only wide disparity is found between the individuals who as a group have a pattern of below the mean performance in each of the scores on positive choice compared with the individuals who as a group have a pattern above the mean in each score on positive choice. They show on Test II a difference of 8 months in length of stay. The difference is attributable to individuals remaining in the — — — positive choice pattern who at the time of Test I had already been a longer time in the community than the average member of Group A; the shorter-residents on the average have moved to other patterns on Test II and shifters into the — — — pattern were for the most part longer-stayers. This finding is reflected also in the greater mean length of stay of the group of subjects who on Test II are below 1 S.D. from the mean of the population in number of individuals expressing positive choice for them. Staying a longer than average time in the community connotes either that the individual is slow in acquiring vocational and other competence necessary to earning a living, or was very much younger than average on entrance, or elects to take a course of training requiring an extra long period of preparation. In the above finding, the subjects belonged chiefly to the first category of long-stayers.

[2] In this connection see Howell's finding, at the college level, that intelligence does not enter into social status (choice-status), and inferentially into leadership, to any significant degree. Charles E. Howell, "Measurement of Leadership," *Sociometry*. V:163-168, May, 1942, p. 166.

Relation to Social-Contact-Range

Whereas no single aspect of positive choice or the three main aspects as a unit show any correlation in the general test-population with the member's age or intelligence, or length of residence, intelligence and length of residence each correlate significantly at .34 with the member's social contact range. (See Table XVI.) It thus appears that there is a small tendency for the individual of higher intelligence quotient to show somewhat more social initiative in making and maintaining contacts with others, and that length of residence with others tends to work in the same direction, the social expansiveness of the individual increasing somewhat with increase in his period of stay with others. The emotional expansiveness of the individual and his social expansiveness were found (see p. 51 and pp. 62-65) to show only the slightest significant relationship $(A_I, r = .22, C.R. 2.48)$ and practically to operate as independent expressions of the individual.

It may be that the individual has more control over the extent of his social expansiveness than he has over the extent of his emotional expansiveness. In the one case, the individual's expression in social-contact-range develops with his length of time with others; also to some degree, according to his intelligence, he develops social initiative in contacting others. In the second case, the individual in his extent of choice for others is practically as emotionally expansive from the start of his stay with others as he is later, and his intelligence does not appear as a determining factor in his extent of choice for others. To some degree, perhaps, the individual may have "command" over his social expansiveness, and little or no "command" over the needs for which his expression of choice for others registers the counterpart. Social initiative in making contacts may show increase on the part of certain individuals only after they begin "to feel at home" in a new community. For a few individuals also their increasing expression of such initiative may be more or less "deliberate" — once having acquired some fair degree of skill in social "exploring," they may increasingly enjoy such behavior and increasingly practice it, if and when they feel like doing so. Certain of the subjects who display considerable "sociableness," again, sporadically, show periods of "nonsociableness." They can be observed to "space" their expression of social expansiveness according to whether it involves using up time and energy they apparently consider they need for matters more important to them at the particular period. This "timing" is hardly ever observable in the expression of emotional expansiveness in the test-population. The extent of the subject's expression of choice for others is apparently not determined, in the same sense, by what other matters are occupying his time and attention. It may be that in the test-population this would not be necessary since the individual's choice expression does not interfere with the fulfillment of plans he may have for himself. In the more complex living and working situation of the adult, choice may not only be "interfered" with but restriction of its expression *appropriate to the* person's desire may even be necessary for the individual who elects certain avenues of work or certain avenues of living.

Leader-position, Average-position, and Isolated-or-Near-isolated-position

Although in the test-population as a whole there is no correspondence between age, intelligence, or length of residence, and positive choice, it might be expected that there would be some correspondence for the individuals who are in leader-positions or in isolated-or-near-isolated positions within the structure. In general, however, the findings are negative: the factor of one or another kind of position in the structure accorded to the individual by the members of the community cannot be attributed to his degree of intelligence alone, his chronological age alone, nor to the "status" of his being a relatively new or a relatively old-resident only. The individuals in leader-positions on Test I show the same average IQ as the individuals who are in isolated-or-near-isolated-positions on Test I. On Test II there is a difference of only 6 points in IQ between the two groups, in favor of the individuals occupying leader-positions. The leader-group on Test I is 9 months older than the isolated-or-near-isolated-group, but the average length of stay is the same for both, 1 year, 2 months.

A trend which may or may not be significant appears, however, in analysis of the factors for the individuals who "move up" and who "move down" from Test I to Test II, eight months later. Ten subjects have a leader-position, as defined, on Test II only and ten others have an isolated-or-near-isolated-position on Test II only. They may have moved up or down from average-positions or other intermediate locations. The group coming to leader-positions are as a group 1 year younger, 11 points higher in IQ, and the period of their residence is 4 months briefer than the group coming into isolated-or-near-isolated-positions. On the other hand, the group of subjects who are in leader-positions on *both* Test I and Test II are 5 months older, only 2 points higher in IQ, and have been for 6 months less time resident than the group of subjects who are in isolated-or-near-isolated-positions on both Test I and Test II. Each group of subjects differ little in these factors, from the group who have average-positions in the structure. By the time of Test II, however, there does appear some tendency for the few subjects who come into isolated-or-near-isolated-positions within the structure to be comprised of individuals who are relatively older in chronological age and relatively older in terms of residence in the community, and also somewhat less "bright" than the few subjects who come into leader-positions at the later period. But the group of individuals who are found in isolated-or-near-isolated-positions relatively early, at the time of Test I, and continue in such positions on Test II, are as "bright" as the group of individuals who are found in average-positions on both occasions or as the group of individuals who are in leader-positions on both occasions. Eventually, it appears, the occupants of a given category of position in the test-community do not remain differentiated as a group by the factor of intelligence. No one category of position in the community appears to serve as a residuum of the "dull" or of the "bright" exclusively, although no individual who is among the least intelligent in the population is found among the members in leader-positions.

Role of High Opportunity for Contacts

A leader-position, as defined by the subject ranking 1 S.D. above the mean of the population in number of individuals choosing him, is found for 37 subjects in Group AB (N = 236). The number of subjects in Group AB who had a "high opportunity" to become chosen (see p. 131) is 33. Thirteen of the high opportunity subjects are over-chosen to the extent of 1 S.D. above the mean. Thus 35 percent (13/37) of the over-chosen subjects are individuals of high opportunity to be chosen, whereas 65 percent (24/37) attain the status of being chosen to a like extent without such exceptional opportunity being provided for them. (The results on Test II are closely similar. Of the 21 subjects at 1 S.D. above the mean in number of individuals choosing them, only 8 are individuals having high opportunity, or 38 percent (8/21); the remaining 62 percent (13/21) have the same position in spite of not having high opportunity.) Or stated in relation to Group AB as a whole, in which 16 percent (37/236) of the membership attain an over-chosen status, 12 percent (24/203) of the members not having high opportunity as compared with 39 percent (13/33) of the members having such opportunity attain the choice-status of over-chosen.

High opportunity to know and be known by others thus does not appear necessarily conducive to the individual's being chosen to a much greater extent than others who do not have such unusual opportunity. Factors other than the one of being placed in a physical situation inviting much social contact must account for the fact that certain individuals are over-chosen. A physical situation favorable to choice may not become a psychological situation favorable to choice unless the individuals involved are able to make it so; conversely, a physical situation not exceptionally stacked in favor of choice may become a psychological situation favorable to choice if the individuals make it so. Individuals to whom others are drawn to a greater extent than average may be sought out or themselves make their own opportunities whether or not they are placed in prominent situations for contacting others. Consideration given to the more subtle factors which may be involved in choice (see chap. IX) also make it appear logical that choice is not found to be disproportionately produced towards individuals by the mere set-up of situations which would permit it to be developed.

Still it may be considered a surprising fact that any relationship at all is found between high opportunity for contact and the choice-status of the subject. One explanation may lie in a tendency for individuals who elect a vocational situation requiring contact with many persons to be individuals who at the same time "feel comfortable" in dealing with others; *i.e.*, they may be attracted to such vocations rather than avoid them because the human contacts which the daily work involves are not a source of difficulty but of satisfaction. Thus it may happen that the enrollment in such vocations becomes to some extent selectively comprised of persons who are more able to draw choice to themselves than is the average individual.

On the other hand, the high opportunity group as a whole and each vocational group within it shows a mean social contact range exceeding that of the test-population of Group AB. In the instance of salesmanship, the students as a group show a mean social contact range of 94.8, a score almost twice as great as the mean score of Group AB, 50.5. The few students of telephone operating are also much above the mean of AB; they show an average of 76.5. On the other hand, the students of beauty culture as a group do not differ from the general population; they show a social-contact-range of 53.4. It is possible that the individuals who elect to study and practice salesmanship are inclined to be in any situation somewhat more socially expansive, as measured by the number of others with whom they initiate and maintain social contacts, than the individuals who elect to study and practice the more manual vocation of beauty culture. (It does not necessarily follow that they are *emotionally expansive* towards a greater number among those with whom they have social contacts. The subject's emotional expansiveness and his social expansiveness, it will be recalled, were found to be practically unrelated. See p. 63.)

In each vocational group, the mean social contact range of the subjects who rank 1 S.D. above the mean in extent of individuals expressing positive choice for them exceeds that of the subjects in the same vocation who do not rank at this point. The finding should be expected as the social contact range of the subject and the number of individuals choosing the subject correlate (r = .40, Group AB).

It appears that increase in the individual's social contact range is facilitated in the test-community by a high opportunity situation for making social contacts in the two vocations of salesmanship and telephone operating, whereas it shows very little increase in the high opportunity situation given by the vocation of beauty culture, despite the latter's providing equally high opportunity for contact. The selective factor may be that subjects who are relatively more expansive socially are drawn to the kind of vocation in which this expression has an importance which it does not have to a like extent in the kind of situation requiring primarily manual skill. The "outlet" which the individual wants may affect his selection of a vocation.

The 20 individuals in the high opportunity group who are not found to be over-chosen show very little difference in age, intelligence, or length of residence from the group of 37 individuals who, with or without high opportunity, are over-chosen. The latter are only on the average 1 month younger, 2 points lower in IQ, and have been a 9 months shorter period in the community. However, the 13 high opportunity subjects who are also over-chosen are 9 points higher in IQ and have been 1 year and 3 months longer in residence than the 20 high opportunity subjects who are not over-chosen. While the single factor of length of residence has been found to play no role at all in the extent to which the individual is chosen, it is conceivable that higher intelligence *and* a longer stay in a community might sometimes operate together so as to result in the individual's becoming over-chosen; his better intelligence might be recognized only gradually and his contribution to the community might also be made only gradually. However, in the present finding, this does not appear as the explanation. The longer length of residence resulted from the individuals generally having come to the community at younger ages than average and hence becoming eligible for the high opportunity vocation only after they had completed the academic requirements and thus been in the community for some time.

Age, intelligence, and length of residence appear not to account to any appreciable extent for the individual differences in choice-status accorded the individual by the membership of the community as a whole. Moreover, an over-chosen status may be achieved by the individual whether or not he is given exceptional opportunity to know and be known by others in his community; but individuals who show an over-chosen status are frequently found in situations involving many contacts. The individual apparently seeks out so far as he can the kind of situation which appears to be compatible with his disposition towards inter-personal contact.

CHAPTER VIII

BEHAVIOR CHARACTERISTICS OF
UNDER-CHOSEN, AVERAGE CITIZENS, AND OVER-CHOSEN

Are personality differences related to the individual's position in the structure of a community? Do under-chosen or isolated individuals show very different personality pictures as compared with over-chosen individuals or as compared with individuals chosen to an average extent? Are there any behaviors which distinguish as a group the individuals who are located in the same "level" of the structure? Are there any behaviors which all individuals generally display to an equal extent regardless of their choice-status? Does the personal factor of the individual's characteristic behavior appear as a determining factor in the extent to which others are emotionally expansive towards him?

Although the psychological result of the augmenting of choice upon choice is not to be understood as resulting in quantitative psychological effects in the same ratio, for the individual who is the focus, there does appear to be a point in the receipt of positive choice that carries with its attainment certain psychological implications for the group of individuals who are found at or above this point in the community under study. Likewise there appears another point in the receipt of positive choice that carries with it certain other psychological implications for the individuals as a group who are found at or below it in this community. The lines which divide each of these groups from the large majority of the population appear essentially different when the behavior of the individuals are compared.

In the community of the study, the behaviors shown by the members of the population towards one another may be studied from several viewpoints. The subjects as they are "interpreted" by the housemother in each housing unit are, so to speak, seen in relation to one another by an adult who is in immediate authority and equally responsible for the welfare and development of each member of her group. The behaviors which she considers commendatory are generally behaviors which further the individual's own welfare and directly or indirectly that of the other members of the group. The behaviors which she considers interfere seriously with the individual's present or future adjustment are generally complained of because they retard the individual's own development or that of the members of the group as a whole or else tend to hinder the carrying out of her plans for the activities of the group as a whole. Hence, an analysis of behaviors on the basis of "complaints" and "commendations" by the housemother of each subject gives a picture of behavior characteristics, on the part of the individual, especially affecting the individual favorably or unfavorably and perhaps also affecting the membership of his group favorably or unfavorably. Further, since housemothers in reporting the behavior picture of an individual may mention behavior which is only occasional rather than characteristic or displayed generally by the individual, "behavior items" in the analysis are included only if reported by the housemother on three or more separate occasions during the six weeks immediately prior to or immediately following Test I and/or Test II in order to relate the typical behaviors during the respective period to the choice-status of the individual. On the other hand, the housemother's behavior is under constant purview by the members of her group and reflects the point of vantage from which they view the actions of the house-mother; the personality of the individual subject is reflected in the interpretation given to the actions and behavior of the housemother. The "behavior items" attributed by the individual to the housemother are included in the analysis likewise if reported on three or more occasions during the period surveyed. The reports were collected by the investigator during the routine of her work as psychologist. In securing these reports, the subject's expressions regarding her relationship to or attitude towards the housemother were incidental to the subject's general discussion. The expressions represent the spontaneous remarks proffered by the subject in the course of consulting the experimenter on vocational or other progress.

The categories used in the behavior classifications are those which appeared obvious upon inspection of the data. To illustrate the nature of the behavior data classified in the analysis, sample material is given under each category used in the classification; in certain instances, the category itself is sufficiently descriptive without examples. Thus, the classification was not preconceived and superimposed upon the data, but was built directly from inspection of the material. (See Table XVII.) The classification was not revised after tabulation of the data; thus it represents the original categories into which the data appeared to classify on first inspection.

TABLE XVII. BEHAVIOR ITEMS REPORTED

Behaviors Complained of by Housemothers (N. =	Choice-Status		
	41 under-chosen	41 average-chosen	43) over-chosen
1. quarrelsome and irritable, chip on the shoulder behavior (initiates quarrels, replies in chip-on-the-shoulder fashion, misconstrues criticisms directed towards self, and the like)	15	3	1

TABLE XVII. BEHAVIOR ITEMS REPORTED (*Continued*)

Behaviors Complained of by Housemothers (N. =	41 under-chosen	41 average-chosen	43) over-chosen
2. nagging, complaining, whining behavior (complains and nags housemother and girls about small matters which majority do not mention, as size of room, its location in cottage, amount of portions served at table, turn in showers, etc.)	8	4	—
3. nervous, jumpy behavior (jerky movements, useless motions, as swinging foot when seated, and the like)	8	4	—
4. aggressive and dominant behavior (getting another individual to submit to wait on her, make her bed, do her "commands," give in to her suggestions when doing a common task with another, and the like)	12	6	2
5. rebellious behavior (refusing to do what is requested by person in authority, and the like)	4	7	11
6. behavior actively interrupting the group's activities (temper-tantrums, walking out when remaining is essential to group's functioning, and the like)	11	—	1
7. behavior passively interfering with group's activities (assuming role of by-stander when active participation is called for, exhibiting lack of interest and enthusiasm sufficient to interfere with group's plans, and the like)	13	1	1
8. behavior showing resentfulness of being criticized (sulks, does not behave pleasantly for some time after being criticized, generally considers criticisms unjust, defends own conduct whether or not justified, and the like)	16	9	8
9. behavior attention-demanding but not praise-seeking (asks questions when she knows the answer, asks for instructions already received, makes requests knowing they cannot be granted, submits work to supervisor prematurely instead of waiting for regular time, persistence in discussing own problems, and the like)	11	5	1
10. praise-seeking behavior (draws attention of staff to minor accomplishments; frequently asks if she is doing well; and the like)	10	4	2
11. initiatory behavior in making innovations without asking permission (behaviors considered as too self-directive and self-confident for the individual's own good, and the like)	2	4	13

TABLE XVII. BEHAVIOR ITEMS REPORTED (*Continued*)

	Choice-Status		
(N. =	41 under-chosen	41 average-chosen	43) over-chosen
12. retaliatory behavior ("getting even" with another individual for behavior considered unfair, as by making caustic remarks, embarrassing her in the presence of others, refusing to lend support expected, and the like)	2	5	14
13. reticent behavior regarding personal matters (does not bring personal troubles to the housemother, as problems concerning her home and family and the like)	3	5	13
14. behavior pernicious in its effect on the morale of the group (spreads untrue rumors detrimental to group's interests, discourages constructive relationship of others to the housemother, encourages others to disregard standard of conduct set by group and by housemother, and the like)	11	—	2
15. behavior resulting in avoidance by others of the individual	8	—	—
Behaviors Commended by Housemothers			
16. cooperative behavior (accepts assigned tasks, readily takes share of responsibility in projects requiring cooperation with others in the running of the house, and the like)	7	28	40
17. behavior marked by evenness of disposition (good emotional control as evinced by lack of crankiness, temper displays, rude retorts, and the like)	6	20	27
18. behavior requiring no special attention from housemother (individual falls in with routines and goes about her business without requiring attention of housemother)	—	21	30
19. behavior making the most of vocational-avocational opportunities (serious in achieving her ambitions, applies herself to vocational courses, takes earnestly her school assignments, and the like)	—	17	31
20. voluntarily does more than own share of work (of own accord, without being asked, does extra work when it needs doing, volunteers help in situations needing extra workers, and the like)	7	18	25
21. behavior showing planning and organization (goes about things in an organized way, makes an ordered attack upon whatever she undertakes, and the like)	—	13	26

TABLE XVII. BEHAVIOR ITEMS REPORTED (*Continued*)

	Choice-Status		
(N. =	41 under-chosen	41 average-chosen	43) over-chosen
22. behavior showing initiative (starts new projects and makes innovations in the ways of doing things, as in the running of the house, its activities, and the like)	2	8	28
23. behavior showing willingness to accept temporary, minor or background roles (as being assigned menial tasks so others can have more prominent assignments, does not act injured when others are given the limelight in activities, and the like)	3	13	26
24. behavior exhibiting ingenuity in changing conduct of "problem" girls (as forestalling tantrums, publicizing to group p. g.'s contributions, helping p. g. to gain recognition, deterring others from excluding p. g. from their activities and the like)	—	8	37
25. behavior exhibiting solicitude towards new girls (as encouraging n. g., showing interest in n. g. by deeds in n. g.'s behalf, fostering an understanding between n. g. and others, and the like)	2	9	39

Girls' Complaints about Housemother

26. does not "encourage" girl ("doesn't encourage me" and the like)	12	3	—
27. does not "understand" girl ("doesn't understand me," "finds fault with me instead of trying to understand me," and the like)	16	5	2
28. exhibits unfair behavior ("gives others more chances than she does me" and the like)	19	4	—
29. does not listen to and consider girls' opinions ("doesn't treat a person like a grown-up"; "doesn't show respect for your opinion, thinks she is always right even if you give evidence for your opinion"; "is against your being stubborn but she herself is stubborn in changing plans for the house when good ideas come up"; and the like)	2	3	9
30. exhibits behavior inconsiderate of the individual when reprimanding ("is sarcastic"; "doesn't come right out with something straightforward"; "has a haughty tone when she's correcting"; and the like)	2	3	11

TABLE XVII. BEHAVIOR ITEMS REPORTED (*Continued*)

	Choice-Status		
(N. =	41 under-chosen	41 average-chosen	43) over-chosen
31. exhibits impatient behavior ("too impatient with girls who can't catch on fast"; "hurries girls who shouldn't be hurried, who aren't quick because they can't be . . ."; and the like	—	7	13
32. displays distrust of girls' use of initiative ("puts a person in her place when they really are helping her out by attending to things for her"; "acts like a girl is intruding on her domain"; "first she develops your initiative and then she attempts to break you down"; "I respect her intentions, why can't she respect my intentions"; and the like)	4	5	14
Girls' Expressions of Housemother			
33. "encourages" girl	15	11	—
34. "understands" girl	19	14	1
35. provides opportunities to improve ("always gives me a chance to improve," and the like)	7	12	2
36. shows courtesy ("never fails to thank you," and the like)	8	8	2
37. exhibits dependable behavior ("never goes back on her word," and the like)	1	13	8
38. expresses sense of humor ("has a great sense of fun and doesn't get angry over nonsense"; "laughs at the funny side of things"; and the like)	11	7	6
39. displays thoughtfulness of the individual when reprimanding ("doesn't scold in front of others"; "chooses words that won't make you hate her"; and the like)	—	5	12
40. shows impartiality in dealing with the group ("doesn't favor one girl over another"; "is fair to the worst girls as much as the best"; and the like)	—	6	12
41. obliges the individual to meet reasonable standards ("not an easy-mark for anybody"; "makes the girl earn special privileges"; and the like)	—	7	15
42. trusts the individual ("trusts every girl so far as she shows herself worthy of it"; "gives you a free hand as long as you cooperate"; and the like)	—	6	13
43. displays consistency in behavior ("never moody and mean just to show she is boss"; "you			

Table XVII. Behavior Items Reported (*Continued*)

	Choice-Status		
(N. =	41 under-chosen	41 average-chosen	43) over-chosen
know where you're at with her, doesn't fly at the girls even if she's feeling bad"); and the like)	1	5	11
44. believes in individual's potentialities ("doesn't act like the girls are no good who won't co-operate and try to spoil things for everybody"; "makes you feel you should try to change people and not just treat them bad in return if they act bad"; "sees so much possibilities in a girl that first thing you know ...she...gets to be different"; and the like)	1	7	17
45. listens to and considers girls' opinions ("allows a person to say her opinion"; "considers what the girls think in making up her mind about plans for us"; and the like)	—	4	13

Non-differentiating Behavior Items

(mentioned in housemother reports)

46. personal habits of behavior satisfactory (habits of cleanliness, neatness, table manners, and the like)	28	25	31
47. moody behavior (shows marked ups and down in emotional tone)	15	14	15
48. generous behavior (shares belongings, services and the like)	20	23	21

Further Items of Differentiating Behaviors

49. visits psychology office in behalf of another individual (instead of self)	—	2	15
50. in speaking about self shows insight into own behavior	7	12	27
51. in speaking about others shows insight into their behavior	4	15	31
52. makes unasked-for suggestions to psychologist for welfare of others	—	6	17
53. complains of another girl's conduct towards her	21	13	4

The analysis is concerned with behaviors found for three different positions of choice-status: the under-chosen, the average-chosen, and the over-chosen.

Under-chosen is defined as placing 1 S.D. below the mean of the test-population; over-chosen as placing 1 S.D. above the mean; and average-chosen as placing approximately at the mean, in number of individuals choosing the subject. The number of under-chosen positions are 41 (19 on Test I and 22 on Test II); the number of over-chosen positions are 43 (22 on Test I and 21 on Test II); for a basis of comparison 41 other positions placing nearest the mean on either test were selected.

Hence, on one test the behaviors of the same individual may be listed under one choice-status and on the second test, listed under another choice-status if this individual has shifted to another category by the second occasion; or the behaviors for a given individual may be listed only for one test if the subject has not placed as under-chosen, average-chosen, or over-chosen on both tests, and may not be listed at all if the subject is found in other than the defined positions on both occasions. The analysis is thus based on the behaviors found to accompany a given choice-status, regardless of what individuals at the given time are occupying the given choice-status.

An examination of whether or not the behaviors of any group of subjects are characterized by differences in one or another direction when the behaviors are classified for individuals according to the respective choice-status they occupy when displaying certain behaviors reveals each of the three positions of choice-status to be distinguished from one another by a greater or lesser incidence of particular behaviors.

The under-chosen appear five times as often as average subjects to show "quarrelsome and irritable behavior," while the over-chosen subjects show only one-third as great an incidence of such behavior as the average-chosen subjects

(Behavior Item 1). The under-chosen show twice as great an incidence of "nagging, whining behavior" and of "nervous behavior" as do the average-chosen subjects, and such behavior appears conspicuously absent for over-chosen subjects (B.I. 2, 3). Similarly, the incidence of behavior described as "aggressive and dominant" is twice as great for under-chosen as for average-chosen and three times as great for average-chosen as for over-chosen (B.I. 4).

The under-chosen, too, appear as showing almost exclusively behaviors which either passively or actively interfere with or interrupt the activities of the group (B.I. 6, 7) and behaviors which are interpreted by the housemother as "pernicious in effect on morale of group" or as "resulting in avoidance by others of the individual" (B.I. 14, 15). But behaviors "showing resentfulness of being criticized" (B.I. 8) are about equally frequent for average and for over-chosen subjects and are nearly twice as frequent for under-chosen as for average-chosen subjects. In "praise-seeking behavior," the under-chosen, again, show a greater incidence than the average-chosen subject, an incidence approximately twice as great as that for the latter, while the over-chosen show least behavior which is so interpreted by the adult (B.I. 10).

On the other hand, behaviors reported as "rebellious" are most infrequent for the under-chosen, about twice as frequent for the average citizen as for the under-chosen, and about three times as frequent for the over-chosen as for the under-chosen (B.I. 5). The over-chosen also exceed both other groups in "initiatory behavior in making innovations without permission," in "retaliatory behavior," and in being complained of for "reticent behavior" regarding personal matters. In such behaviors they are conspicuous by an incidence about three times as great as for average subjects, while the under-chosen show only about half as great an incidence as the average subjects (B.I. 11, 12, 13).

On the part of the over-chosen, the frequency of a "getting-even" type of behavior between themselves (among other over-chosen) and attempts to circumvent an adult may reflect the community of interest and competition in which they are active. Towards the adult, the behavior is likely to take place in situations providing the individual with no other "successful" outlet and the individual acts out of resentment to restriction on use of initiative; towards peers, the matter can be directly attacked. The lack of a similar degree of retaliatory behavior by average-chosen or by under-chosen towards themselves or towards the over-chosen may reflect the fact that there is not sufficient (or equally earnest) competition to give occasion for such behavior to arise.

In regard to the greater "reticence" of the over-chosen, there appears no ground for assuming that the explanation lies in their having no "troubles" or even fewer personal worries than the rest of the population; their failure to seek the housemother's attention and aid to the extent expected by her may perhaps be referable to a greater ability on their part, as compared with the average citizen's, to "accept" such worries, an ability which may be partly accounted for by their possessing better perspective on them provided by their greater interest in other persons outside themselves.

Behaviors considered "commendatory" by the adult (*i.e.* the housemother) form a counterpart to the above findings. The under-chosen appear to be distinguished from average-chosen subjects not only by a smaller incidence of such behaviors but also by an apparent lack of displaying certain behaviors commonly credited to the average-chosen. While the incidence of "cooperative behavior," "behavior marked by evenness of disposition," and "behavior marked by voluntarily doing more than own share of work" (B.I. 16, 17, 20) is only about two or four times greater for average-chosen than for under-chosen, the incidence of the individual's displaying "behavior requiring no special attention from housemother," "behavior making most of vocational and avocational opportunities," and "behavior showing planning and organization" (B.I. 18, 19, 21) is conspicuously lacking for the under-chosen; and in these behaviors the average-chosen show from one fourth to one half smaller an incidence than do the over-chosen.

Further, "behavior showing willingness to accept temporary minor roles" has an incidence twice as great for over-chosen as for average-chosen subjects; it also appears very much less frequently for under-chosen as compared with average subjects (B.I. 23); and the differences in "behavior showing initiative" are even greater between the three groups of subjects (B.I. 22). However, the behaviors which most outstandingly differentiate between under-chosen, average-chosen, and over-chosen are found to be "behaviors exhibiting ingenuity in changing conduct of 'problem' girls" and "behaviors exhibiting solicitude towards new girls"; in such behaviors the over-chosen show an incidence over four times greater than that of the average-chosen, and the display of these behaviors by the under-chosen appears rare (for B.I. 24, incidence 0, for B.I. 25, incidence 2).

The under-chosen show in common many varieties of behaviors the effect of which may tend to separate and draw individuals apart rather than to bring them together (B.I. 1, 2, 3, 4, 6, 7, 8, 9, 10, 14). The average-chosen show somewhat less than half as great an incidence of such behaviors, and, on the other hand, about twice as great an incidence of behaviors the effect of which may tend to bring individuals into constructive relationship with one another (B.I. 16, 17, 18, 19, 20, 21, 22, 23, 24, and 25). Further, in the very behaviors in which the average-chosen outrank the under-chosen, the over-chosen in turn are found to exceed the average citizen by approximately twice as great an incidence. Thus, it appears as much a matter of what behaviors are rarely exhibited by the under-chosen as it does a matter of what behaviors they frequently show which may account for their holding the choice-status of under-chosen in the community. Likewise, it is notable that the average citizens are not in any sense *average* in all constructive or "reputable" behaviors — they approach the over-chosen in a number of such behaviors (see B.I. 16, 17, 18, 20) — but rather that the sum-total of their behaviors taken as a whole redounds to their remaining average contributors to the community life: the incidence of behaviors having a negative import for inter-personal exchange (in common work and living) (see B.I. 1, 2, 3, 4, 9, 10) appears to offset those having a positive import sufficiently in the case of such individuals to "hold them down," as it were, to an average status.

In turn, the statements of the subject regarding the housemother, when classified according to their "intent, whether commendatory or adversely critical," reveal notable differences according to choice-status of the subject.

The under-chosen appear as viewing the housemother in terms of her personal relationship to them as individuals, as they see this relationship to be. (B.I. 26, 27, 28, 33, 34.) They reveal themselves to be almost completely limited in their thinking regarding the housemother to a "personalized" plane. The average-chosen subject shows a wider scope, appearing to view the adult not only in this light but also in terms of her conduct towards the group as a whole, while the over-chosen subject appears to think of the housemother almost totally in terms of her conduct towards the entire membership. Thus praise of the housemother taking the form of "encourages me" or "understands me" shows an incidence of 34 for under-chosen, 25 for average, and but once for over-chosen. Similarly complaints about the housemother which take the form of "doesn't encourage me," "doesn't understand me," "is unfair to me," show an incidence of 47 for under-chosen, 12 for average, and but twice for over-chosen.[1] On the other hand, praise of the housemother which takes the form of "displays thoughtfulness of the individual (any individual) when reprimanding," "shows impartiality in dealing with group," "obliges individual (any) to meet reasonable standards," "trusts the individual (any)," and "believes in the individual's potentialities" (B.I. 39, 40, 41, 42, 44) show twice as great an incidence for over-chosen individual as for average-chosen, and no incidence at all for under-chosen; and "displays consistency (see examples) in behavior" is also given as praise twice as often by over-chosen as by average-chosen and but one incidence appears for the under-chosen (B.I. 43).

In two expressions of commendation of the housemother, the average subject exceeds others: "exhibits dependable behavior" shows an incidence of 13 for average, 8 for over-chosen, and but once for under-chosen (B.I. 37); and "provides opportunities to improve" is six times as frequently given by average-chosen as it is by over-chosen, and about twice as often by average- as by under-chosen (B.I. 35).

[1] It should be recalled that intelligence showed no correlation with choice-status so that these differences in "thinking" cannot be accounted for by differences in intelligence level among the subjects in each of the three positions of choice-status.

The explanation is suggested that the over-chosen assume housemother *should* exhibit such behavior, and hence she may not draw praise on such account. (*E.g.* Why should a housemother go back on her word? or Why shouldn't a housemother provide opportunities to improve?) The average- and under-chosen may be, too, a more "grateful" or less critical group. This explanation seems to gain support from the great frequency of "shows courtesy," given in commendation by under-chosen and average-chosen four times as often as by over-chosen. Similarly, the under-chosen appear more "glad for" the housemother's "sense of humor" than do the average- or the over-chosen subjects (B.I. 38).

On the other hand, the over-chosen show three times as great an incidence of "listens to and considers girls' opinions," as praiseworthy comment on the housemother, than do the average-chosen and no incidence appears for the under-chosen (B.I. 45). A wider base of criticism generally is shown by the over-chosen: the frequency of "does not listen to and consider girls' opinions" (B.I. 29), "exhibits behavior inconsiderate of individual when reprimanding" (B.I. 30), and "displays distrust of girls' use of initiative" (B.I. 32) is three times as great for over-chosen as for average subjects, and still less frequent for under-chosen. Similarly, "impatient behavior" (B.I. 31) forms the basis of adverse comment not at all by under-chosen, but fairly often by average citizens and twice as often by over-chosen as by average citizens.

The lack of such criticism of the housemother on the part of the under-chosen cannot be explained by absence of impatient behavior towards them as individuals for it is mainly because of such behavior towards them in particular as well as towards individuals generally that the over-chosen criticize the housemother. The explanation is suggested that the under-chosen do not see impatient behavior as such, but consider the housemother's conduct more in terms of "gives others more chances than me," etc. (B.I. 28), or else see it on a "personalized" basis.

There thus appear several differences in the manner of evaluating an adult in authority which distinguish the three groups of subjects having over-chosen, average-chosen, and under-chosen positions of choice-status in the test-population.

The over-chosen appear generally to view this adult in relation to all members of the group and to "judge" her accordingly. Their statements imply as much resentment of a housemother's intolerance or impatience with the less adequate citizen as if this attitude were directed towards themselves. They are apparently in no sense "blind to" her shortcomings even on occasion when such shortcomings may not directly affect them as individuals. They show an impartiality and an impersonal attitude both in their commendation and their criticism which surpasses that shown by the average citizen or by the under-chosen citizen. The two latter groups appear largely concerned with how the housemother treats them as individuals rather than with how she conducts herself generally towards the group as a whole; for the under-chosen especially, but also for the average subject, the housemother appears to be thought of by them on a personalized plane: her relationship to them as individuals. The thinking of the over-chosen appears not only not to be limited in this sense but to show evidence of a greater emotional maturity on their own part reflected in their resentment of the housemother for distrusting the individual's use of initiative and unwillingness to consider the individual's opinion, and the like, as well as in their appreciation of her trusting the individual, being consistent in her behavior, believing in the individual's potentialities, showing willingness to listen to opinions, being impartial, obliging the individual to meet reasonable standards and the like.

The question arises whether the impersonal attitude of the over-chosen, as compared particularly with the under-chosen, reflects a greater need on the part of the under-chosen for "affection" from the housemother, a need which hardly can be presumed to be so great on the part of the over-chosen since they have, so to speak, affection to spare, coming to them from their peers. The question arises also whether the individual in order to be impartial and impersonal in his estimate of others when he is himself a part of the situation must be fairly secure in his relationship to the members of the group as a whole, in which he is a participant. The evidence appears to indicate that for the adolescent, at least, a choice-status of under-chosen to the *extreme* extent here used in selecting under-chosen subjects in this analysis (1 S.D. below the mean of group) carries with it outlooks and personalized attitudes which may be indicative of considerable insecurity, as well as conduct which reflects emotional immaturity as well. As the individual's choice-status "rises," behavior trends also "rise" in the sense that there is more and more evidence of adult-like behavior and outlooks which indicate that the individual is seeing himself more in relation to all other members of the group than simply to the person to whom he is directly responsible. Whether change in choice-status or change in the individual's behavior occurs first, this research cannot suggest; it would seem, however, that they have a very close development and are most certainly interactive at all points.

Non-differentiating Behaviors

On the other hand, certain other behaviors show no relationship to the choice-status of the individual. Marked "ups and downs" in emotional tone apparently do not affect the extent to which the individual is chosen by others: moody behavior shows an approximately equal incidence for under-chosen, average- and over-chosen subjects (B.I. 47). Thus moodiness, *per se*, does not appear as a factor which may act either adversely or favorably upon the individual's choice-status; evidently its role is not crucial in inter-personal relationships. Similarly, "generous behavior," such as sharing possessions, services, and the like, does not appear to differentiate between the individuals who are average-chosen, under-chosen, or over-chosen; it shows practically the same incidence at each level of choice-status (B.I. 48). "Satisfactory" personal habits of neatness, cleanliness, table manners, and the like, comprise also a kind of behavior which does not apparently either foster or discourage choice on the part of others towards the individual (B.I. 46). It would appear that the three behaviors found to be non-differentiating are behaviors which, whether the individual stands "high" or "low" in them, will not determine in one direction or another the placement of the individual among the under-chosen or over-chosen or average-chosen citizens in a community.

Further Differentiating Behaviors

In addition to the foregoing behavior analysis, a classification of behaviors exhibited by the subject in conferring with the psychologist reveals choice-status to be distinguished by a varying incidence of certain behaviors both in respect to the individual's situation and in respect to his relation to the situations of the others. For inclusion in the analysis the behavior must have been exhibited on three or more separate occasions by the subject. Since this analysis concerns the subject's behavior in a different setting, apart from that in which it was observed by a housemother, the findings bear further significance for an understanding of behavior.

The initiative of the over-chosen, so frequently both commended and complained of according to the viewpoint of the housemother, is further reflected in two other behavior expressions: three times as frequently the over-chosen subject, as compared with the average-chosen subject, made "unasked-for suggestions to the psychologist for the welfare of the others" (B.I. 52). This form of behavior was noted not at all for the under-chosen subjects. Further, "visits to the psychology office in behalf of another individual (instead of self)" were made approximately seven times as often by over-chosen individuals as by average-chosen, and not at all by under-chosen subjects (B.I. 49). On the other hand, "complaints (to the psychologist) of another girl's conduct towards her" were most frequent on the part of the under-chosen, only half as frequent on the part of the average-chosen, and rare for over-chosen (about one third as frequent as for average-chosen, B.I. 53). The explanation is suggested that relative lack of facility on the part of the individual of of average-choice-status, or of less than average-choice-status, in dealing with others may take the form of complaining about them.

Moreover, occasions on which the individual displayed insight into her own behavior (in conferring with psychologist) show over twice as great an incidence for the over-chosen as for the average-chosen subject, while the average-chosen show almost twice as great an incidence as is found for the under-chosen (B.I. 50). The results are supported further by similar frequencies for occasions when the subject "in speaking about others shows insight into their behavior" (B.I. 51). (For examples of such remarks as are considered "insightful," see italicized words, pp. 191-194.)

It will be recognized that the lifting out of behavior "items," for the purpose of ascertaining characteristic tendencies, disregards the relative position such items may have within the total setting in which the behavior was displayed and in consequence cannot describe the personality of individual subjects. The analysis aims solely to discover whether choice-status tends to be characterized by different "quantities" of behaviors.

On the other hand, the question may well be, at least for certain kinds of behavior, not whether there is more or less of such behavior found for a given choice-status, but whether or not there is *any* such behavior found to accompany a given choice-status. The difference may in some instances be rather a qualitative difference that provides the crucial variable.

It will be recognized, too, that estimates of behavior characteristics based on housemother reports only take no account of the subjective differences between housemothers in viewing behavior displayed before them. Behavior which one housemother would construe as non-commendable and as requiring assistance to "alter" another housemother might construe as commendable and to be encouraged. *E.g.* one subject might be considered by her housemother as exerting too much initiative "in matters which were none of her business" and "not knowing her place"; the same behavior on the part of another subject might be considered by the latter's housemother as "exceptionally helpful." The classification of the behaviors also reflects the housemother's viewpoint in other ways. It is of interest, for example, that the housemothers report "dominant and aggressive" behaviors more frequently for the under-chosen, but do not often so interpret the behaviors of the over-chosen. It is as if the *manner* of exerting their influence, on the part of the over-chosen, is so well "disguised" by finesse of one sort or another, that really dominant and aggressive behavior, coming from them, is not so thought of by either their peers or their housemothers. Yet it is their suggestions which gain a hearing and are frequently utilized. A study of the individual personalities of the subjects, however, reveals the behaviors described are not unduly distorted by housemother-bias.

CHAPTER IX

LEADERSHIP AND ISOLATION

In various directions, the evidence points to a certain stability in inter-personal relationships of choice, positive and negative. The analysis has stressed this stability. But within the "architecture of relative permanence" there is constant movement: the positions of individuals are continually shifting in an "upward" and "downward" direction (and even remaining on a certain level over a long period registers the fact that the individual has been replenishing relationships which are severed by some members leaving the population of the study). What appears as stability of structure is actually the *slowness* of this continuous movement within the structure.

The reasons for this stability and this slowness of flux within the structure appear in the behaviors distinguishing choice-status. Individuals who are isolated from choice by other members for them show in the trends of their behavior tendencies to conduct themselves in ways which imply a marked lack of orientation on their part to the elements of the total group situation; frequently they not only fail to contribute constructively to the group but hinder by their behavior the activities undertaken by other members. Especially by their "externalizing" of private feelings of irritability and the like they subtract from rather than add to the general tone of the social milieu about them.

Individuals who are over-chosen by the expression of choice from other members for them show, in the trends of their behavior, tendencies to conduct themselves in ways which imply an unusual sensitivity and orientation on their part to the elements of the total group situation; to a very much greater extent than the average member, they constructively contribute to enlarge the social field for participation of other citizens, to encourage the development of individual members, to make possible a wider, richer common experience for all by their innovations altering the *status quo* of things as they find them; they are thus creative improvers of others' situations as well as their own and in exercising such leadership are at the same time chosen as the most wanted associates by the membership. Especially by their "internalizing" of private worries, anxieties, and the like, and by their public display of high *esprit de corps* they enhance the general tone of the social milieu about them.

Choice appears as an expression which is not only a response of attraction towards an individual but a response which may, in a sense, be considered "earned" by the person chosen. The isolates are individuals who in a community numbering about four and a half hundred persons do not actively "win" the attraction of any other members to them; conversely, the leaders are individuals who in the same community are eminently successful in "winning" the attraction of other members to them.

It might be conjectured that individuals who are "sent" into isolation or "elevated" to leadership respectively by the membership of the community as a whole might in each instance be found to resemble one another *as a group* in their respective personality attributes; the findings, however, reveal both isolates as individuals and leaders as individuals not only to resemble but to differ markedly in personality from one another as they vary from each other respectively as a group. While many points of overlapping appear in the personalities of leaders *as individuals*, and similarly, for isolates *as individuals*, real differences in personality also appear to characterize the members of either group respectively as *persons*. For illustration of the nature of personality differences between isolates (and also of near-isolates who are chosen by one individual) and of typical motivations given in expression of rejections towards them on Test II, a résumé of the personality-picture with accompanying rejections are given for a number of such subjects. The isolated subjects selected for illustration were likewise isolated on Test I; the two near-isolated were in one instance isolated and in the other, near-isolated on Test I. Similarly for illustration of the nature of personality differences between leaders, a résumé of the personality-picture for each of a number of such subjects is given, with a few examples of choice motivations towards them. The selected leaders were also over-chosen on Test I.

Isolates and Near-isolates (*chosen by one*)

Among the subjects no isolate and but one near-isolate appears who is not rejected by a relatively large number of individuals. The near-isolate, chosen by one person and rejected by no one, is Amelia. As there were no motivations of rejection expressed towards her, remarks regarding her gathered in other contexts are included.

AMELIA [1, 2]

(near-isolate: chosen by one; rejected by none)

IQ 96; age 17 years 8 months; length of residence 1 year 9 months; Test II

Appearance. Small in stature and features; straight black hair; blue eyes; expression practically devoid of animation, almost apathetic;

[1] All names are fictionized.
[2] See Table VII, p. 80.

voice low and monotonous, very slow speech tempo; gentle, shy manner; overly polite and unassuming.

Personality-behavior picture. Extremely passive and unassertive in reactions; says very little about herself or others; rarely volunteers information; makes no requests of others yet invites their imposing requests upon her; has to be deterred from doing work of others; is indiscriminate in offering her services to others; appears to crave affection and to seek outlets for her affectionate feelings towards others by doing "kindnesses" (in the form of tasks which are mainly menial or uninteresting) for anyone who happens to be near her; makes herself promiscuously available for duties so that whoever cares to may impose upon her invariable good-nature. Shows no initiative in exerting pressure on others to obtain what is her due in return for her labors. Is almost painfully unassuming. Very impressionable and suggestible. Shows practically no insight into herself or the motives of others in respect to their conduct towards her. Conforms to school rules without questioning. Uncritical to the point of being gullible. Appears not to be able to endure anyone's not thinking well of her; excuses her waiting upon others by saying, "I did it because I thought she would be mad at me if I didn't." Apparent difficulty in marshalling herself to take a stand on conflicting issues; consequently is considered "wishy-washy" by other girls. Actually her behavior is consistent (a "yes" to everything) but it is interpreted by peers as vacillation — sometimes standing for this and sometimes for that; this produces a feeling she cannot be counted upon to act as a situation calls for one to act. Frank, naïve, and uncircumspect in general behavior but harbors some awareness of others' lack of appreciation of her; this is shown indirectly in her typical remarks about over-chosen individuals (whom she herself chooses exclusively): "When you do her a favor, she doesn't forget it; she does something nice back for you and other girls don't seem to think about it." Timid, unexpressive, "uncrystallized" personality; calm and restful but gives impression of being sad because of lack of animation. (Sociogram, p. 111.)

Remarks towards Amelia:

"She hasn't any learning ability at all. You can't teach anything to her. As far as her ways go, she has a lovely way about her. She likes to be everybody's maid. When there's anything to do, she's right on hand to do it. It makes me feel sick for anybody to be such an easy-mark; I just don't like to have anything to do with her."

"She stays by herself. She'd drop anything to do anything for anybody else no matter what it is or who it is. That's her worst enemy, her habit of doing favors senselessly."

"She's pitiful, doesn't stand for anything, at least not for anything I've been able to find out; always being somebody's maid, always doing something somebody asks her to do."

"She gets along all right with the girls by doing a lot of favors. Sometimes they are favors a friend wouldn't do, like other people's work for them. She can't say 'no;' maybe she thinks she has a good character, for myself I call that way no character at all."

"If she can't do the big things, she'd just as soon do the little things because she says you have to start that way. She gets along with people but they tease her because she doesn't fight back. She's so quiet that if I talk with her, it's mainly a conversation with myself; I wouldn't get anything out of being associated with her."

"There's nothing definite about her. She never takes sides on issues that come up. She's slow and sort of not interesting. There's nothing against her but nothing in her favor much either. You don't feel she's around hardly. She's a little silly; she'll let people put things over on her. She's not responsible. She'll get herself in such a position that she has to take the blame, like a foolish good sport would. It's almost as if she has no self-respect the way she lets people get her to do things for them. Otherwise the girls don't bother with her much, but she doesn't catch on. They really don't seem to take to her; in my opinion, they take her for a ride. She has no special friends like the rest of us."

From the point of view of one not a member of her group, it is not readily understandable why an individual having the personality of Amelia should be near-isolated by her peers. Amelia behaves offensively towards no one; instead she is obliging to the point of being at everyone's beck-and-call. She is shy, gentle, unassuming, and generally uncircumspect. The remarks of her peers indicate, however, that such behavior makes them feel pity for her but that pity in itself is not sufficient grounds for positive choice; on the other hand the fact that they apparently feel sorry for her may account for the fact that they express no rejections towards her.

Lack of choice for her appears related also to her failure to win the respect of others mainly on account of her indiscriminate "waiting upon" anyone who is near her and allowing them to give her the role of a servant in the group; secondly, to her failure to take a stand based on decisions made by herself rather than giving a "yes" to each question asked her — her suggestibility being in consequence interpreted by her peers as "nothing against her but nothing in her favor much either." The repercussion of the presence of her personality in the group appears to be close to nil; neither positively nor negatively does she appear to affect the general behavior or choice reactions of other members. Amelia as a person in the psychological structure of the group might be called an *neglected* isolate.

The near-isolate Ruth, who is chosen by one individual, appears, unlike Amelia, to have a personality which is definite and winsome but, also unlike Amelia, is highly insincere and circumspect in dealing with others.

RUTH

(near-isolate: chosen by one; rejected by seven)

IQ 99; age 15 years 11 months; length of residence 2 years 1 month; Test II

Appearance. Above-average height; medium weight; good posture, rather graceful; small, delicate, pretty features; attractive coloring with curly, crisp reddish hair; straightforward, trusting, appealing expression. Well-poised. Voice resonant; speech marked by very clear, almost clipped enunciation; talks freely in interesting, effortless manner.

Personality-behavior picture. Self-confident, capable, realistic, ambitious, but "unprincipled;" easily wins rapport with and the confidence of others with whom she comes into contact and then uses their attraction to and trust in her for purposes they had not intended she should.   Shows marked lack of integrity in her relations to others.   Tries to "climb" by playing up her own achievements and playing down those of others.   Gives an impression of naïveté but is actually highly circumspect and capable of considerable scheming to gain her ends quickly.   Temporarily can produce discord in a group by carrying remarks confided to her.   Appears to deliberately aim to produce discord out of resentment towards other individuals being looked to to direct activities; seems unable to tolerate others having a more important role than herself and contrives to disrupt their plans.   Carries out her designs unostentatiously, and until they have been traced to her it is not evident she has been the originator. Gives extremely plausible explanations which appear authentic until further investigated.   When told that another person has been hurt by her conduct, responds, "People make me tired being so sensitive."   Always appears self-possessed and certain of herself.   Competent but self-centered and unreliable, potentially harmful in her influence, insensitive.

Rejections towards Ruth:

"She has sort of deceitful ways about her.   She does things on the side and nobody knows about it.   Maybe I think she's worse than she is but I don't want to be with people I can't trust.   I get feeling uneasy like they might lie about me or something, and Ruth is not exactly truthful."

"Ruth's just a case of too bad, too bad.   She's so charming and pretty and smart and has such nice manners, but Oh my! what a blow when you think she's OK and then discover what she really is.   She simply has no sense of honesty at all.   I don't mean she takes things — I mean she takes your trust in her and then acts just the opposite.   She looks like gold and turns out brass, or rusty iron would be more like it; anyway, I have no use for her; nobody can have.   She pretends to be what she isn't.   A 100 percent hypocrite.   Sponges on other people's efforts; tells the housemother she did some piece of work when maybe she did only a tiny part of it. Always out for credit and not for the thing itself, seeking a reputation.   She has the reputation but not the sort she thinks.   You have to check on everything she says.   When you catch up with her, she always has a handy alibi, and when you look into that you find she's exaggerated even in the alibi.   I told her several times that if everybody did as she did there wouldn't be any confidence in people because nobody could trust anybody else. She makes me so mad I guess I am hard on her. She always wants to have the lead but on account of how she is, she's not in demand; it's a shame really, what a mess she is."

"She has a way of getting people to think she's helping them and then she goes behind their back and tells some staff member everything they've told her. She's cooked her goose on this campus. She plays people against each other, that's mostly what I have against her. Tells me that Jacqueline wants something done and I do it and then find out Jacqueline never even talked to her about it, that it's really something she herself wanted. There isn't a straight-forward thing about her. She's quite advanced in her school work which makes her think she's advanced in everything else; she's dense, you can tell her and tell her and she still doesn't change. She's a rotter and wants to be important but people aren't as dumb to her ways as she thinks."

The motivations of Ruth's peers in rejection of her indicate that she is in disrepute with them because of her violation of standards of conduct which the membership consider minimal for cooperative living together. The lack of choice to her appears related not to a lack of capacity on her part to establish rapport with others but to her having repeatedly shown disregard of and distorted the "trust" others place in her before they become aware of her capacity for duplicity; it appears related, too, to her failure to respond favorably to others' admonitions to "better" conduct — "You can tell her and tell her and she still doesn't change." The fact that Ruth casually thwarts the members' attempts to make her "change" may account for the harshness of their condemnation of her.[3]

[3] It would appear that Ruth, nevertheless, possesses potentiality for attaining a leadership position under other circumstances, e.g., in a community less characterized by face-to-face contact between its members and, hence, one in which concealment of insincerity of conduct generally may more readily be accomplished. It should be noted that occasionally, as in the instance of Ruth, rejection appears as a counteraction following discovery that a much wanted relationship of rapport is seemingly impossible to establish. Rejection may thus reflect resentment of the individual who could belong to the "inner circle" but "mysteriously," as if disinterested, passes it by.

The isolate Jessie presents a simpler personality picture.

JESSIE

(isolate: chosen by none; rejected by 17)

IQ 83; age 13 years 8 months; length of residence 1 year 8 months;
Test II

Appearance. Chubby and small but very muscular physique; brown wavy thick hair kept dishevelled by habit of running fingers through it; pasty complexion but very red lips; beautifully-shaped blue eyes; expression almost desperate, watching other person as if she expected some dire thing to happen; manner rough; voice very low, almost a whisper, except when angry.

Personality-behavior picture. Petulant, quarrelsome, easily upset, given to pouting and sullen defiance of reasonable requests; seldom reports what, if anything, is bothering her at the time until she first has exhibited a temper tantrum; apparently makes little effort to control temper, displaying it even on very inauspicious occasions (as during a party). Has a habit of staring which is annoying if not distressing to other girls. Seldom verbally communicative except during temper outbursts; then expresses notions that indicate she considers herself persecuted and hated by those around her. During such periods of uncontrolled excitation, will kick and fight and scratch, apparently with intention to harm others. On other occasions, when not angry, can become so excited as to cause general commotion by her activities though her evident intention may be to cooperate. Extremely resistant to suggestion; wants to have her own way even in a group where falling in with common effort is needed. Appears to feel others are forcing her to do things their way; frequently gets attention by behaving in such manner that she cannot be ignored. Apprehensive, aggressive, self-centered, suspicious and ill-at-ease with contemporaries.

Rejections towards Jessie:

"The only thing I don't like about Jessie is that when something doesn't go her way she just gets up in the air. She is bound she is going to get it. On account of her disposition I don't want to be with her. She refuses to do anything anybody asks her to do. She herself can never see anything to do; if she wanted to sit down she would sit down, even if there was a pile of work around her to do. She just doesn't care."

"She likes to do things the opposite what others like to do whether it's right or wrong. She's stubborn and she has an awful rotten disposition. She's always flying around in tantrums. She'll give you something one day and take it back the next. She just does funny things to pick a fight. You see her doing something and tell her about it and she will say she didn't do it when you are standing there."

"She goes around with a look on and makes you feel that you have done something. She goes around with an expression in her eyes. She's always on the outs about things, antagonistic-like, acts as if other girls were against her when it's herself who's against everybody."

"She has a fierce temper. She just lets it run right away with her. She's terribly nervous. She stands in front of you and sways back and forth or bites her hands, the knuckles."

"When she gets into a rage, I always have a feeling she is dramatizing getting mad; I mean I don't feel she's mad herself. She likes to make people afraid of her. I said so to her and she said, 'Do you think I could?' If you ask her to do something, maybe she'll do it and maybe she won't, and also she doesn't care how it's done."

Jessie, unlike Ruth, shows no duplicity; she directly expresses herself in temper tantrums and similar behavior when matters do not apparently go as she would wish. Petulant, quarrelsome, and easily upset, she appears rejected because she is, at least in part, felt by her peers to be aggressive and attempting to dominate them by "scaring" them into fear of her; secondly, her contrariness when asked to cooperate is interpreted by her peers as stubbornness. It is of interest that while it is said in rejection of Jessie that "she refuses to do anything anybody asks her to do" and "herself can never see anything to do . . . would sit down even if there was a pile of work around her to do," it is said in pitying disparagement of Amelia, "when there's anything to do, she's right on hand to do it . . . makes me feel sick for any-body to be such an easy-mark." The personalities of Jessie and Amelia appear to illustrate in this respect opposite extremes in cooperative conduct neither of which is considered by fellow-members to be desirable.

The isolate Mary presents a personality-picture which differs radically from those of either Amelia, Ruth, or Jessie.

MARY

(isolate: chosen by none; rejected by 12)

IQ 77; age 15 years 3 months; length of residence 2 years 2 months; Test II

Appearance. Medium-sized physique inclined to over-weight; bushy, curly brown hair falling over face; round hazel eyes; jovial grin and constantly laughing expression; lounging posture as if rolling along when walking, restless motions when sitting, tosses head particularly when talking. Voice loud and discordant; cheery, lively manner; appears always to be amused by something.

Personality-behavior picture. Makes herself immediately at home in any group and acts as if she never suspected that others might consider she has barged in upon them. Incessant talker; conversation rambling and superficial in emotional tone. Seems to articulate every thought or observation that occurs to her and to find them all "delightful" enough that others would wish to hear them; wears an almost ecstatically happy expression as she talks; appears to be blithesomely unaware of others' feelings in respect to her; is so voluble that she is often asked to stop talking; on such occasions does not seem to feel "hurt" but soon begins again to talk in a stream. Has an active imagination and elaborates on simple happenings; but fantasies appear pointless because she chooses her audience and occasion indiscriminately. Aggressive and self-assertive, very affectionate and demonstrative in a boisterous manner, as if blissfully happy and unable to control exuberant expression. Works and plays in a hit-or-miss fashion, appearing unable to tackle a task or a game in an organized way. Is easily distracted from whatever she is occupied with and inadvertently tends to distract others without apparently realizing she is doing so. Shows little orientation to elements in a situation. Frequent laughter, in consequence, appears unprovoked. Insight practically lacking.

Rejections towards Mary:

"Mary doesn't have many good things about her that I can see. She never can find anything to do, just wanders, never has anything on her mind. And she's so fidgety I get tense all the while she's around; I hardly can stand to be near her, with her constant smile and talking."

"She's terribly silly. She talks about things that haven't any meaning and then she'll laugh. Everything is funny to her. It gets on a person's nerves, a phonograph that never stops. You can't get away from her no matter what you do."

"She's always talking and never gets anywheres. No matter what you do you can't stop her. She tags after you if you tell her you have things to do. I don't see any signs of ambition in her and I have never seen her concentrate on anything; she doesn't seem to get interested in getting ahead."

"Mary's attitude of doing as little as she can as fast as she can annoys me. Maybe it's not her attitude but it's the result of how she is I'm speaking about. She has her good points all right but I'm against the kind of way she does what she does. Also nothing about her appeals to me. Her voice is harsh and it bothers me; her walk just grates on me, she's so sort of uneasy. And mostly I can't stand her acting like she had something to be laughing at every minute when nothing funny's going on."

"When a girl is entertaining someone, she'll continually walk up and down past the guest and if not invited to join the group, she invites herself. She's just heedless that way."

In contrast to Jessie especially, Mary is *always* communicative, cheerful, amused with herself and the present situation, exuberant and out-going. Nevertheless, she is rejected by many and unchosen. The motivations of rejection to her indicate that her peers interpret her behavioral expressions of superabundance of good spirits as evidence that she is "silly," and her over-flow in speech as "always talking and never gets anywheres"; her failure to perceive the more serious outlook of others leads them to want to be rid of association with her as she appears to distract them from the matter at hand.

Again, the conduct standards set by the members as desirable appear not to be met by Mary whom they reject also as not showing "any signs of ambition" and never seen to "concentrate on anything" and "doesn't seem to get interested in getting ahead."

On the other hand, while Mary is invariably a pleasant person, Margo appears isolated and rejected by many even though she is a colorful personality.

MARGO

(isolate: chosen by none; rejected by 16)

IQ 85; age 17 years 9 months; length of residence 2 years 4 months; Test II

Appearance. Tall, slender stature; straight, wispy black hair; deep-blue eyes; sharp features, aquiline nose; high color; expression anxious and tense; generally gives impression of being emotionally overwrought about some immediate situation; sometimes calm, then appears capable, energetic, and very attractive in an exotic way; voice deep except when excited, then high-pitched, very emotional in tone; manner confident and assertive.

Personality-behavior picture. Shows marked swings in emotional expression, at times dejected, again excitedly happy; during either period is on the defensive towards persons around her. Much given to fantasy and other mental constructs in which she has a heroic role. Reacts by being violently offended when interpreted by other girls as fabricating. Is interested in cartooning and caricature; shows talent for spotting and "taking off" the inconsistent behavior or peculiar idiosyncrasies of others; does this occasionally in their presence when deed may embarrass the person in question (as speech of girl who has projecting teeth); will not allow with good humor similar jokes on self; bursts into spell of weeping under such circumstances. Very unrealistic in her ambitions and jealous of others who appear to be on way to achieving theirs. Appears to feel she is not superior and is not satisfied not to be. Shows a degree of talent in use of words. Writes stories which are well organized and packed with dramatic incidents which are feelingly related. In no other behavior or expression of thought trends, does she show a sense of organization. Is precipitous, almost startling in her behavior towards others while apparently seeking to win their esteem. Reacts hysterically if others speak of her conduct disparagingly to her. Imaginative, self-assertive, self-centered. Very greatly over-active and restless. Inclined to brood.

Rejections towards Margo:

"Margo is just terrible. She's a regular pest. She acts silly. She thinks she's being comical but she carries it too far. She clowns but she does it in a way it hurts people. She doesn't seem to understand that she shouldn't do those things. She works hard but if she has a disagreeable job to do, sometimes she thinks she is being imposed upon. She always seems afraid she'll do more than another person does, more than her share I mean; and she even seems like she's afraid somebody will get more than she gets — I even think she eats more than she's hungry for for that reason. When she talks, she always picks people apart, just gossipy."

"She's awfully nervous; she bites her nails, wiggles, and can't stand still. Hardly nobody gets along with her."

"She doesn't keep anything to herself and if you give her an inch she takes a yard. If you tell her something she'll add something on and then repeat it. She goes from laughing to crying very easy."

"She has nice manners when she's calm but she's mostly nervous all the time. If you say something to her that she doesn't care to hear, she'll start shaking all over. Like if you say she's a liar, she'll start shaking all over and biting her nails and crying. If you say she can't do something she wants to do, it's just the same way — she gets nervous like that."

"If she thinks a job is too dirty, she won't do it and puts up a fuss; she wants to have only the clean jobs. She's entertaining I will say but she's awful careless *how* she entertains."

"It's not a nice thing to say about her but I don't think I would like to be associated with her. Every time she comes around, she makes me nervous. She just bites her nails right down and has a way of swinging herself back and forth. She has a habit of talking only about disagreeable things. I try to avoid her as much as possible. I share only the necessary conversation with her. She doesn't have very much company with the girls. When she comes around, they all move away."

The lack of choice to Margo and the many rejections of her appear related to the fact that her moods carry her to extremes of conduct which the members of the group are at a loss to cope with and hence do not condone in common living together; first, they evidently feel distraught and uncomfortable, unable to deal with her on an understanding basis; second, they apparently come to resent her because of their protective or solicitous feelings for the persons among them who may be the object of her talent for caricaturing. Moreover, Margo's lack of a simpler variety of humor is emphasized by her unwillingness to accept fun directed in turn at her or the face-to-face criticisms of her peers — she "goes from laughing to crying very easy." Certain members also appear to see in her a tendency to be careful not to do more than her share of work and to consider as "dirty" (so to speak, below her) an occasional menial or unpleasant task assigned to her; such behavior apparently goes against the standard the members consider "right."

It should be noted, too, that whereas Mary is adversely criticized as a person who "talks about things that haven't any meaning and then she'll laugh; everything is funny to her," the implication is that Mary talks in fun, innocently and senselessly, whereas Margo is considered as having "a habit of talking only about disagreeable things" although both individuals are avoided by members of the group.

The isolate Vera shows a personality-picture which hardly at all resembles that of any other isolate or near-isolate in the community. In contrast to Ruth especially, Vera appears to care greatly to contribute to others both her ideas and her affection and to be extremely appreciative of capacities which other persons possess, particularly in social facility in which she realizes herself to be lacking. Since her motivational responses in choice reveal much of her outlook and feeling for others, three of her statements in choice of others (all leaders) are included.

VERA

(isolate: chosen by none; rejected by 18)

IQ 118; age 14 years 9 months; length of residence 2 years 6 months; Test II

Appearance. Petite figure; pale complexion; dreamy, thoughtful, rather sad expression; slate-blue eyes; nose small and retroussé seeming out of proportion with rest of face. Gives a first impression of being self-absorbed, timid, somewhat withdrawn; in speech, however, shows herself highly articulate. Voice confident and well-modulated but increases in tempo the longer she talks.

Personality-behavior picture. Diffident and hesitant in approach to peers but readily enters into conversation with an adult if she feels the adult responds adequately; in such conversation conducts herself, with considerable social grace, as a peer of the adult, showing no tendency to place more "value" on the latter's point of view than on her own; appears to delight in such exchange but does not seek it unless the adult opens the way for her to do so; able in making articulate her opinions in such situations.

Shy and retiring in manner when observed in a group, wears an expression suggesting she is entertaining private thoughts and is "not among those present" except when the main focus of attention, as when others are listening to her; then becomes very animated in expression and seems to be swept away by desire to make listeners grasp the importance of what she is saying; a curious increase in tempo of speech accompanies increase in general emotionality the longer she talks; when listeners indicate they understand, animation sharply subsides and she becomes quiet and apparently again ab-

sorbed with private thought trends; when listeners indicate misunder-
standing, lack of interest, or difference of opinion, an expression as
of anguish or physical pain passes over her face, lingers a while and
then her expression takes on again a look of private occupation. She
does not give in at once except to a reaction of lack of interest; towards persons who argue back, she vehemently argues in return, becoming so excited that discussion is rudely ended by one or another
participant.

Always requires overt demonstration of warmth of reception when
talking to others; otherwise apparently feels others are disinterested.
Never known to talk to peers about self or others; discourses with
them only about ideas and expresses herself in a vocabulary that lacks
humor and is described by peers as "dictionary stuff." In tone of
talk with peers, in contrast to that with adults, there is a marked
absence of a casual touch or of a spirit of fun. Is characterized by
other girls as "an intellectual," "ethereal," "doesn't know how to be
herself." Is avoided by others apparently because of their feeling
uncomfortable in her presence.

Often tries to get others to incorporate her original ideas into
activities; is almost completely unsuccessful in such attempts. Occasionally gets one over through a round-about route — telling someone who then tells another until someone puts it into operation.

While showing pronounced lack of social facility to make other
members of the group appreciate her potential contribution, gives
repeated evidence of exceptional insight both into herself and peers.
Very appreciative of other individuals and gives no evidence of entertaining feelings of self-pity when similar appreciation does not
greet her. Never complains of other individuals' treatment of her.
Sensitive, discriminating, but emotionally over-intense in her reactions. Ambitious, patient, studiously inclined. (Sociogram, p. 106.)

Rejections towards Vera:

Average citizen: "She is quite a boaster. She can do what somebody
else can't do, *she* thinks, boasting about her brilliance.
If she's so brilliant, I say it should show up without her
telling about it. Of course she doesn't say right out
'I'm brighter than you are,' but the way she expresses
herself you know that's what she thinks even if she does
go around with a long face. Personally I never bother
to speak to her. Jean does though, but then she's fortu-

nate, 's got a large heart, room for everybody no matter how nasty they are. Jean tells me I am narrow-minded. For the time I act different but soon Vera gets on my nerves again and I just stay away or walk off from her."

Jean: "She is quiet, odd, different from most girls. She's quite a brilliant girl but she has a tendency towards dumbness. She's quite bright in school and she gets along good but when she gets around someone, it seems as though she is asking dumb questions or arguing on points that don't matter — like how a thing should be said. It seems as though her remarks come out without her thinking what the other persons will think of her insinuating they don't know much vocabulary. She doesn't think at the time, but later she will admit to me that she didn't know how rude she put it. She doesn't think as fast as she talks. Vera and I don't think along the same lines at all. What interests the rest interests me, but she figures very few things are interesting and mostly only her own ideas. I have to admit she is clever on thinking things out but I can't help feeling Vera is a snob. Sometimes she isn't tactful and shows she hasn't much respect for people who can do only little tasks and then of course when she wants them to cooperate with her on a project they refuse and are mean about it."

Above average but not over-chosen: "Most all the time she seems to be above everybody and that gets my goat. I have to hide my feelings not to be fresh to her. She says a thing and you don't know how to take it. She's kind of cutting sometimes and you can't tell whether she means it or not. I don't think it's conceit; I think she doesn't know *how* to put manners into talking to a person."

Another leader: "I think what's wrong with her is she's got a perfection complex. Always talking about ideals. She's pleasing to talk to at times but then at other times little things seem to tear her apart. Her personality is not suitable I think. She can't put herself on a level with a person; she's too far-away or something."

Jacqueline: "It's hard to get Vera in on things because other people don't feel right with her. When she begins to talk on subjects, she is so earnest, it's like her life depended on you getting the point of what she's saying and you don't feel good because you feel she cares too much so you want to keep her off controversial subjects, where if she would just say things plain and not so strong you could reach some understanding. It's practically impossible to get anywhere in a discussion if she's in on it because if she believes a thing she can't stand it if you don't believe it. Her ideas get thrown out because she can't stand the open air on them. She's sort of on the blue side and I can't let myself get too interested in her or I'd have to neglect all the other girls for her."

*Average
citizen:*   "She gets off the subject when you're talking to her or else if she stays on it she talks in such peculiar language that nobody knows what she means really. Jean says she understands Vera but I think she says that so we'll give Vera a chance to try out some of her crazy ideas. That's where Jean has another guess coming because we're not going to support plans of Vera's when Vera puts on her sensitivity act when you simply say maybe, 'How about talking so a person can tell what you're saying?' She antagonizes a person to such an extent that hardly anyone will congratulate her when she deserves it, she's so painful to cooperate with. Two times Jean played a trick on us; she let Vera plan two events and didn't tell us and everything went so smoothly you'd think Jean had done it all herself the girls were so enthusiastic. But all the same we didn't like Vera better for it because we're against her ways on account of her pride in herself."

Vera's statements about her choices:

Jacqueline: "Jacqueline is altogether wonderful. She has an original mind, and she shares her mind with others. I am like her in how I think but I'm not like her in other ways because nobody is interested so much in my ideas. She knows how to make people *want* to listen to her. I feel glad for weeks after talking to *her* for a few minutes."

Jean: "Jean's the most perfect girl I ever met. My heart goes out to her so. She makes you feel a part of things.

Even when everybody puts you down, Jean it is who comes along and lifts you out of yourself. She's one of the girls you can talk to — she listens to you and you feel she isn't doing it just to be nice but that she really is interested in what you say. She never thinks that everything is hopeless when you're discouraged and feeling let-down. Jean tries to make you better than yourself. Sometimes she goes in for telling me the good points about the school to make me content here. She talks most as much as I do when I once get started, only she talks more quiet than I do. She explains things in different ways, she can even hold a nice conversation with the girls. She makes them feel right in their place. That's what I wish I could. Jean has a keen way about her, just seems to draw people around her."

Olga: "Olga's like an older sister; she knows the answer to every question you want to ask, and I am never afraid to ask her. She helps you in every sort of way. You can carry on a conversation with her so easy. She is frank and so affectional. She will still like you if she liked you regardless if you get into a lot of scrapes. She's someone you can put your confidence in. She isn't exactly intellectual but she's awful nice all the same and she has a way about her — when you tell her something so serious she can make it so light for you. She has a way to relieve your worries so much. Why, even a little thing, when you have a grudge against a girl, she can reason it out for you. She isn't angry at you from one minute to the next. She's very dependable. You can count on a smile from her."

The motivations for rejection of Vera indicate that Vera's over-emotional manner when talking is disconcerting to her listeners and that her tendency to express herself in a bookish or unfamiliar vocabulary to her peers leads many of them to consider she attributes to herself a superiority which she does not consider them to possess. Whatever actually motivates her behavior towards other members of the group, she is credited by them as behaving so as to make herself incomprehensible to the average member and resented by them as "a boaster," as seeming to be "above everybody" as "too far-away," as having too much "pride in herself," and the like.

She is pictured by the two leaders Jean and Jacqueline as a person whom it is difficult to introduce into the activities of the group. The leader Jean appears to have concluded that Vera is fundamentally "a snob," a person who not only "shows" but really "hasn't much respect for people who can do only little tasks" and hence a person who does not "think along the same lines" as herself — Jean describing herself as one who is interested in "what interests the rest" and Vera as one who is interested "mostly only in her own ideas." The leader Jacqueline appears less vehement in her rejection of Vera and implies that she regrets Vera's "ideas get thrown out because she can't stand the open air on them"; Jacqueline seems to wish Vera "would just say things plain and not so strong" in order that "some understanding" could be reached. Jacqueline's statement indicates she wards off becoming "too interested" in her since the alternative would be that she would "have to neglect all the other girls for her."

The personalities of the isolates and near-isolates show, with but one exception (Ruth), the common characteristics of a marked incapacity for establishing rapport with other persons; they appear actively to repel choice and invite rejection to such extent as they cause "psychological discomfort" to others. Occasionally, too, the isolation of an individual appears to result from deliberate shunning of the individual as a reaction to misuse or "betrayal" on his part of rapport when established (Ruth); or, again, the individual may be isolated because his personality offers nothing to others which is sufficiently valued by them generally to draw choice to him (Amelia). No one personality-pattern accompanies isolation or near-isolation in the population of the test-community.

Leaders

The findings on leader-individuals likewise reveal wide individual differences in personality. Their reflection in *ways of behaving* show leadership to be definable by *a manner of interacting* with others.

The simplest personality picture shown by a leader is that of Olga. In certain respects she resembles the isolate Mary: Olga, too, is talkative, affectionately demonstrative, perfectly at-ease with others, emanates good will, and shows little tendency to "judge" or criticize those around her. In other respects she resembles the near-isolate Amelia: Olga, too, is quick to volunteer to help others in their work. In difference from Mary, however, her talking is oriented to the listener and in difference from Amelia, her generosity in helping others is not taken advantage of by them or considered a sign of "weakness." Further, unlike either Mary or Amelia, her behavior appears to reflect a personality which is "at peace" with itself and the world and emotionally equipped to raise the "morale" of others by her equanimity and the effectiveness of her approach to any situation.

OLGA [4]

(Leader: chosen by 19; rejected by 2)

IQ 85; age 15 years 11 months; length of residence 1 year 8 months; Test II

Appearance. A big, large-boned, awkward girl; wide, plain face; pleasant, interested look; stringy blond hair; blue eyes; smiling ex-

[4] See Table VIII, p. 81.

pression quick to break into laughter. Gives the impression of being irritation-proof, never on-the-outs with life or with those around her. A perfectly at-ease manner. Pleasant voice.

Personality-behavior picture. Completely unself-conscious. Never appears to think of what impression she is making on others or whether she is making any impression; direct and frank to the point of naïveté. Indiscriminately affectionate manner towards everybody, whether her friends or others, and whether newly met individuals or old acquaintances; very demonstrative. Solicitous for the physical well-being of others, generous to a fault. Talkative, always full of news; interested in whatever is a-foot, whether work or fun events. Works rapidly at own task, then jumps in and helps those nearest at their work. Her continuous good-heartedness does not appear to be taken advantage of; is not asked to do things for others; it is she who volunteers; others won't ask her because they know she'll consent and they just "like her so much they don't." Appears to regard with equanimity the realities of a situation whether others are likewise calm or are anxious and disconcerted. Quick to take tension out of situations; this quickness not intentional apparently; frequently when her action has resulted in taking tension out of the situation, there is evidence that she was unaware that the situation was tense or that her behavior eased it. Readily gets into a conversation; no respecter of "persons"; talks to "important" officials as if they were old-time friends. No finesse whatever, just the essence of naturalness, "a human being." Treats everyone as peers, with no discrimination. Not at all suggestible to ideas or actions of others not agreeing with her sense of "rightness." Always gives the other person the benefit of the doubt; if the other person disillusions her, she immediately tells her what's what and gets very angry. Many individuals react to her faith in them by not violating it, even though they act otherwise to others. Lack of a greater number of rejections to Olga appears to result from her vast simplicity, a simplicity, however, which does not reflect great lack of intelligence but rather a lack of "judging" others, which they in turn feel and are glad for. Has no overwhelming ambition; seems not fraught with the idea that what she does must be done because it is so important; instead seems to attend to task at hand because it's there to be done. Emanates complete and apparent forthrightness and good will to all around her.

Excellent sense of security; mature, though naïve, in her reactions. Will ask the reason why if not fully comprehending rules or directions. Definitely knows her own mind and will state her case if she thinks things are not fair or unintelligent as planned by staff. Admired by other girls for storming "the lion's den every time reasons aren't as plain as the nose on your face." An asset and a constructive influence in any group, "makes you believe in people, to know her."

Without deliberate finesse, without advance planning, the confident, enthusiastic, positive attack that Olga brings to the immediate problem at hand is infectious to those participating in the same situation, alters in a constructive direction their emotional outlook upon it, and results in renewed efforts on the part of the co-participants who out of respect for her effectiveness apparently feel challenged. Olga appears to have earned a role of leadership also because she seems to epitomize simple "humanness," "warmth," and "rightness" (yet does not make others feel they are less "good" than she is), together with practical capability and a capacity for "speaking up" for the group and for herself according to her own sense of what is "fair." She does not moralize or harbor resentment of things she does not approve; instead, she takes up the matter directly and at once with the persons involved (whether staff or girls) and is not hesitant to show her anger if satisfactory explanation is not given.

Yet observation of Olga does not reveal any indication that she is aware of her influence upon others. The leadership she exerts appears as an "unconscious" kind of leadership — the result of naïve, uncircumspect behavior but behavior which within the group in which it occurs seems to harness the energies of other members and to crystallize in its expression personality attributes respected if not aspired to by them.

The leader Edith contrasts sharply with Olga in personality. She is a "logical," deliberate person, not like Olga one who intuitively seems to act perspicaciously but one who instead thinks out each course of action she undertakes, weighs her words and "wastes" few of them. Unlike Olga, too, she is undemonstrative, almost distant in her manner.

EDITH

(Leader: chosen by 17; rejected by 3)

IQ 96; age 16 years 9 months; length of residence 1 year 10 months; Test II

Appearance. Slight in build, average height but seems taller; hair straight, colorless blond, hair-dress elaborate, fashioned with care; blue eyes; even finely-cut features; expression serious but relaxed; manner rather distant and prohibitive of easy approach, the opposite of ingratiating; has a nimble way of walking, as if not touching the ground; carriage and gestures in general also light and delicate; voice soft and well-modulated, tempo slow; never hurried in expressing herself.

Personality-behavior picture. Is direct and severely simple in conversing; in giving her opinions first states what other points of view there are, then states her stand; is so "logical" and practical, so independent and persuasive, that she appears to crystallize the opinions of other members of the group and to play a strategic role in deciding issues and shaping attitudes. Her presence in a discussion seems to set its "tone." Very deliberate in her behavior; cannot be rushed into "taking sides." Seldom proffers her suggestions until rest of group have had their "say." Acts as a consultant of other girls on non-personal matters chiefly, as the merits of different vocations, the settling of disputes, etc., but does not appear to be sought after for sympathy. Uses no excess of words in expressing herself and terminates conversation as soon as decision is reached; neither seeks nor gives much companionship to others.

While she appears overtly to exert herself socially very little towards others, she readily establishes rapport with and treats everyone who "consults" her with a like respect and is herself treated by her peers as if she were an expert more apt than others among them at handling a variety of matters and situations (although she is not the most intelligent member). This role she appears to fulfill so adequately because of a decided unconcern on her part regarding opinions of other girls if these appear "no good" (regardless of the "importance" of the individuals in question); frequently uses witty remarks to bring others including staff into line with her decisions; has a way of smiling very suddenly and fully, almost like laughing, just at the moment when she arrives at the main point of what she is saying — this appears to lighten the sharpness of her definite manner of expressing herself. Unusually self-assured, unusually insightful and emotionally mature; highly practical in her approach to problems. Appears equally calm under diverse circumstances; patient; never impetuous either in speech or manner. Consequently gives impression of being much older than she is.

Like Olga, however, Edith shows similarly a capacity for taking a stand on issues and holding to it. Like Olga, also, she is not a "respecter" of persons but is equally democratic and consistent in her treatment of all members of the group. Unlike Olga, though, her leadership is almost exclusively that of the "expert" who is called upon in crises "formally" to help others reach decisions.

The leadership Edith exerts appears an *impersonalized, deliberate* kind of leadership resulting from her exercising of her capacity for impartially arbitrating matters and weighing the pros and cons of opinions on issues as they arise — a capacity in which she surpasses that of most other members. It would appear quite likely that Edith, in contrast to Olga, is well aware of her strategic role in the group.

The personality of the leader Jacqueline differs greatly from that of either Olga or Edith. She appears to possess a great capacity for deep and understanding rapport with others; is empathic in her feeling for the "whole" person of another, and all her relationships to others appear to be on a person-to-person basis which she cultivates out of interest in the individual *as an individual.*

JACQUELINE

(Leader: chosen by 22; rejected by none)

IQ 114; age 17 years 2 months; length of residence 2 years 5
months; Test II

Appearance.   A supple, lithe physique excellently proportioned;
pretty features; expression winsome and contemplative; large lumi-
nous brown eyes, tan complexion, wavy dark brown hair.   Fine
colorful speaking voice.   Well-poised.   Manner gracious.
Personality-behavior picture.   Very self-aware and equally well
aware of others.   Feels others' moods practically as if they were
her own; emphatic in her reactions to people; seems to understand
"the whole person" of the individual; rapidly gets into rapport with
a wide range of individuals, seems to "experience" them; appreciative of other individual's troubles, problems, or special gifts.   At the
same time "objectively" withholds over-sympathetic reactions although she is very sympathetic; likewise withholds overly critical
reactions she has to others.   Censures and praises "therapeutically."
"That was wonderful what Jean did on field day, but soon she'll
be too important for this place if people don't stop telling her so."
Exceptionally articulate verbally as well as mimically.   Particular
facility in "tuning" her words to the person with whom she is talking.   "Gets away with" the suggestions and criticisms she gives others.
Is herself very conscious of the impression she is making upon others
whom she cares to impress favorably; will go out of her way and
undergo great sacrifices to make the adult or other girl realize her
worth.   Tenacious.   Will undergo more than necessary rather than
ask to be relieved, whether it is work assigned to her or a situation
causing her acute emotional distress.   Aspiration level high and ability likewise high.   Wants a lot of recognition and succeeds in getting it in a bonafide, well-earned way.   Cares nothing about the
kind of recognition anybody can earn; it must convince her that she
has accomplished more than another could accomplish.   When she
has excelled so very much beyond others that the few whose good
opinion is important to her know her quality, then a simple word or
look is all she wants from them.   When commended responds, "Oh
that wasn't anything, I wanted to do it; it wasn't hard."   Never
asks privileges and favors not given without the asking although she

knows they would be granted. Unusually appreciative of any "nice thing" another person may do for her and shows her appreciation in unusual ways. Shows exceptional esthetic appreciation of nature, literature, and painting, but not of music. Longs "to see the beautiful other countries of the world;" content to remain 3 years to finish high school and vocational course giving her suitable earning capacity. Is very ambitious for others as well as for herself. Confides only to one member of the staff, although she must know she is on good terms with all of the staff. Hides any disappointment she may have; displays an evenness of disposition covering a variety of moods, well-controlled. Takes in the nuances of a situation, astutely sizes up the participants, and then re-makes it without a dissenting voice protesting; shows such tact and subtlety in dealing with others that they hardly realize she has "managed" them and they appear to think they changed their minds themselves. Has a humorous way of stating what she has to say and a buoyancy in walk and manner. Cares nothing about clothes, practically not at all about "dolling-up;" because of her walk and stance, however, looks well in almost any kind of clothes. Not self-conscious about appearance.

Only a fairly good sense of security; will probably not have a really sound sense of security unless her efforts redound in later life to recognition of a sort removing all doubt where she stands in respect to others. Has exceptional integrity. Proud. (Sociogram, p. 108.)

Motivations of choice by Doris [5] (*herself a leader, present Test I only; IQ 117*) *for Jacqueline:*

"When she came first she used to feel superior to us but I took that out of her. She is buoyant and picks you up and she's dramatic and when she tells about something she almost lives it. We click on all kinds of little things. *She has great ideals* and she fills you with ambition. I think she is awfully smart, she has read so many

[5] This protocol is included although given by a subject who was present for Test I only, since it throws light on the behavior and "thinking" of leader individuals. Words credited as insightful are in italics; see p. 162. All protocols in the study were recorded verbatim by the experimenter in interview with the subjects within two to four days of the test. The subject was asked: "Why did you choose X to be in your — group?" and "why did you choose not to have Y in your — group?" It was understood that statements were confidential. No effort was made to urge the subject to expand on her spontaneous statements, however brief or inarticulate. Instead, if she seemed unable to explain beyond a meager remark, the experimenter said: "That's quite sufficient; I just want to be sure I have the record for your choices right." Interest in giving motivations appeared great regardless of the verbal ability of the subject.

books. You can always expect to have exciting things happen if you spend an evening with her. To her nothing is impossible either. You can be just desperate and she'll make you feel foolish to yourself.

"We are the closest of friends. We feel free with each other and you know you don't always feel free with people. All the time I knew her, she was always honest in all her dealings. We get into mixups together and she'll stick it out. *She gives you advice in a way that makes you think for yourself, not that she thinks it's right just because she says it.* And just to see her breezing along sort of breezes you along with her. She tilts her head in the door and says 'Hello, lady!' (to housemother) and comes down the corridor saying 'Hi, Doris!' She's efficient and when I'd be scared to death when we were putting on a big luncheon for guests and I'd say, 'Are you sure we're doing right?' she'll say, 'Positively.' Goodnight, so much self-assurance she has.

"We're both reserved about important matters but when we get together we aren't reserved. It's rather a privilege to be intimate with her. *While we* (the group) *have a way to take things practically, she tries to broaden things out* to cover the whole country, like a philosopher would. She does it also because she reads Greek writers that wrote a thousand years ago. But I think *it's her nature though to like to be lifted up* from this world and stay out a while, and then come back again. She'll tell you what Demosthenes had to say about the thing you're talking about. She goes far above a lot of girls, not that she goes above myself. At club, Alice was trying to explain something in her simple way, and Jacqueline explained by deeper things that most girls don't understand, and she uses her vocabulary to a very great extent so sometimes I am asked what she meant. You see we don't have all girls of equal intelligence in the house, some of them are jealous therefore, if they don't get her right.

"She used to sit by the hour and let me stream my sob-stories out to her and she could sort of add a word here and there *so you'd scarcely know it until you got to see her point of view and not your own any more.* I might say, 'I'm not going to do the same things over and over again' and she'd say, 'Well, you always do do the same things over and over' and I'd say, 'Yes, you do, don't you?' And it would seem different and all right that it was this way. (Reference is to routines of the institution.)

"*Jacqueline can lead and not make the girls feel they are being overpowered but rather that they are doing things of their own accord.* She herself *doesn't refuse to do things even though she doesn't like to, only in case it's unreasonable. And she is never a person to advertise.* She tells me things she doesn't like about everyone but to no one else. I guess the girls think she can't *see faults but she certainly can.* She is very *compassionate,* she can feel 'no' but she *won't say 'no' unless it's better for a girl not to help her out.* She has a motto, 'Never help the helpless,' by which she means not being hardhearted really, though it sounds that way, doesn't it? I didn't realize how bad it sounds before but it works out good. The idea is *you shouldn't consent to help a girl, even if she's a new girl, if she doesn't do first as much as you think she should do,* because if you do she will get the idea it's your place to help her and her place to be helpless and that way you work in a circle, and later you can't get out of helping her because she really stays helpless, I mean she doesn't get confidence of her own. Some girls think you are mean not to but they respect you and when you do they forget that they thought you mean before. *Jacqueline doesn't have to work hard to make friends.* She arrests attention by the dignity of her, walking straight with her head up, to see her you think walking is important. She recognizes originality and when ideas come to me she puts them over. In the beginning I wouldn't have said a thing very often; then she came and wasn't here long till I got more interested on account of her. I'm quiet but quick to make decisions, I think it out fast, and then she goes to it fast.

"We arbitrate, Jacqueline and I. She is jealous a little but has good points to overwhelm it. When she does suffer from feeling sad she comes to my room. I don't try to talk back but read and listen to her and that soothes her. *She acts more sure of herself than she really is and is under a terrible strain* and then you can sense that she is tired out and goes to her room to be alone. When she is angry she'll go to her room and cry it out and not produce the anger in public like some girls. She feels she should help everyone and *that makes her feel more confident.* To her I could tell what I want to be and she'll comprehend it, and she is farther in High School and knows things that Olga doesn't know. She can *understand things and can decipher what you mean and not just sympathize.* There are not many girls who I feel understand me and then you can't confide in them but Jacqueline does."

Motivation of choice by Doris for Alice a near-isolated, chosen only by her: [6]

"My deepest interest in Alice is mostly pity because she is so lonely and has no friends. . . She's kind of comical really — you have to praise her for every little thing before she goes on to the next thing. . . But when her mind gets working on things she's suffered, she's years older than you are and that depresses you because you've enough troubles of your own. *Her heart gets easily broken, she can't stand to be scolded at all. If anyone does, she feels they don't like her. She has never been able to put faith in anyone as long as she's lived,* and that's one reason I wouldn't break faith with her myself." (Sociogram, p. 110.)

Jacqueline's motivations of choice for Doris on Test I:

"Doris brings all her troubles to me and calls me sister and I would do the same only I feel I have to act different like I was older, though I'm younger. She'd never tell the other girls what goes on in her mind, only to me. She has unique qualities. You know you can depend on her, there is never a doubt in your mind. I like the way she'll argue with a girl to get her to change her mind about a thing and she'll dare to do anything. Sometimes I look up to a person and sometimes I look down, but Doris I can hold on a level with myself. She has a point of view about life, that the future will tell what is in you more than the past. That's how she tells me I can be about the past — that you don't go backward if you understand this about life. Something's very fine about her which most girls don't have. She doesn't feel superior though she has reasons to feel so and she doesn't put herself forward. She isn't too modest either, she is just right. That's the most important quality anybody can have. Also I liked her the first day I saw her. She ironed a dress that day for me. I decided she was ladylike, talented and cheerful. Nothing ever ruffles her and if she does have anything wrong with her, she'll go to her room and not make the other girls feel bad too, although she has a temperament and you have to be careful how you treat her. Just living with her you get so you like her. Besides I like about her how she appreciates things you make up, tap-dances and stunts.

"Also there's Edith, she's a lot of fun and pleasure to me too, but

---

[6] It is of interest that the one choice Alice receives on Test II is given her by an over-chosen who had been a friend of Doris while the latter was in the community.

I'm more attached to Doris. Edith and I often join forces and get someone in a room and make them snap out of anything they are in. She is always the same way, not at all moody in any way and I like this about her so terribly much. She isn't touchy and doesn't seem to have a temper. She is very playful, that's like me."

The leadership exerted by Jacqueline is that of a personality recognized by other personalities in the group as gifted intellectually and emotionally to aid them to cope with their individual needs and problems as well as able to "lead" without making others "feel they are being overpowered but rather that they are doing things of their own accord." Unlike Edith who is given the role of an "impersonal" counselor by her peers, Jacqueline's efforts hold a personal significance. "She gives you advice in a way that makes you think for yourself, not that she thinks it's right just because she says it." Lack of rejections expressed towards her appear explainable by her great finesse in dealing with others. Sympathetic and "objective," unusually astute in human contacts, ingenious, resourceful and appreciative of talent, Jacqueline appears as a person who is an artist in stimulating the development of others, fostering their welfare, and interpreting their unexpressed needs to other persons.

In contrast to the leaders Olga and Edith, Jacqueline has many moods. Her techniques for controlling them are revealed as going "to her room to be alone" or letting a friend "read and listen to her and that soothes her." It will be recalled that the moodiness of the isolates was most often publicly displayed.

The leader Jean shows a personality picture which lacks almost all of the subtleties and nuances characteristic of Jacqueline. Yet Jean is nevertheless, through a different manner of behavior, found to exert leadership.

JEAN

(Leader: chosen by 24; rejected by 2)

IQ 112; age 17 years 2 months; length of residence 2 years 3 months; Test II

Appearance. Athletic, well-proportioned physique, square shoulders; bounding walk; alert bright blue eyes; pert, confident, merry, look-you-through expression; a poised-to-go posture; bright gold hair very curly and tangled; complexion covered with freckles so as to appear quite dark. Gives immediate impression of adequacy, tense-ness, and jovial outlook. Attractive resonant voice. Manner somewhat arrogant. Speech and gesture have a decisive quality.

Personality-behavior picture. A dynamic, strong personality, very self-aware, and apparently little aware of others as individuals; camaraderie manner, loud, cheery, and friendly towards others, chiefly as a group. Skips the verbal efforts of person-to-person rapport that other leaders make or seek to make with others. Calls out to a roomful of girls as she enters, "How's everybody?" in a manner that makes them all feel equally "near" to her. Seems to get a "group-response" rather than a person-to-person response for the most part. Pitches into things without hesitation; epitomizes "fresh-ness," vivacity, gayety, and urge for endless activity. The group often appears to be interpreted in her conduct; others would like to have the "nerve" to do as she does. Never once was known to "wait on" other girls' needs or to bid them to wait on her wishes; the latter is not necessary as they seek to wait on her often against her desire; they seem to want to serve her, just to be near so much "life." Her satisfactions appear to lie in what she does, the outlets she gets, doing what she wants to do (and there is always something she wants to do), rather than showing dependence on whether or not other girls or staff members think her accomplishments worthy of comment. "She thinks she's good" and nobody need bother to praise her. "Wonders why we get down if we get low marks." She herself seldom praises others, even her choices, for their achieve-ments. Life is to be lived and you live it and you don't worry about it, is expressed in her lack of dwelling on her own situation or that of others. Lives actively, participates fully, with never a thought as to whether she has captured the front seat and most de-sirable role or not. But no one takes these from her very often.

Everybody appears to enjoy her performance in play and in work. Is sincerely dismayed if her "usurping" is brought to her attention. "How was I to know Margaret wanted to do it? She didn't say so. Shouldn't she speak up and tell me? Nobody has to be bashful telling me something. I tell you what — I'll say delicate like, 'Margaret, you take a shot at it,' next time. Then I'll pray she won't keep us waiting all day for her to get started. Like the rest of them, *never* in a hurry." In speech, is dramatic, quick, seldom at a loss for words, spontaneous, and witty in repartee; never offended at jokes directed at her; immediately enlarges upon them, making herself twice as ridiculous as the joker did; a person who is very easy to caricature who wins others' esteem by her lack of touchiness when she is the object of such attempts. Highly entertaining member of any group. Large-minded in her talk about others; will not tolerate "fussiness" and "putting down" girls who are obviously not very cooperative or in other ways have the disfavor of the group; says, "Live and let live; you're not so perfect yourself if you want my opinion." Her presence in any group seems to bolster the members' confidence and enthusiasm.

Frequently considered by adults as on the erratic side, "a wild girl," but to her peers she's "it." Very effective in a group relationship to 15 or 20 or 30 or to the whole population. Her leadership appears to be of a magnetic sort; her manner, attitude, and actions are infectious to many of the individuals functioning with her; without a direct person-to-person effort on her part to enlist supporters to her "plans," spontaneous support is forthcoming.

Good sense of security; healthy-minded; realistic, frank individual with a confident optimism and enthusiasm.

Motivation for choice by Jean for another leader, Catherine:

"Our friendship lasted as long as we've been here but she is moody and so am I, so at times we'd stay away from each other. It is always there though at times it is more vigorous than at others. The same things disgust us and the same things delight us. We get a lot of comfort from each other. She is good to even the people she doesn't respect and will lend them things. I don't go so far as that myself. She has a temperament and you have to be careful how you treat her. When she's had an argument with someone she'll go in and play the piano for hours. I thought it must be good to have an outlet for your feelings and she says it does help a lot.

When she'd stop playing she'd be all smiles again. Catherine is awfully sympathetic and can't stand to see anyone in pain, and she has a lovable disposition. She is able to do so much for the girls and I admire her for that."

The personal concern and solicitude of Jacqueline for others is lacking in Jean's approach. Instead the leadership Jean exerts appears as that of a vivid, strong personality who imbues others with desire to lend support to her plans through bolstering their energies and interests by her own tireless enthusiasm for activity. Dramatic like Jacqueline, but brusk and not hesitant to censure others openly and crudely (unlike Jacqueline), she exhibits a camaraderie manner to all members of the group such that each member seems to feel equally "near" to her and equally invited to participate. Due to her tolerant inclusion of all, she abruptly thwarts the efforts of persons who wish to exclude members in disfavor with them. She exerts a "classless" leadership in the sense of seeing no differences, no "classes"; like a recruiter to a cause that needs many supporters, she is primarily not so concerned with others as persons as she is with action. When she speaks up for herself, it is speaking up for the group, but unlike Edith, it was not after she had personally asked others' opinions; her opinion was simply their unexpressed opinion.

The leadership displayed by Jean in the group might be termed a *group-approach*, so little does it appear to be bound up with a *person-to-person* response between herself and individual members; instead she appears to ask for and gets a group response hardly at all based on individualized verbal efforts at gaining rapport with each member separately.

The leadership exhibited in the group by Olga, Edith, Jacqueline, and Jean appears in each instance to reflect a manner or "style" of leadership — a particularized style which is directly traceable to personality attributes of the individual leader. Actually, however, the "success" of a given "type" of personality in demonstrating leadership in the test-community appears dependent upon the fact that the population itself is comprised of so great a variety of personalities that no one personality "type" can win an exclusive lead over all other "types." Each leader becomes a leader through making a contribution to the membership — a contribution which all members do not equally want or need. There is frequently very little over-lap between the individuals who "support" one leader (as Jean) and those who support another leader (as Jacqueline). Jean's appeal seems chiefly to persons not so readily "reachable" by the articulate personal methods of Jacqueline; the subjects who are most withdrawn socially apparently do not feel it necessary to talk with Jean but still may get from contact with her a companionship which is understanding if not verbally expressed in the same manner as Jacqueline is able to "attune" her words to the individual.

Whereas the leaders to no less extent than the average citizen reject the relatively non-contributing (or "destructively" contributing) members of the community, only they as a group are distinguished by the observable control they overtly display of such feelings towards them. The average citizen does not generally so well "inhibit" her feelings of annoyance or disregard in the same manner, and for this exhibition may be called "to account" by the leader. (*E.g.* see p. 181. "Jean tells me I'm narrow-minded.") This may be due either to a lack of recognition on the part of the average citizens of the nature of the isolate's "internal" problems, or to a greater lack on their part of capacity to control their feelings towards individuals to whom they similarly are not attracted. To the average citizen, the isolates and near-isolates generally are "nuisances" interfering with the smooth running of things and detracting from the amount of attention the leader has to give, absorbing disproportionately the leader's time and energies, so that she has thereby less at her command to expend for all members.

In this situation, the leaders appear to stand as mentors "protecting" the isolates and *at the same time* as mentors protecting the average citizen from her own tendencies to exercise aggressive behavior towards the "helpless." The average citizen perhaps "unconsciously" accepts such thwarting — recognizing it as "justifiable" — but at any rate overtly revamps her "style" of behavior at least when the leader is present. (*E.g.* see p. 181. "For the time I act different but soon Vera gets on my nerves again and I just stay away or walk off from her.")

It may be that to the leader personality all members are relatively "imperfect" including herself (see pp. 181-182, 191-195, 197) as demonstrated by her statements concerning herself and others, and that according to the degree to which she considers the individuals "responsible," she "holds" them to certain standards. This "holding to" she applies even more severely to herself. Instead of producing resentment because of such conduct, the average citizen appears to consider it an indication that the leader "respects" the latter's capacity "to do better;" *e.g.* see p. 181. "She tells me I'm narrow-minded."

It is as if the leader, having an understanding generally surpassing that of the average citizen, recognizes in the "most inadequate" members of the population limitations which such individuals cannot readily overcome and hence limitations which should be taken into account in everyone's dealing with them. (See Doris' statement on Jacqueline's "philosophy" of "never help the helpless" until they have done all they can do for themselves, only after which point is it apparently desirable to give "help." Evidently the poorest adjusters in the group very soon reach, in the leader's opinion, a stage in which they "require" such aid.) It is as if they come to view such members of the population as "patients" not to be treated in the same fashion as those capable of showing more competence. Even Jean, who was seldom one to temper her words "in speaking her mind," could be observed to express herself in a different manner in speaking to such individuals.

The universal characteristic of the leaders in this study may be a "logical" carrying out of their larger insight into the needs of persons generally and at least partially a reflection of greater emotional maturity on their part than appears to characterize the average member. In any case, the average citizen appears to feel "challenged" and reacts positively to "bawlings out" given by a leader, while the "less able" citizen appears only further discouraged by such tactics on the part of others towards her, a reaction to which the leader appears willing to accede. (*E.g.* see p. 194. "Her heart gets easily broken. She can't stand to be scolded at all.") In consequence, there appears little mystery in the fact that the isolated and near-isolated (also newcomers, see pp. 86-89) are found to direct many more of their choices towards the leaders than towards other members. The rejections the leaders express for them are "disguised" in every-day living by kinds of conduct which such members have a right to interpret as real interest in them; the rejections the average citizen expresses are not so well covered up by tactful or equally considerate behavior (nor, of course, is the average citizen in a position to bring as much in the way of "benefits" —she cannot so easily "make" others "let in" the "unwanted" nor so successfully "make them feel a part of things" since she is not "leading" activities to the same extent).[7]

In part, too, choice to the leader appears to involve a matter of the unique nature of what transpires between the chooser and chosen — the "lift" the leader gives, the "encouragement," the "new view of things," the "belief in himself." Individuals not so strategically located in the structure, individuals who may not thus be so "psychologically aloof" or "high" in the estimation of the chooser, may not in consequence be able to cause him to "look up to" what they have to say in the same way as he seems to cherish the remarks of the leader. (*E.g.* see p. 182. "I feel glad for weeks after talking to her for a few minutes.") "Close" friends may sympathize but the leader-individuals seem to have a sense of "where things stand" to such an extent that their advice is the more sought-after advice, a sense of whether to encourage or discourage a course of action for outcomes lying far ahead of the immediate occurrence. (*E.g.* see pp. 191-195.) The time the individual spends in talking with the leader may not be so long as that he spends in talking with others generally, but the result upon his own behavior of a given conversation may be more profound and more lasting.

---

[7] Monema E. Kenyon suggests a further explanation: that the leader may hold greater appeal to the isolate (or near-isolate) because the former may represent "what he would like to be," a sort of "wish-fulfillment" (conscious or otherwise); on the other hand, the citizen who is nearer to average in his psychological position in the group may have adequate satisfactions coming to him in his immediate setting — hence, that there would be less likelihood of his "looking so far afield."

In a population so large as that of the test-community, the varieties of leadership are manifold. Nevertheless, in personality a number of characteristics of leaders stand out as common attributes. Each leader "improves" from the point of view of the membership, through one method or another, the social milieu. Each widens the social field for participation of others (and indirectly her own social space) by ingratiating them into activities, introducing new activities, and by fostering tolerance on the part of one member towards another. Each leader shows a feeling for when to censure and when to praise and apparently is intellectually and emotionally "uncomfortable" when others are "unhappy" or "left-out."

No leader is invariably a "pleasant" person (like the isolate Amelia); instead each is definite in her stand and will fight for what she considers "right." The leaders are apparently not "perfect" beings; on the contrary, in their conduct towards their supporters they are frequently severe in their criticisms; but the average individual appears to depend on this very severity, this holding them to accomplishment and insistence upon "fairness." The leader Jean would on occasion walk into a group and bruskly remark, "Let's get going — what are you all waiting for — let's get at it." Her response would be a laugh from the members of the group and their jumping into action.

Moreover, each leader appears to succeed in controlling her own moods at least to the extent of not inflicting negative feelings of depression or anxiety upon others. Each appears to hold her own counsel and not to confide her personal worries except to a selected friend or two; even among leaders between each other this very careful reticence is usual. Each appears able to establish rapport quickly and effectively with a wide range of other personalities [8] and to win their confidence. Each appears to possess to a greater or less degree unusual capacity to identify with others to the extent of feeling solicitude for them and to act in their behalf. By one manner of behaving or another, each leader lightens the "burdens" of other members of the group.

By contrast, the isolates and near-isolates appear relatively "self-bound," unable to bridge the gap between their own personalities and those of other persons. In this respect, each appears herself in need.

Both leadership and isolation appear as phenomena which arise out of individual differences in inter-personal capacity for participation and as phenomena which are indigenous to the specific social milieu in which they are produced. Individuals who in this community appear as leaders may or may not be found to be leaders in another community of which they later become a part; likewise individuals who in this community appear as isolates may or may not be found in another community later to also remain isolates.

Nevertheless, it would appear that there are certain qualities in the personalities of the leaders which once these have become an integral part of the individual's personality pattern (such a quality as freedom from self-concern sufficient to enable him to be concerned with matters affecting many others than himself) are likely to remain since they reflect a high level of emotional growth and maturity and thus may be expected to act favorably upon his future relationships with persons in other groups. Similarly, it would appear that certain qualities in the personalities of the isolates (such

[8] Even though a particular leader may appeal especially to individuals who have some personality-trait in common (*e.g.* Jean to the "withdrawn"), within any such group the variations are still, of course, enormously complex.

a quality as inability to observe and orient one's self to the elements of a situation and the persons comprising it) unless outgrown may continue to act unfavorably upon the individual's future relationships in other groups. The "why" of leadership appears, however, not to reside in any personality trait considered singly, nor even in a constellation of related traits, but in the inter-personal contribution of which the individual becomes capable in a specific setting eliciting such contribution from him. Similarly, isolation appears as but the opposite extreme on this continuum of inter-personal sensitivity between the members of the group and the individual.

PART THREE

THE NATURE OF EMOTIONAL AND SOCIAL EXPANSIVENESS

CHAPTER X

Personality and Inter-Personal Relationships

The individual differences which this research has disclosed in the social and emotional projection of individuals towards one another provide an insight not only into the nature of the choice process as it operates between individuals, but also an insight into the dynamics of personality tapped by the choice process. The social expression of the individual, as measured by his initiative in seeking and maintaining contacts with other persons, is found to differ essentially from the individual's emotional expression, as measured by his choice behavior. The individual is revealed as having *a limited emotional range* or *repertoire* for reacting to others by positive choice or by rejection and this emotional repertoire shows only a very slight relation to his social projection in contacting others.

The individual in his exercise of choice and rejection of others does not significantly depart from his characteristic range according to the manner in which the situation in which he is is structured in respect to him (by the extent of others' choice or rejection of him). On the contrary, the individual's capacity for emotional expansiveness appears as a relatively constant characteristic which is not so elastic that he can readily extend or reduce its expression according as others "want" or "don't want" him, are receptive to him or are inexpansive to him. The range of the individual's emotional reactions appears *stable within his repertoire of expression*. Whether the structure of the situation in which he finds himself invites choice from him or rebuffs choice by him, he appears impelled to find an outlet in expression for others which is determined more by his own need for and response to others than by theirs for him. The individual's choice behavior, *in contrast to his social expansiveness*, appears as an expression of needs which are, so to speak, so "central" to his personality that he must strive to fulfill them whether or not the possibility of fulfilling them is at hand or not. The extent of negative or positive "press" exerted by others towards the individual appears not to affect the extent of his need for others, as measured by the extent of his own negative or positive choice behavior towards others. The individual, moreover, shows not only a characteristic repertoire in choice expression towards others but in turn is himself the focus of a significantly consistent amount of choice and rejection, *viz.*, a characteristic expression which represents his *stimulus-value* to others.

Among the many ways in which the psychological structure resulting from choice behavior on the part of the members of the tested population may be described, this research finds it may be most accurately envisioned as *an equilibrium in flux*. The movements which take place continually within it are compensatory movements which do not disturb the total structure *viewed as a totality*. This tendency of the total structure to retain its characteristics from one time to another *even though the respective positions of its carriers* (the members of the population) alter from time to time is one of the highly significant facts to be realized in the understanding of the inter-personal structure of the community and disclosed by comparison of the *same* community at distant time points. The shifts "upward" and "downward" that are recorded in the choice-status of individuals in the population are, so to speak, *bound* to occur since interaction cannot be static; the surprising finding is that whatever changes occur for *individuals* the total structure is not significantly different.

It is, no doubt, the *reflection* of this broad characteristic found by this research to describe the total structure of the population's inter-personal relationships which is also revealed when the constellation around *one given individual* is examined. In the latter instance, too, this relatively small constellation of inter-relationships is found to have significant internal consistency in its composition about a given individual who is its focus (chap. VI). Such findings suggest that by persistent investigation of the inter-personal structure arising through human interdependence and interaction a more precise knowledge of such societal phenomena, commonly viewed as outside the possibility of investigation, may be gained. Moreover, by subjecting the gathered data to orderly analysis, a systematic body of knowledge might come to provide insights into society's structure and the conditions under which it assumes one or another form.[1]

In the little community studied in the present research, both isolation and leadership were found to be products of inter-personal interaction, and not of attributes residing *within* the persons placed in the respective choice-status by the membership. A social process of interaction involving a certain manner of behaving *by and towards* the individuals respectively so isolated or so "lifted" to leadership was found to form the very basis of the isolation and of the leadership. No simple variable, such as the length of time the individual had been in the community or his chronological age relative to other members or his intelligence or even his greater op-

---

[1] H. H. Jennings, "Sociometry and Social Theory," *American Sociological Review*, VI:IV:512-522, August, 1941.

portunity for contacting others, appears to account for the particular choice-status accorded to him. Instead, the reciprocal interplay maintaining between the individual and those in the same field *and constituting the individual's personality as the latter view him,* appears the underlying basic explanation of isolation and leadership. The personalities of such individuals, viewed by the investigator, also reveal from this "objective" standpoint (*i.e.,* that of an outsider) similar "estimates" to those given by co-participants in the field; but the more significant finding is not what kind of personality is likely to be isolated or what kind of personality is likely to be a leader (judged impartially by the investigator in study of such individuals) — the more significant finding is that personality *per se in so far as it is reflected in social structure* is the capacity for interplay with other personalities, for responding to and for being responded to, in a reciprocal situation, the field in which the individual is in common with other individuals. Personality attributes accompanying isolation and personality attributes accompanying leader-positions, though they are found from an "objective" estimate to be widely contrasting, do not constitute a formula for either isolates or leaders; *within* either group the individuals vary in personality greatly from one another and *between* either group the individuals show also frequently personality variables in common. The urgent fact in either instance is the reaction to and the interpretation given to the respective behaviors exhibited by the individuals *and the latter's* characteristic manner of reacting to and interpreting the behaviors of fellow-members. Then it is seen that G. Murphy's [2] exposition of personality as not simply organism but as or-

[2] Gardner Murphy, "Personality and Social Adjustments," *Social Forces,* XV:472-476, 1937, p. 473.

ganism in a situation is further experimentally validated by the findings of this research. From situation to situation, the personality is re-defined, and the re-defining is reflected in the choice-status found for the individual from time to time.

Exploration of the simpler forms of biological organisms presents us with a picture similarly complicated. Weiss has vividly pointed out the field character of organization, biological and social, for individual cells — the fact that they "owe their fate . . . to the operation of forces and conditions to which they become subject in the course of development." [3]

Similarly, the physicist finds that a knowledge of electric charges does not provide an understanding of their action; it is the description of the electromagnetic field between the two charges and not the charges themselves which is essential, the action being determined by the field.[4] Thus the field concept for physics is no longer merely "a means of facilitating the understanding of phenomena from the mechanical point of view." [5] In the construction of the field, *viz.* the lines of force, "our entire knowledge of the acting forces can be summarized." [6]

The field setting in the present research is the individual's *social space*. It describes the area in which the individual interacts or strives to interact with other persons and they with him. Each individual's social space is found to cover a varying area or sphere of other persons. The "evoking power" [7] of certain individuals to marshal to themselves

[3] Paul Weiss, *Principles of Development*, p. 289. 1939.
[4] Albert Einstein and Leopold Infeld, *The Evolution of Physics*, p. 157. 1938.
[5] *Ibid.*, p. 157.
[6] *Ibid.*, p. 135.
[7] The expression "evoking power" and one which follows, "press," are borrowed from the insightful contribution of Henry A. Murray *et al.*, *Explorations in Personality*. 1938.

the emotional expansiveness of those around them appears very great. In other instances, the individual appears conspicuous for the lack of positive choice expressed towards him.

The study indicates that exploration of the field in investigation of behavior can clearly reveal the significance of environmental factors in relation to individual characteristics. The choice-status of a given individual is seen to result not alone from his individual characteristics nor alone from the environmental factors to which he is subject but from the interaction of his individual characteristics *with* the individual characteristics of those about him, those *in his field, i.e.* who have psychobiological relevance to his behavior (and for whom he has such relevance). Again, in a different sense, environmental factors are seen to play a negligible role. The individual's extent of emotional expansiveness towards others is seen to be *his individual* characteristic, a characteristic which finds consistent expression without relevance to the environmental factors which may exert "press" for or against its fulfillment.[8] It may be postulated that the concept of need comes nearer to describing emotional expansiveness than does the concept of trait. The individual is actually expressing how many persons he feels the need for in his life situation. We may judge it to be a trait, since the individual does not vary significantly from time to time in the extent of his expression towards others, but he, the individual giving the information, is himself of course not consciously displaying a "trait" nor aware of his consistency.

The field also reveals a number of psychological "laws" of another sort. By and large, it is seen that the positive at-

---

[8] It is as if the individual must conceive of himself as "wanted," must not "see" the rebuffs which are being accorded him; he may not have to rationalize his situation for it may not be apparent to him.

tractions of individuals to one another far outweigh the rejecting or repelling feelings active between them in the test-community where they share a common life. Moreover, the inter-personal structure which comes to exist is characterized more by stability than by flux and displays a typical form, *viz.* has the same general outline at different times (regardless of the fact that different individuals may at different times be found to occupy various positions of choice-status). The balance in proportions of this structure at different time points in spite of the different positions ("upward" or "downward") of its individual carriers can thus be aptly described as an equilibrium in flux.[9] The question may be raised: Why does the field exhibit such a structure? The answer appears to lie in the different inter-personal capacity of individuals to draw choice to themselves, different capacities which maintain their respective differences in this respect *even as the group as a whole develops* in such capacity.

Within this structure, the phenomena of leadership and isolation appear as side by side phenomena that are born of the press exerted by field forces which are specific other persons acting upon the individual; in the one instance, individuals are propelled into positions of leadership through the response which greets their extraordinary capacity for

---

[9] It should be noted that this interpretation refers to the *total structure* produced by choice behavior and not simply to constancy in number of certain positions of choice-status, *e.g.*, number of isolates, number of leader-positions, number of reciprocations, etc. The writer has elsewhere reported that the extremes in position are consistently found to about the same extent upon re-test of the *same* population ("Structure of Leadership," *Sociometry*, I:99-143, July-October, 1937, p. 122). J. H. Criswell has also reported confirmation of such findings ("Social Structure Revealed in a Sociometric Retest," *Sociometry*, II:69-75, October, 1939, p. 74) and moreover noted that the degree of cleavage in a given group tends to remain constant. The importance of the present findings consequently lies in the fact that they do not concern only one or another aspect of structure or extremes in choice-status, but the *total structure in every respect considered as a whole.*

inter-personal contribution *in specific situations* and, in the other instance, individuals are propelled into isolation through lack of positive response to their inter-personal contribution *in specific situations*.

Study of the behavior attributes accompanying high and low choice-status gives a view of individuals who differ respectively in capacity to contribute to the needs of others, to interact with mutual appreciation and benefit. It is seen that the individual's personality at a given moment reflects the field forces with which it is interacting and affects those field forces.

Leadership appears as a process in which not one individual has a major role but in which relatively many share. The specific avenues of rapport which bring one individual into contact with a particular "constituency" (selection of other persons) may not resemble those which relate a second individual to the persons who are drawn to him. The several-ness of leadership appears related not alone to different capacities on the part of the leader-individuals but to the personality differences within the population; the latter are so wide that no one individual apparently can bridge the gap to rapport with others to a degree sufficient to earn choice from a majority of members. The superior capacity which one individual may have to recognize and respond to the needs of others does not show itself as a generalized capacity which may relate him to *any other individuals*. It appears in the special sensitivity between the individual and *specific* other persons, resulting in interaction between them. The concept of an individual being "a leader" (as contrasted with other individuals who are not "of this type") is, in this sense, without confirmation from the findings of the present research. The forces residing in a particular group and the expression they require evidently come to fruition according as the group contains within itself members through whom it can find outlets of representation; in the test-community, these forces are various and demand manifold expression. It is hardly likely that in larger communities and nations a less complex inter-personal structure of leaders is natural for their expression. Nevertheless the leader-positions judged by a stringent criterion are, in the test-population, limited in number; they appear to be so limited because the number of persons who are drawn to exert exceptional efforts in behalf of other members (in a manner which the latter recognize as constructive and representing their interests) are relatively few. It would seem that even as "standards" in this respect rise in a population, individual differences keep pace with the needs and leadership remains a many-sided process.

CHAPTER XI

THE RELATION OF CRITERIA TO
LIVING-WORKING SITUATIONS

Does one situation, as working together, produce more or less positive reactions of choice than another situation, as living together? Does choice behavior in one situation, as working together, resemble or differ from choice behavior in general in another situation, as living together?

The present analysis examines the findings in relation to two criteria used by the subject as the base for choice and rejection: living in the same housing unit (L) and working in the same vocational (work) group (W). (See p. 37.) The individuals to whom the subject reacts may be chosen on one criterion or for both, rejected for one criterion or for both, or chosen on one criterion and rejected for the other criterion. Hence the analysis refers to the gross number of positive or negative expressions for inclusion of others for *living* or *working* and differs from the major report which is concerned entirely with the number of different individuals chosen or rejected (see p. 44).

The volume of positive expression of choice for L exceeds by close to one third the number of positive expressions of choice for W made by the subject for other members of the population. On Test I, 832 choices for L are given and 605 for W. The volume of rejections for L also exceeds appreciably the volume of rejections for W given by the subject: 426 and 363 respectively. Positive choice and rejection *towards* the subject consequently follow the same trend. On Test II, this trend is continued. (See Table XVIII.)

TABLE XVIII. SUMMARY OF CHOICES AND REJECTIONS ACCORDING TO CRITERIA OF *Living* AND *Working*

Test I	Chosen by the subject		Rejected by the subject		Choosing the subject		Rejecting the subject		Reciprocating choice by subject		Reciprocating rejection by subject	
N. 133	L	W	L	W	L	W	L	W	L	W	L	W
Median	5.80	4.16	3.02	2.55	4.70	3.57	1.58	1.45	1.27	0.80	0.17	0.16
Mean	6.26	4.55	3.20	2.73	5.84	3.83	2.74	2.33	1.76	1.06	0.47	0.35
S.D.	3.01	2.56	1.99	2.34	4.70	3.02	3.69	2.66	1.94	1.44	1.06	0.70
r	.61		.55		.80		.77		.75		.71	
All reactions	832	605	426	363	777	509	364	310	234	141	63	46

Test II	Chosen by the subject		Rejected by the subject		Choosing the subject		Rejecting the subject		Reciprocating choice by subject		Reciprocating rejection by subject	
N. 133	L	W	L	W	L	W	L	W	L	W	L	W
Median	6.38	5.12	3.14	2.80	7.27	5.85	2.26	2.02	2.29	1.44	0.33	0.29
Mean	6.71	5.61	3.36	2.86	7.91	6.08	3.39	2.89	2.80	1.80	0.72	0.62
S.D.	3.00	2.65	1.98	1.83	4.99	3.96	3.64	2.99	2.13	1.46	1.15	1.03
r	.70		.75		.91		.87		.72		.76	
All reactions	893	746	447	381	1052	808	451	385	373	240	96	83

Table XIX. Summary of Correlations on Choices and Rejections
According to Criteria of *Living* and *Working*

N = 133.

	Test	r	Zr/σz
Number chosen by subject on criterion of *living* and number chosen by subject on criterion of *working*:	I	.61	7.87
Same:	II	.70	9.64
Number choosing subject on criterion of *living* and number choosing subject on criterion of *working*:	I	.80	12.21
Same:	II	.91	16.97
Number reciprocating choice by subject on criterion of *living* and number reciprocating choice by subject on criterion of *working*:	I	.75	10.32
Same:	II	.72	10.08
Number rejected by subject on criterion of *living* and number rejected by subject on criterion of *working*:	I	.55	6.87
Same:	II	.75	10.32
Number rejecting subject on criterion of *living* and number rejecting subject on criterion of *working*:	I	.77	11.34
Same:	II	.87	14.81
Number reciprocating rejection by subject (mutual rejection) on criterion of *living* and number reciprocating rejection (mutual rejection) on criterion of *working*:	I	.71	9.86
Same:	II	.76	11.07

In view of the finding that L is thus consistently the more productive of reaction among the subjects, it is further notable that reciprocation of reaction (either positive by positive or negative by negative) is also consistently greater on L than on W. The positive reciprocation of the subject for L on Test I is 28 percent of the individuals chosen (234/832) and on Test II is 42 percent (373/893). The positive reciprocation of the subject for W on Test I is 23 percent (131/605) and on Test II is 32 percent (240/746). The increase from Test I to Test II is thus 14 percent for L and 9 percent for W.

A similar trend is shown by the results on negative reciprocation. For L the increase in number of individuals mutually rejecting the subject compared with the number rejected by the subject from Test I to Test II is 6 percent, *i.e.*, a rise from 15 percent (63/426) to 21 percent (96/447). For W the increase in number of individuals mutually rejecting the subject compared with the number rejected by the subject from Test I to Test II is 9 percent, *i.e.*, a rise from 13 percent on Test I (46/363) to 22 percent on Test II (83/381).

Thus reciprocation of positive choice and reciprocation of rejection increase on both criteria from Test I to Test II, eight months later. It is notable that L shows a greater relative gain in positive reciprocation than in negative reciprocation while W shows a trend in the opposite direction: the increase is 14 percent on L and 9 percent on W for positive reciprocation; the increase is 6 percent on L and 9 percent on W for mutual rejection. This finding results in spite of the relatively greater increase on W than on L in number of positive choices made by the subject from Test I to Test II, and also in spite of the relatively greater number of both positive and negative reactions given on L compared with W on both tests.

In the test-population the results indicate that living together in the same housing unit is provocative of more positive reactions and of a greater likelihood of the individual being reciprocated by those to whom he is attracted than does participating together in work. The living situation also produces more likelihood of the individual rejecting others to a larger extent than does the work situation but not necessarily also finding himself reciprocally rejected to any greater extent (in proportion to the extent to which he rejects others) than in the work situation. It may be that the living situation is implicitly more vital to the individual than a vocational situation in the community of the study.

There is found a significant correlation between the number of individuals chosen by the subject for L and the number chosen by him for W: $r = .61$ for A_I and $.70$ for A_{II}. The extent of the subject's expansiveness thus carries over from one situation to another and is also consistently maintained from Test I to Test II, eight months later. This is likewise found for the extent of his rejection of others: $r = .55$ for A_I and $.75$ for A_{II}. The correlations are still higher between the number of individuals choosing the subject for L and the number choosing him for W: $r = .80$ for A_I and $.91$ for A_{II}. The number rejecting him on L and the number rejecting him on W correlate at about the same level as appears for positive choice to him on the two criteria: $r = .77$ for A_I and $.87$ for A_{II}. About equally high correlations are also found for reciprocation of the subject's positive choice expression on L and on W ($r = .75$ for A_I and $.72$ for A_{II}) and for reciprocation of his negative expression on L and on W ($r = .71$ for A_I and $.76$ for A_{II}).

It thus appears that the individual who attracts relatively more or relatively fewer in one situation attracts more likely than not relatively more or relatively fewer in another situation among individuals who are in a position to know him in both situations. The subject's desirability [1] to others as expressed in choice to him does not appear to be limited to one situation; nor does his evident lack of desirability as shown by the extent to which he is rejected appear limited to one situation, under circumstances in which he is generally available for various roles in a community. Further, the indi-

---

[1] This term is preferred by the writer to the term "acceptability" because the latter seems to connote a passive or tolerant attitude merely. *Choice* expressed by one individual towards another registers an *active wanting* of the chosen person as an associate. For similar reasons, the writer considers the term "popular leader," as often employed in the literature, to be a misnomer. Wide discrepancy is found on comparison of data taken on the basis of a "popularity vote" and data based on sociometric testing. (See the writer's "Structure of Leadership," *Sociometry*, I:I:99-143, 1937, p. 133; the data on popularity were "votes" cast for "The one I consider is most popular.") It may be that "popularity," as commonly understood, is based on qualities which appeal at a distance and may become flat when related to a criterion to be utilized in a life situation. Leadership shows itself to be in essence a reality test. The leader comes face-to-face with persons and situations and may aid in bearing or interpreting realities. He has to "pass" a proximity test on the basis of demands related to the needs of others. Hence the term "supporter" would seem more fitting than the term "follower" to imply the active reciprocity involved in leadership.

vidual's own expansiveness is shown not to be bounded by a situation of one kind. The relative extent of his expansiveness appears to carry over from one situation to another of a very different kind. Moreover, his capacity in respect to being reciprocated by others is highly correlated in whichever situation he wants to be associated with them.

The choice process in both its positive and negative aspects is seen to be affected by the situation in which it emerges. The situation of living together produces a greater expression of both positive and negative reactions. Yet in the work situation mutually negative reactions between individuals arise to just as great an extent in proportion to the total negative reactions in that situation as in the situation of living together. In both situations the positive aspect of choice predominates over the negative aspect and even as the volume of positive and negative reactions expressed towards the subject increases,[2] the positive aspect is still ascendant over the volume of negative expressions towards him.

The situation of common living appears to encourage wider positive inter-personal response, the members of the population showing themselves to be more expansive towards one another in this situation than in the less "flexible" situation of work. The finding may reflect a less complete or less intimate knowledge on the part of the individual of others with whom he works as compared with the kind of knowledge and subsequent understanding of them he may gain in

[2] The test group are the focus of more reactions on Test II as they have become an "older" part of the membership of the community, similarly as college students who are seniors are as a group the focus of more reactions than are the freshmen as a group. The "older" members *as a group* are apparently more widely and better known through the accumulative effect of longer participation in the community. The first experimental evidence that moving to a "higher" college class in general affects choice-status on the campus favorably is to be found in the work of Vreeland. See F. M. Vreeland, "Social Relations in the College Fraternity," *Sociometry*, V:151-162, May, 1942, p. 154. Such results, too, may be taken as evidence of norms of reference within a group affecting the action of choice behavior. See esp. Newcomb, p. 335.

the diversified living situation. The work situation also may be less relaxing and allow less individual variation in adjustment to its demands, thereby fostering greater "social distance." [3] It may also be more stringent in its requirements that the individuals share more equally the responsibility for common functioning, whereas the living situation may allow individualizing of responsibilities in accordance with the personal tastes of the person. The contribution of each individual to the common living may be almost infinitely varied. At the same time, the living situation in general may call forth more communication, verbal and otherwise, from the individuals. Work, on the other hand, provides in itself a direct focus for the attention and interest of the individual; in a living group, observation of others can hardly be avoided nor the hearing and reacting to the talk of others even if the individual should not wish or be interested to do so. The need of the individual for inter-personal relationships appears as great early in his stay in the living situation as it does later when it meets with more satisfaction in terms of mutual response. The situation of living with many others appears one which is apparently so stimulating as to elicit from the individual a volume of positive response towards others which does not become significantly greater as he stays longer in the group.

The most imposing and favorable fact of the findings in its implications for inter-personal relationships generally is how greatly the total positive reactions between individuals surpass their negative reactions [4] whether in a living situation or in a working situation.

[3] E. S. Bogardus, "A Social Distance Scale," *Sociol. and Soc. Res.*, XVII:265-271, January–February, 1933.

[4] It is of interest that between total strangers Barker finds an even greater proportion of positive to negative responses. Roger G. Barker, "The Social Interrelations of Strangers and Acquaintances," *Sociometry*, V:169-179, May, 1942, p. 178.

PART FOUR

SOCIOMETRIC DIFFERENTIATION OF GROUPS

CHAPTER XII

THE CHOOSING PROCESS IN INTER-PERSONAL RELATIONS IN LEISURE-TIME

How does the choice process operate in informal aspects of community life, not determined by considerations such as living in a common housing unit or working in a common vocational unit? Do the phenomena so far analyzed in this volume also appear, in very similar manner, for this population when their choice expression for leisure time association are examined? Does the individual show himself to be more or less expansive towards others on this criterion? Does he meet with more or less mutuality in his positive expression for spending leisure-time with others? Are those members of the population who are chosen much above average on the criteria of living or of working together also well-chosen for leisure? Does leadership carry similar connotations in both settings?

Does the individual show again the consistency in choice behavior which is found to characterize him in his response to others in a collective situation of living or working [1] with others?

Moreover, from one time to a later time, does the choice process show a significantly different expression in leisure situations from the characteristics it shows in common living or working situations? What, if any, importance does the individual's position in respect to choice from others for leisure hold for his choice-status within his official groups for

---

[1] It will be recalled that common living means a single room in a housing unit of 20 to 28 individuals (see p. 36); the work groups usually were comprised of from about 7 to 15 individuals. (For test instructions, see pp. 32-33, 33n.)

work or living Can he, for example, be in leisure a center of many choices while he is little wanted as a co-worker in any work situations?   Or, vice versa, does it appear that the individual's choice-status may be high in the latter and contrastingly low in the former?

What, if any, correlations are found that bear on the mental hygiene of inter-personal living, both in formal and informal roles, on the part of the members of the test-community?

The method of analysis is developed to examine the nature of inter-individual expression of choice for leisure, and to compare the findings with those for common living or common working together.

Method of Analysis

The method of analysis of the data given on the criterion of *leisure* is a comparison of the number of different individuals reacted to positively (chosen) or negatively (rejected) by the subjects, with the number of different individuals reacting positively or negatively to the subjects, and with the number of different individuals who reciprocate the subjects' choice or rejection.   The results of this analysis are given in Table XX and Table XXI.

Second, the method of analysis is concerned with a comparison of these results with the results found on the criteria of *living and/or working*, given in Table I (p. 46).   Correlations between the latter and leisure-time are given in Table XXII.

Third, the method of analysis is concerned with the amount of overlap on any criteria (living, working, leisure) in number of different individuals chosen by the subjects or choosing or reciprocating the subjects.

Fourth, directions taken by choice expression by or towards the subjects are examined.

Fifth, the motivations for choice are considered.

For convenience of presentation, the criterion of leisure and/or recreational time (see pp. 32, 37, and 44n) will be referred to simply as *leisure;* likewise, the criteria of living and/or working will be referred to simply as living-working, to indicate wherever the data on these two criteria are combined in the analysis. It will be recalled that Chapters I to X are concerned with these combined data only and thus did not require re-mentioning of criteria; see p. 37. Up to this point, then, the one exception is Chapter XI which compares data on living with data on working. The problem of comparing data on three criteria at once is so complex that only for analysis of overlap among these criteria are such results separated in the present chapter. There is one exception to this statement: for comprehensiveness of presentation, it is found occasionally necessary to include the findings on each criterion independently treated as these may bear on a particular point important to the analysis.

Throughout the analysis [2] results on leisure will usually be presented first, followed immediately by comparison with the results on living-working.

Context of the Leisure Criterion

Leisure-time, to the population under study, comprised time *for being with* whatever persons the individual wanted to seek out; or he could, if he wished, spend all or much of such time alone. The test-community had organized recrea-

---

[2] It will be recalled that the entire population comprise the field for choice: on Test I, 443 and on Test II, 457 individuals less one, the chooser; and that the test-group comprise, for the analysis, 133 individuals who were present for both Test I and Test II, eight months later. See pp. 34, 35, and 45.

tional programs which were scheduled at regular times, but leisure-time came for any individual when his schedule contained no planned work, study, or play. Thus *leisure,* as here designated as a criterion for sociometric choice, means in choice expression the individual's decision for or against simply being with particular other members of the population in the time at his disposal, which time could be filled as the individual saw fit, according to his inclinations, perhaps in a certain manner on some occasions and in other ways at other times.

Moreover, having chosen another individual, the individual was not obliged thereby to see either a little or a lot of that other individual in terms of leisure-time spent; it meant only that the organized and planned programs were to be so arranged that the leisure-time choice-structure *could* function, *i.e.,* that conflicting schedules for vocational work and academic study and various recreational programs which might coincide so as to keep apart individuals who wanted time for seeing one another would be re-arranged in timing so that *such opportunity* would be maximized, in case the individual wanted to see those he had chosen. Thus, the leisure choice expression was not to be carried out by assignment to "leisure groups," in the same way the choices for *working with* were carried out in re-arrangement of membership in the work groups or as choices for *living with* meant re-assignment of house members. (See p. 28, fn. 3.)

This distinction was considered important in order to enable the members of the population to maintain their social life, in this sense, spontaneously and fully at their own command, *i.e.,* not to "institutionalize" informal mingling by setting up informal-choice-groups. (In the light of the findings, this factor of freedom for structuring one's leisure

according to one's own wishes appears important, and, perhaps, even crucial to the quality of spontaneity exercised in
the choice behavior of the population.)   In this connection,
it is worthy of note that very rarely were individuals observed
to build up a "set" program for themselves during their leisure-time.   Even those who did, in the sense of playing
cards together rather regularly or "going-in-for" book discussions or practicing archery often, were observed to do so
with *only a few* of the other individuals they had chosen and,
also, observed not to maintain the activity selected consistently and exclusively during their leisure with them.   For
example, archery practice might be accompanied by a "gab-
fest" in which the individuals became so absorbed that the
practice was stopped or postponed and then might not be
taken up again for several weeks.

All of these aspects, obviously, are significant for any interpretation of the choice expression on the leisure criterion for
the present test-population.   Mention is given them here as,
of course, *leisure* may in other contexts carry different connotations; and to emphasize the lack of possibility of gen-
eralizing from the present findings to some future findings
which may come from use of the leisure criterion in a context
which, for example, might mean choice action for a more
specific recreational program of game playing where the factor of skill for the activity on the part of the individual would
affect his choice behavior.

Living with carried, in the test-community, many collective situations within which the individual had to share group
life with others.   Although each individual had a single
room, bathrooms, living room facilities and dining rooms
were for the use of the group membership of the house as a
whole.   Similarly, care of the house was a common obliga-

tion; in consequence, wherever any one individual did less than others in this respect, the comfort and exertion of many might be affected. Moreover, the willingness of the individual to fall in with the wishes of the membership generally when his own wishes were in another direction might and often did affect the atmosphere of the house for all. *Working with*, in the test-community, also carried numerous "in-common" pressures, often less subtly expressed than in the context of *living with*.

Thus, leisure-time presents a setting of contrasting interest for the study of choice behavior.

Positive Choice by and towards the Subject

On the criterion of leisure the choice behavior of the subject towards others and of others towards him, as measured by volume of choices given and received, shows on both Test I and Test II no significant correlation: $r = .08$ on Test I and .11 on Test II. See Table XXI. Thus the extent of positive expansiveness in choice expression for association in leisure shown by the individual is not found to be met by a corresponding extent of positive expansiveness towards him. It will be recalled that the criteria living-working shows similar results, on Test I the correlation being very small but significant and disappearing on Test II (see p. 53).

On the other hand, the extent to which the individual's choice for others is reciprocated by them correlates at both periods fairly highly with the extent of his choice for others: $r = .40$, Test I and .45, Test II, and significance is at the .01 level of chance. It is noted that practically the same level of correlations is found for living-working (see p. 50).

Again, as in the latter context, a much higher correlation appears for leisure between the extent to which the individ-

ual's choice of others is reciprocated by them and the extent
to which he is chosen by others: r = .73 for Test I and .70
for Test II.

Thus, whether for leisure or for living-working, the individual who tends to form mutual relationships is apt to be
shown greater expansiveness by others generally than is the
individual who does not or does to a smaller degree.   Moreover, to a lesser extent, the individual who is himself more
expansive tends to find mutuality of response.   But sheer
quantity of expansiveness in choice on the part of the individual shows no relation to the volume which others express
towards him.

Positive and Negative Reactions, Singly

Between Test I and Test II the positive expression of the
subject *for others* correlates at .54; between Test I and Test
II the negative expression of rejection of others by the subject correlates at .40, and both coefficients are above the .01
level of significance.   Both correlations are higher than those
found for living-working (r = .37 and .27 respectively, see
p. 56).

Thus for leisure grouping, the individual's performance in
choice expression for others on the two occasions, eight
months apart, shows somewhat greater consistency than his
performance for the more formal settings, although he also
shows consistency in the latter.   Or to state it conversely,
the individual shows himself to vary more from his own
previous performance in choice expression (in both positive
and negative reactions towards others) for the more formalized setting of living-working than he does for leisure-
time association.

It is to be noted also that, as a group, the subjects show no

TABLE XX. SUMMARY OF CHOICES AND REJECTIONS

ACCORDING TO

CRITERION OF *Leisure-time*

TEST I AND TEST II.

The choices and rejections are taken from the total population: 443, Test I; 457, Test II.

	Chosen by the subject		Rejected by the subject		Choosing the subject		Rejecting the subject		Reciprocating choice by subject		Reciprocating rejection by subject	
N. 133	Test I	II	I	II	I	II	I	II	I	II	I	II
Median	3.87	3.97	.80	.71	2.83	2.97	2.00	2.95	2.86	2.90	0.27	0.30
Mean	4.08	4.31	1.04	1.10	3.55	3.92	2.43	3.33	2.89	3.10	0.60	0.71
S.D.	1.65	1.90	1.43	1.66	3.43	3.60	2.10	2.32	2.11	2.37	1.03	1.11
r		.54		.40		.72		.13		.61		.75
All reactions	543	573	138	146	472	521	323	443	384	412	80	94
D/σD	1.64		.43		1.42		3.75		1.18		1.10	

significant change in the number they choose or in the number they reject; the critical ratio of the difference between the correlated means on the two tests are for positive choice by the subject, 1.64 and for negative choice by the subject, .43 (see Table XX). Thus, whereas the individual subject is not highly consistent in increasing or decreasing his choice expression on the two occasions, resulting in low correlations, the typical change is non-significant.

The positive expression of others *for the subject* on Test I and Test II correlate at .72. However, the negative expression of others for the subject on Test I and Test II shows no significant relation: r = .13, C. R. = 1.45. The comparable correlations for living-working are .66 and .65 respectively. (See p. 57.)

Table XXI. Summary of Correlations on Choices and Rejections
According to Criterion of *Leisure-time*
between Test I and Test II

N = 133.

	r	Zr/σz
Number chosen by subject on Test I and number chosen by him on Test II	.54	6.71
Number rejected by subject on Test I and number rejected by him on Test II	.40	4.71
Number choosing subject on Test I and number choosing him on Test II	.72	10.08
Number rejecting subject on Test I and number rejecting him on Test II	.13	1.45
Number reciprocating choice by subject on Test I and number reciprocating choice by him on Test II	.61	7.87
Number reciprocating rejection (mutual rejection) by subject on Test I and number reciprocating rejection by him on Test II	.75	10.81
Number chosen by subject and number choosing him: Test I:	.08	
Same: Test II:	.11	
Number chosen by subject and number reciprocating him: Test I:	.40	4.71
Same: Test II:	.45	5.39
Number choosing subject and number reciprocating him: Test I:*	.73	10.32
Same: Test II:*	.70	9.64

* N on Test I = 112, on Test II, 118; *i.e.* 133 less the number of unchosen. In calculation of the coefficient of correlation (Product-Moment), such individuals are omitted as they could not have reciprocations if they received no choices.

Note: The critical ratio of Zr/σz at 2.58 (or above) indicates significance at the .01 level of chance; the ratio at 1.96 indicates significance at the .05 level of chance.

For leisure-time, moreover, there is found a significant change in the number of individuals who reject the subject from Test I to Test II (C. R. = 3.75) and no significant change in the number of individuals who choose them (C. R. = 1.42). It will be recalled that for living-working association the findings are just the reverse, the subjects as a group receiving a significantly greater amount of choice and an insignificantly greater amount of rejection, from Test I to Test II. (Yet on neither criterion does the subject himself alter to a significant extent in his choice or rejection of others on the two occasions.)

Thus the question arises: Why *in leisure-time association* are the subjects rejected to a significantly greater extent on the second occasion and why are they not chosen to a significantly greater extent on the second occasion?

The results may suggest that in the informal situation of leisure, as compared with more formal settings of housing or work units, the individual can not as readily "promote" relationships, in the sense of winning others to finding him attractive enough for choice. In working or living together, the individual's behavior as a group member may count and advance his position. He may find numerous opportunities within the range of the activities to make himself useful to group endeavors.

In the leisure setting, it may be that the individual simply "cares about" the other individual as a person in a more total sense and there may be little he can do about either gaining or losing a relationship with him. Similarly, there may be little the second individual can do about his own response to the first individual. The base of feeling in many instances may be less within the realm of control and at the same time less within the possibility of "change" regardless of either individual's conscious or overt effort.

The results may also suggest that the choice behavior of rejecting is possibly less "rational" for leisure association than for a work context. It may be more apparent to the individual why another does or does not reciprocate him in a work situation and much less perceptible to him in the leisure setting. He may more readily "see" why another individual objects, for example, to his work habits and therefore less resent his attitude towards him. Since it is vastly more difficult for any individual to account for another's not caring for him personally in whatever manner he would like, more anxiety may be produced with some accompaniment of hostile feelings. Moreover, it may become a "touchier" matter for discussion and consequently less often ventilated and clarified. Thus, when an effort is made to "win" the friendship of another person and this meets with lack of success, the individual may more deeply resent not gaining the response he wants, and, feeling there is little explanation for such outcome, may "place the blame" upon the wanted individual.

In the group setting of common housing or common vocational situation, on the other hand, neither choice nor rejection may be, in a like sense, so vital to the individual's deeper feelings, or, perhaps, as much beyond his control. If a co-worker does not respond as one would wish, since the *level* of response need not tap one's own peculiarly individual needs and tendencies to a like extent, there are many others to whom it is possible to turn. In leisure, the selection may possibly be a "personality" choice almost exclusively—thus there may not be other individuals who can quite take the place, or substitute for, the wanted individual.

Proportion of Positive to Negative Choice

The gross number of positive choices expressed by the subject for different individuals on Test I is 543 and on Test II, 573. (See Table XX.) The gross number of rejections expressed by the subject for different individuals on Test I is 138 and on Test II, 146. Thus on both occasions tested, the positive expression for participating with others in leisure-time is practically four times as great as the expression of rejection.

While the trend is in the same direction as choice expression for living-working, it is noted that in the latter case the proportion of positive to negative volume is two to one (see p. 59).

However, in gross amount of positive and negative reactions, the leisure criterion shows a much smaller volume than does living-working. In the latter context the subject chooses approximately twice as many (1045, Test I; 1116, Test II) and rejects over four times as many (587, Test I; 571, Test II).

Two criteria combined would by chance be expected to hold more choices than one criterion, but even when considered singly (see Table XVIII) each is found to produce more choices than the criterion of leisure. On Test I, the total number of choices given for living is 832 and for working, 605; on Test II, 893 and 746 respectively. Similarly, the negative expression is much smaller for leisure than either for living or working considered singly. On Test I, the total number of rejections given for living is 426 and for working, 363; on Test II, 447 and 381 respectively. Thus, of the three criteria, leisure shows a significantly smaller volume of positive and negative choice behavior.

In terms of the average chooser, the positive expression of choice for leisure shows on Test I a mean of 4.08 individuals chosen by the subject and on Test II a mean of 4.31 individuals chosen by the subject. The comparable results for living-working are on Test I a mean of 7.86 and on Test II a mean of 8.39 individuals chosen by the subject. Thus the typical individual is about half as expansive in the number of persons he wants for leisure-time affiliation as he is for more "official" settings in the life of the community. He also expresses on the average less than one fourth as many rejections for leisure (mean = 1.04, Test I; 1.10, Test II) as he does for living-working (mean = 4.41, Test I; 4.29, Test II). Thus also in negative reactions, the individual's expression is consistently different in the two instances and much smaller in volume for leisure-time than for living-working.

The individual is found to differentiate between leisure-time and common housing or common work context in the volume of his choice behavior, both positive and negative, on Test I, and this finding is apparently not a passing phenomenon: he maintains approximately the same volume in number of individuals he responds to by choice or rejection, on the respective criterion, at one time and at a later time (8 months apart, Test II).

Proportion of Positive Mutuality

The number of individuals reciprocating the subject's choice to them is 384 on Test I and 412 on Test II. Thus 71 percent of the individuals chosen by the subject on Test I (384/543) and 72 percent of the individuals chosen by him on Test II (412/573) reciprocate the subject's positive choice.

The comparable percents on the criteria of living-working are much smaller: on Test I, 31 percent and, on Test II, 41 percent of the individuals chosen by the subject reciprocate his choice for them (see p. 59). Thus compared with the findings on leisure, the proportion of reciprocation to choice expended for living-working is roughly about half as great on both occasions of testing. In contrast also, on the second occasion, a gain of 10 percent in proportion of reciprocation is found for living-working and practically no gain (1 percent) for leisure.

Mutuality for leisure is, of course, more marked, since fewer choices are given and on one criterion, than in the choice expression for the combined criteria living and/or working, which together present a more heterogeneous base for expression. It is therefore in point to note the findings on the latter two criteria considered separately. (See Chapter XI, pp. 218-24.) This analysis reveals that neither living with nor working with produces so great a proportion of mutual response to choice expended as the leisure criterion shows. (The percents are 28 and 42 respectively for living on Test I and Test II respectively, and 23 and 32 on Test I and Test II respectively for working.) It also discloses that between the two occasions of testing, eight months apart, there is a greater gain in positive mutuality to choice expression given for the situation of living with compared with that of working but for both contexts increases are found.

While for leisure-time a smaller amount of choice for others is expressed by the subject than for association in work or housing, this smaller amount is found to meet with a very much greater proportion of reciprocation—a proportion which does not significantly increase with length of stay in the community. On the other hand, in choice expression for

work and/or living contexts, the individual shows a significant gain at a later time in the amount of mutuality that
meets his own expansiveness.

Individuals Reciprocated and Chosen

The findings just reported relate to the total volume of
choice expended and the volume of reciprocation meeting it.

In terms of number of individuals who find some mutuality in choice expression towards them the findings on Test I
show approximately no difference between the criteria.
Twenty-five or 19 percent (25/133) on Test I are unreciprocated for leisure; 16 percent (21/133) are unreciprocated
for living-working; on Test II the respective findings are 15
percent (20/133) and 9 percent (12/133).

Thus while about the same number of individuals show no
mutuality in either context for choice on Test I, a greater
gain in number of individuals reciprocated on Test II, eight
months later, is noted for living-working than for leisure.

The results contrast further in the number of individuals
who are unchosen on either occasion. As was noted earlier
(see p. 47 and p. 79), of the 9 individuals (or 7 percent:
9/133) who are found unchosen on Test I for living-working, five (or 4 percent: 4/133) remain still unchosen on
Test II. These findings compare with 21 individuals unchosen on Test I (or 16 percent: 21/133) and 15 individuals unchosen on Test II (or 11 percent: 15/133), for leisure. Thus a little over twice as many are chosen by no
one for leisure association as compared with work or housing
situations on Test I and, eight months later, although the
number of unchosen is found to decrease in both contexts,
more individuals remain unchosen for leisure than for living-
working.

It is to be expected that there will be more unchosen on one criterion than on two criteria combined. But when each criterion, living with and working with, is considered separately, the leisure criterion still is found to produce more unchosen than either living with or working with. On Test I, the number of unchosen for living are 12 and for working, 18; on Test II, 6 and 7 respectively.

It is as if evoking choice towards one's self as a wanted associate may be more difficult in the "freest" and most informal setting than in one where group factors in the situation require a more formalized regime. The latter apparently acts as a mediator between the individual and other individuals as well as a censor of the "kind" of interactions they may have.

Proportion of Mutual Rejection

The number of individuals reciprocating by rejection the subject's rejection of them is 80 on Test I and 94 on Test II, or 58 percent (80/138) on Test I and 64 percent (94/146) on Test II.   The increase of 6 percent compares with a like increase of 7 percent for living-working (see p. 59).

While in the latter respect the findings are in the same general direction as appears for living-working, the proportion of negative reciprocation to rejection expended is several times greater for leisure-time.   The comparable percents on the criteria of living-working are 16 on Test I and 23 on Test II.   (See p. 59.)

Thus although the individual rejects many fewer persons for leisure-time association than he does for living with and/or working with, the majority of those he rejects also reject him.   On the other hand, for work or housing situations, only a minority return rejection to his rejection.

Mutuality: Positive and Negative

The mean increase from Test I to Test II of both positive reciprocation and negative reciprocation is a non-significant increase in both instances (C. R. = 1.18 and 1.10 respectively). The results contrast with the significant increase for both positive and negative reciprocation from Test I to Test II for living-working (see p. 59).

The number of individuals who on Test I and on Test II reciprocate the subject correlates at .61 for positive choice and .75 for negative choice. The comparable results for living-working are for positive mutuality a less than significant relation and for mutual rejection a correlation of .33.

It appears that, in contrast to his expression for association in the more official life of the community, on the criterion of leisure-time the individual is highly consistent in maintaining the volume of mutuality, whether positive or negative, that characterizes him at one time to a much later time in the same community. For the more formal groupings considered together (housing and work units), the performance he shows in achieving positive reciprocation is markedly irregular (see p. 60), suddenly increasing as he starts to find success in such relations, thus resulting in lack of correlation. More regularity in performance at the two test periods marks his mutual rejection of others for living or working with in the same situation, although here, too, the correlation is much lower (r = .33) than for leisure-time.

It is as if the individual "learns" or at any rate "improves" in the choices he makes for the more official group settings, *i.e.* improves in the sense of gaining greater mutuality as shown by his "better" performance on Test II and hence shows little or no consistency. Or to put it conversely, within the leisure-time setting for relationships, he shows at an early time a performance which is apparently "maximal" for him and which so well represents what capabilities he has to form such reciprocal relations, that he differs little in the amount and kind of such performance he shows at a later date. This remarkable consistency suggests, of course, many possible interpretations. The area of official group life appears as one in which, to some extent at least, relating to others, as measured by mutuality of choice expression, may be "learned." A similar inference from the findings is not indicated for relating to others with mutuality in informal leisure-time.

Overlap Between Choice for Leisure and Living-Working

It will be recalled that the test-group of subjects number 133. The field for choice by the subject or towards him is the entire population (443, Test I; 457, Test II, less 1, the chooser). In the case of a given criterion, each choice made by the subject is for a different person. He may, however, choose all or many or few of the *same* individuals from criterion to criterion.

The number of choices made by the subject for leisure-time is 543, on Test I. Of this number, 28 percent (152/543) represent individuals whom the subject also chooses to live with in a housing unit, and 8 percent (44/543) represent individuals whom he also chooses to work with in a common vocational situation, making a total overlap of 36 percent. Fifteen percent (82/543) are chosen by the subject for all three contexts: living with, working with, and spending leisure with.

Thus the smallest overlap is between leisure and working and the greatest is between leisure and living, as criteria for sociometric choice. But the largest volume of choice expression for leisure does not overlap with any other criteria, 64 percent (347/543) of choices being for leisure only.

On the average, the individual chooses four individuals for leisure (mean = 4.08). Of these four, it is usual for about two-thirds to be wanted by him for relationships in leisure-time exclusively rather than for association in official groupings of the community.

The percents just given represent the *currently* wanted associates along one or another avenue of group life in the community. The findings should be seen in relation to the particular moment in time when the expressions of choice are given. Thus, for example, while the subject is found to want concurrently in his work unit 8 percent of the persons he chooses for leisure, this should not be interpreted as indicating that the individual finds extremely few individuals in his work experience with others with whom he would *at any time* develop an interest in spending leisure. That such a deduction cannot be made is suggested by a further finding: among the individuals whom the subject chooses for leisure on Test I are 108 or 20 percent (108/543) who had at some time prior to Test I been in a common work situation with him. Findings on Test II show a similar trend: 25 percent (146/573) had been at the time of Test I in a common work situation with the subject. Examination of the comparable data on this point on the criterion of living in the same housing unit reveals only 2 percent and 4 percent respectively. The choice field in both contexts was approximately of like size: the average subject's volume of previous associates in work was 36 and in housing, 29. Being formerly an associate in a common living group does not appear to increase the percent of persons who will become selected by a chooser for relationships during leisure appreciably beyond the per-cent of such selection which he concurrently shows.

It appears, then, that in the test-community, living and working with others are, in this respect, experienced differ-ently: the individual apparently chooses for leisure with as great expansiveness towards his present associates in a com-mon housing unit as he is to show towards them later when he and they may not be sharing this situation; but, towards his present work associates, the extent of expansiveness he shows for inclusion of them in his leisure-time is much less than he shows later after they and he have ceased sharing work re-sponsibilities.

Several hypotheses might be raised as possible explana-tions of the findings. It may be that the individual "takes the chance" of testing out, in the living situation, because of the greater range of behaviors that can be given expression within it, those of his colleagues whom he thinks might be likely to give him the kinds of relationships he wants in lei-sure, whereas he may feel less free to do this in the work situation. In the latter, he may see in the smaller range of behaviors on which attention can be acceptably focussed (be-cause of the pressure of "jobs," "training," and "job-con-duct"), more likelihood that he will be rebuffed for "wasting time" in exchanges of a person-to-person nature that may not fit in with the group-roles expected of the members and by them of each other to meet the common objectives.

It could also be that in the work situation, since it can more readily act to restrict the individual's spontaneity, his emo-tional expansiveness, as a part of that spontaneity, is also reduced in the area of letting one's self come to know others as "persons" or becoming thus known by them. Only later, when the work factor is removed, does the individual's potential spontaneity ultimately re-appear towards his associates, elicited by freedom from considerations of carrying a work-role with them.

It may also be that living in a common housing unit represents a mixture of group pressures and freedoms from group pressures such that the individual experiences within it in living with others a fusion of possibilities for choice expression, both for group-role associates and for personal-role associates. While obviously every group-role is carried by a person and consequently much that is unique to the persons involved will appear in their group-role interaction, nevertheless in *living together as a group of people* (in the test-community, 20-28 persons per housing unit; see p. 36fn) the imaginary line between group-role and personal-role between members appears less clear-cut (or less apparent) than in the situation of working together or in the leisure situation.

In the leisure situation, no tangibly common objectives need constrict the individuals to a similar extent or in the same manner that is the case in the work situation, where "adjusting" or "not-adjusting" is of primary importance not only to the individual member but to his colleagues since his behaviors are linked to group-ends furthered or hindered by his interaction with other members (see pp. 37, 231-32). Thus, on the one hand, leisure might be considered a criterion for choice which lies at one end of a continuum, at the other end of which is the criterion of work, and somewhere probably towards the middle of which is the criterion of living in a communal unit. The extent of overlap or non-overlap in choice selection for the different criteria may conceivably be an indirect sign of how the "atmosphere" in the respective grouping is being experienced by the members.

In summary, after the individual is no longer working with

particular persons, he becomes much more likely to consider them for leisure relationships.   In other words, it appears that working with others acts as a deterrent to the development of informal inter-personal response *during* the period of work association, but that *later*, when the individual is no longer in the same work situation, he then "picks up" from among his former work associates a considerable number with whom he becomes inclined to form inter-personal relationships on a very different basis, as spending leisure-time together.   The individual does not "postpone" the forming of relationships for leisure sharing of time with persons he comes to know in a living-together situation in the manner he reveals he does towards work associates.

Thus, one difference in choice behavior on the part of the individual towards others appears referrable in part to the specific context in which he and they have been exposed to inter-personal contact.   Certain contexts for interaction (as work situations) appear to act in a retarding way upon the individual's tendency to develop relationships of an informal, perhaps "personalized" sort; other contexts (as common housing) apparently do not to any significant extent.

Factors affecting Overlap in Choice Structure and Closed Formations

Inspection of the proportion of overlap in choice expression among the housing groups reveals three groups which show twice as many overlapping choices as are found for the average housing group.   Further inspection reveals that within each of these three groups the overlapping choices show many "closed formations," *i.e.*, the "banding together" into a cohesive structure within which the members choose one another.

For an explanation of these phenomena, the behaviors praised or complained of by the person-in-authority were inspected. (See pp. 144-163.) Only one of these appeared to a marked extent to differentiate between the three groups and other housing groups. "Rebellious" behavior is mentioned as a complaint approximately three times as often, per group, in the three instances than in the case of other groups.

When it is recalled that initiatory behavior may be regarded as rebellious behavior depending upon the person-in-authority witnessing that behavior, it may be inferred that the housing groups differed greatly in the amount of *living space*, that is, in the amount of "what it is all right to do," for its members. While admittedly this is a rough and meager index to "atmosphere," it appears of all the more importance in a further finding.

The individual's tendency to carry into his housing group his leisure-time relationships is found to be unequally spread as a general phenomenon in each of the three groups—even though the conditions of group life may be assumed to have been generally the same for the membership as a whole. Instead, the overlap and closed formations here and there in a given structure of the particular group as a whole are found to involve a selection of individuals. Tracing their positions in their work group, it is found that this selection is of two kinds: (1) individuals who show relatively low sociometric status in terms of choices received and hence individuals who might be presumed to be less able to "adjust" to a regime that was more restrictive generally, and, (2) individuals who show very high sociometric status in terms of choices received in their work group (as well as in their housing group) and hence who might be presumed to be more able to adjust to a "repressive" regime but simply do not intend to do so, instead bolstering their rebellion through "doubling up" on their interrelationship patterns within the group in question.

Thus the hypothesis might be suggested that individuals who are in a position to "suffer most" from a rigid regime (since they show least facility to integrate themselves in an inter-personal setting), and, on the other hand, individuals who are in a position to comprehend most what may be the significance of a rigid regime, for all (since they show most facility in relating themselves to others in groups), *are in both instances* barometers of group atmosphere—*i.e.,* the most likely members of the group to show in their choice behavior signs of registering reaction.

It may be further hypothesized that the individual requires *the kind of* group atmosphere which will enable him freely to form a group-structure related to activities and "principles of living" to which he and other members of the group genuinely can acknowledge allegiance; if he is denied this, he will tend to set up a protective-to-him inter-personal structure and try to re-make the regime as if in his opinion, perhaps, it otherwise might crush him.

At least one of the conditions under which he appears to do this is when he feels he and other members are not having sufficient "say" in how and what activities shall be carried on, as estimated by the number of his behaviors complained of as "rebellious" by the person-in-authority. When the individual apparently feels (whether justified or not) that the official regime of which he is a part is not allowing a way of life he feels would be appropriate, he transplants into it and superimposes upon it, as it were, person-to-person, private-content, interrelationships which under more satisfying-to-him circumstances he ordinarily maintains for the most part outside of it. It might be said that the individual in such cases "reverts" back to concrete dependence upon specific other individually-oriented relationships, putting these ahead of group-role relationships.

Correlations between Leisure and Living-Working

It is of interest to examine the relationship between the subject's expansiveness in choice of others for leisure and for living-working, and similarly, the expansiveness of others for him across the criteria, to ascertain whether there are any concomitant developments or whether no correlations appear. (See Table XXII.)

The number chosen by the subject for leisure and the number chosen by him for living-working show a small but significant correlation which is maintained at about the same level on both occasions of testing: $r = .27$, C. R. $= 3.08$, on Test I, and $r = .26$, C. R. $= 2.96$, on Test II. The number choosing the subject for leisure and the number choosing him for living-working correlate at .43 on Test I and .52 on Test II.[3] Thus there is apparent somewhat more consistency in extent of positive choice reactions towards the individual across contrasting criteria than the individual shows in the extent of his positive choice reactions for others; this consistency shows a slight increase at a later period when the individual remains in the same community, but the individual maintains about the same level he exhibits on the first occasion tested, eight months before. The individual who is relatively more often or less often chosen for leisure will to

---

[3] It will have been noted that the correlations are higher between reactions by and towards the subject for living and for working considered independently instead of together, which may be an indication that these criteria have more in common than living-working, considered together, and leisure-time. See Chapter XI and its Table XIX.

a considerable extent be found similarly located in respect to extent to which he is chosen for living-working situations.

The trend towards correspondence in kind of choice-status is further indicated by the correlation which appears between the number reciprocating the subject for leisure and for living-working: r = .62 on Test I and .55 on Test II. Thus there appears greater consistency across criteria in the extent to which the individual is reciprocated on Test I than in the extent to which he is chosen, but the level of correlation becomes the same (.52 and .55) by the time of Test II.

Table XXII. Summary of Correlations on Choices * between Criteria
of *Leisure-time* and *Living-Working*

N = 133.

	Test	r	Zr/σz
Number chosen by subject for leisure and number chosen by him for living-working:	I	.27	3.08
Same:	II	.26	2.96
Number choosing subject for leisure and number choosing him for living-working:	I	.43	5.11
Same:	II	.52	6.40
Number reciprocating subject for leisure and number reciprocating him for living-working:	I	.62	8.06
Same:	II	.55	6.87
Number reciprocating subject for leisure and number choosing him for living-working:	I	.84	13.57
Same:	II	.89	15.80

* On rejections, the only significant correlation between these criteria found is that between number rejected by subject for leisure and number rejecting him for living-working; r = .42, Test I; r = .49, Test II.

The highest degree of correlation is found between the number reciprocating the subject for leisure and the number choosing him for living-working: r = .84 on Test I and .80 on Test II. (It should be noted that the correlation is much higher than that between the number reciprocating and the number choosing the subject, for living-working, although here it is also high: r = .70 on Test I and .67 on Test II. See p. 53.) In this connection, it is notable that of the individuals choosing the subject for leisure only about one third at the same time select him for living-working; thus the high correlation cannot be taken to mean that a consensus of opinion is present in the response of individuals to him, for the individuals involved are in two-thirds of the instances different individuals. How he interacts with others in living-working may be unknown to most of the individuals who choose him for leisure.

Any explanation of this finding may be tied up with a further finding. While no significant correlations appear between the negative expressions by or towards the subject across the criteria of leisure and living-working, for the aspects just considered, there is found a fairly considerable correlation between the number rejected by the subject for leisure and the number rejecting him for living-working: $r = .42$ on Test I and .49 on Test II.

The results across criteria, both on rejection and on positive choice, may be interdependently based. It appears that the individual who tends to form mutual positive relationships in leisure with those individuals who seek such response from him is at the same time highly likely to be much wanted (even though mainly by different people) as a member of work or living groups. Thus it may be that his facility for getting the response he wants to himself as a person in informal associating provides (or at least is present possibly to offer) an emotional support of inter-personal security that concomitantly acts as a bulwark to enable him to so behave with others in formal work or other official groups that he attracts many members in choice for him as a colleague. On the other hand, it appears that if the individual tends much more than most individuals to reject a great number of people in a context of associating in leisure, he tends to be himself highly rejected as a colleague in the official groups for work or living. Those who reject him, again, are for the most part not the same individuals he has himself rejected for leisure. It is as if something of his "attitude" is sensed by many persons who have little or no first-hand knowledge of it. This finding is the more interesting since no correlation is found between number rejected by the individual for living-working and number rejecting him for living-working. (See p. 54.) Apparently, then, he is an individual who does not himself perceive, or at any rate, direct the volume of his rejections along the same line of group life that is producing it towards him, *i.e.*, along the same criterion for rejection.

On the other hand, it will be recalled that this does not obtain for mutuality of rejection within the living-working context considered as a unit; here there appears a high correlation between the extent to which the individual is rejected and the extent of his reciprocated rejection (see p. 54), but, in this context too, only a slight correlation between his rejection of others and the amount of mutual rejection (see p. 54).

Thus, the gross amounts of rejections which the individual projects towards others or which others direct to him do not correlate on the *same* criteria, but, strangely enough, do correlate to a fairly considerable extent across the criteria of leisure and living-working.

It is as if an index to being much rejected in work or other official group life is to be found in the individual's own extent of negative projections in his informal life with others. In brief, that the individual's performance on one criterion (his amount of rejection of others for leisure exchange) is more linked with the performance of others towards him on other criteria (their rejection of him for living-working) than are either his or their performance within the given criteria considered singly. Thus the individual who rejects relatively many for informal association tends himself to be rejected by relatively many for living-working situations. This finding is of particular interest as most of those who so reject him may not know him in a purely informal context. Whatever enters into the individual's being negatively received as an associate for living-working may possibly be found also to be a factor in his relatively greater negative expansiveness towards others in informal situations.

Interlocked Importance of Criteria in Sociometric Structure

The extent to which a given criterion for choice expression arouses the individual to exercise choice expression along its direction might, on cursory survey, seem to provide one index of the criterion's *choice-interest*. However, the sheer volume of choices given by the individual on a particular criterion as compared with the sheer volume he gives on another criterion, it appears from this study, is not an indication that the former is necessarily more important to him. In fact, as the individual's social atom—the pattern of inter-personal choice and rejection emanating between himself and others in the whole context of his living—is studied as one unit, it appears that no one criterion singly holds an importance such that from its expression the expression on other criteria can be predicted (*e.g.*, from amount of choices made by the individual for living-working, to amount of choices he will make for leisure situations, the correlation in this instance being slight). Certainly if a criterion were employed and hardly any subjects took choice action in respect to it, this might well be evidence that it held very little interest—the subjects showing themselves unable (or perhaps unwilling) to *warm up* to its context for inter-personal collaboration.

However, the mere fact that a sociometric criterion may

elicit a great volume of choice actions—choice decisions for or against association with other members in the particular population for a particular kind of situation, whether spending of leisure time together or working in the same work unit—appears not, in itself, to indicate what sort of importance it has, nor, indeed, even that it is *as* important as other criteria which call forth a much smaller volume of choice expressions. The problem appears one of great complexity. But among the findings which throw some light upon it is the extent and kind of overlap between criteria which characterize the subject's expression. By comparison of such findings *with* the correlations between the individual's performance on different criteria, the *interlocking importance* of different criteria is made evident; moreover, it becomes clear that *kind* of interaction, *e.g.*, mutual as compared with unreciprocated, may be a more critical factor than quantity of interaction, both for the individual's choice-status and the choice-structure of the community as a whole.

Direction of Choice Expression

Subjects who are found to be chosen well above average (*i.e.* by twelve or more persons, see p. 78) for living-working, it is noted, received on Test II on these criteria a disproportionately large amount of choice from newcomers, individuals who had entered the community after the time of Test I. The latter give to the well-chosen ten percent of the subjects 59 percent of all the choices they express for the test-group of subjects.

Examination of their choice expression for leisure reveals, on the other hand, that they give not only fewer choices to them, but a disproportionately small amount of choice—only

4 percent of all the choices they express even though the well-chosen constitute ten percent of the subjects.

The finding raises the possibility that the well-chosen themselves may show more expansiveness towards the newcomers for living-working situations in official group life than for leisure association, and that such reaction to them meets with resentment from the newcomers. However, examination reveals the newcomers to receive from the well-chosen approximately the amount of choice which would be their due by chance alone: namely, 12 percent of all their choices for leisure are given by the well-chosen to the 66 newcomers who represent 14 percent of the total population ($66/457$ less 1, the chooser).

Thus, it would seem not that the well-chosen are not receptive as a group towards the newcomers for leisure association but perhaps the latter *do not believe them to be*. Some substantiation for such a notion appears in a further finding: of the 12 percent of their choices directed by the well-chosen to them, only 1 percent represents first choices. This raises the possibility that lack of a more nearly similar level of response on the part of the potential receiver of choice on the criterion of leisure is "not good enough" so far as the chooser is concerned. In such case perhaps he would prefer to turn elsewhere.

This appears to be precisely what the individual does. The "elsewhere" is not very far afield from his own position: it is predominantly to those members of the community's population who have approximately the same choice-status for living-working situations as the chooser himself shows on Test II. In other words, although he directs a predominant amount of choices towards a relatively few well-chosen individuals for living-working, when he is choosing for spending leisure-time with others he seldom selects these very individuals, shifting instead to those who are more nearly within his "sociometric-class" in the official life of the community.

The "why" of these discriminations is in several respects suggested by the differences which can be noted in the motivations the individual gives for his choice behavior on the different criteria.

Motivations expressed for Leisure Choice vs. Official Grouping

It is of interest that a fuller insight into the meaning of choice motivations for living-working (see pp. 166-205) also appears when choice motivations expressed by the subject for leisure are reviewed.

In the analysis of living-working, the motivations given by the subject are included in case studies of individuals for the light they throw on two extremes of choice-status, isolate- or near-isolated positions and leader-positions.   (See p. 114.)

The present data, instead, are selected to illustrate how the individual differentiates in his expression of choice motivation for leisure association in contrast to living-working. Emphasis is on the qualitative differences which appear and the trends thus indicated.

It will be recalled that in the context of housing and working situations, the individual's expression in choice favors those who in interaction carry forward societal arrangements or conditions for advancing group life of the sort he feels "should be."   And, on the other hand, that the individual shows, by withholding of choice or by active expression of rejection, disfavor towards those individuals who block or retard such group life as he apparently considers appropriate for living together or working together in a group regime.

In this sense, the individual may be said to take a "group-view" or "group-role-view" [4] in his giving or withholding of choice, through the considerations which appear to enter into the manner in which choice is won or earned from him. The view of group-role-of-member appears to be the deciding factor in the spread and focus of choice and rejection—depending upon the individual's estimate of how a potential-choice-receiver will (or has or can) affect the conditions of living and working between the individual chooser *and* other members. What might be called a group-reference-base is implicit and often explicit in the operation of the choice process as examined in communal living and working situations in the community under study.

It is seen, too, that even between groups which are similar, in the sense of being both official in place, time, regularity of meeting and many other factors, the individual discriminates in the exercise of choice and rejection according to the nature of group life—allowing in one (living together) greater flexibility than in another (working together). At the same time there appears a high correlation between the individual's choice-status in each and a high degree of consistency in his expansiveness towards others in each, indicating that there may be much more in common between these two cultural settings than between the latter *and* the leisure-time context of association, from the standpoint of the individual who is a member of the population under study.

Aside from the differences in sociometric patterning between living-working and leisure grouping, just reviewed (see pp. 232-58), the motivations given by the subject suggest that in the psychology of choice behavior, the indi-

---

[4] It is to be understood, of course, that within such an all-over view, many varieties of roles appear.

vidual's emotional projections towards others take, in the two instances, courses differently oriented.

In the work and living groups, the motivations given for the choice structure almost invariably reflect some degree of helpfulness, improvement, or aspiration, *in addition to* whatever element of enjoyment is suggested. In brief, there is implied an *altering* of how the individual now sees himself, to be achieved by his associating with the chosen person because he can "gain" thereby or because the chosen person assumedly has "qualities" he would like to have, and, to some degree also, out of sheer appeal as "someone *I* could help." By comparison, the motivations which appear to underpin the leisure-time structure do not show indications of having a base which, in this sense, is so "flattering-to-the-chosen."

Even the most cursory inspection of the choice motivations for leisure discloses a much more intimate view of the chooser and, indirectly, of the chosen than is the case for living-working. Yet the chooser does little analyzing of his feelings, his tendency being a sort of all-over acceptance centered apparently around a theme no more concrete than "enjoyment." This enjoyment the chooser seems to assume is mutual between him and the other person, and on a very "like" plane.

"You'll think this is a crazy reason but it's the truth. She likes noise like I like noise. I'm always holding myself in in the house, don't yell around or nothing. Susan and I race all over the place in our free time—from the store to the ravines—we get some use of our energy. She's in salesmanship and has to be *just so* with customers, like I do with my patrons in the beauty shop, you could burn them if you didn't watch out. Most people are just too quiet or too dead to suit us, not enough fun. When we're alone we take cracks at even the ones we like, we say 'seems like they're dead on their feet,' and stuff like that, even when we like them—partly we're silly but some of it we really mean. Why not live while you're alive?"

A kind of exuberance of feeling on the part of the chooser towards the chosen is often suggested and at the same time there is little indication that the chooser makes much critical analysis of the relationship as compared with the extent to which he appears to analyze relationships for participating in official groups; instead his statements are relatively simple "announcements" of feeling. Also while a kind of over-all enthusiasm appears evident, the chooser does not go into "ecstasies" about how wonderful the chosen person is in a manner similar to that which is noted, in many instances, in motivations given for living-working (see pp. 191-195). Perhaps in the latter settings a greater "social distance" lends a kind of enhancement to relationships as compared with what appears to be a notable "psychological closeness" between the chooser and the chosen for leisure-time association.

In the leisure-time grouping, the subject appears to visualize himself as getting a feeling of being fully significant for his own sake.

"Y-y-you see, it's like this—I st-st-stutter and sheshe thinks it's cute. I can be myself with her. Lots of people in my house try to help me over st-stuttering but Janet says, 'don't bother, it's cute the way you talk.' I'm always glad to see her, especially when I've been in the house all day, like Sundays—they keep at it so much it makes me feel they won't think much of me if I don't get over it."

He appears to seek to establish with others an interrelationship structure where there is a minimum of restriction placed on the kind of exchange he can get and give and, conversely, a maximum of freedom to be "himself" without being urged by others to "improve" or "to be different" from what he is— whether it is a matter of overcoming stuttering or being "too loud" or, in other instances, being "too serious about religion."

For example, a subject who excludes from the purview of either housing associates or work associates what she considers most important in her life, "my religion," says of her first choice for living in the same house:

"Paula helps the housemother to see a lot of things; if she misunderstands somebody and they won't speak up for themselves, Paula has a way to open it up just like it was about herself—that's how much she cares. Who wouldn't want to be most of all in the same house with her?"

Of her first choice for leisure, she says:

"Gloria has deep thoughts like mine, on religion. I wouldn't say she *has* as much religion but she doesn't think it's crazy that I do. I like to think about the saints and talk about them as if they were right there with Gloria and me. She can imagine how I feel and she gets religious feelings too. She doesn't tell anyone what I tell her either, it's just between us and God. My Gracious, what if Paula knew about it! She is sort of worldly and she'd want *to cure me*, I bet anything. And it isn't something you want to be cured of, it's wonderful to be close to God, you have to strive after it. I tell you it's a struggle sometimes. I think Paula would think I was upset; of course it isn't easy but it is like having a guide-line to your life, if it starts slipping away you *want* to reach out after it. I don't mean Paula isn't somebody God would like—it's more, well it's more that she's just got to live a lot longer to get to find out all her self-confidence and real nice ways, like I was just telling you about her, come from God and not from herself. *I know* because one day I was going to explain to her and she argued. She said, 'What's the matter with you, Caroline, don't get me tangled up in mysteries. If I get sympathetic with someone it's that they deserve it, God hasn't anything to do with that.' You see why I figure like I do."

To the leisure interaction the individual appears to lend an articulation of his most personal view of life, while his more "societal" view, in the sense of keeping group-situations in mind, is aired in the direction of motivations as a group member in living and working situations.

Throughout, in the motivations he gives for his choices for leisure association, he tends to develop a philosophy or view of life peculiarly his, as relatively distinct from that of the next individual, and this he appears willing to have surveyed or criticized by but few of the very persons he chooses for work partners. At any rate, it is apparent in the motivations expressed that he discerns it may be inappropriate to exchange with co-workers in a like manner the same content of ideas and attitudes and temperamental expressions which he apparently feels he may entrust to leisure associates of his own choosing.

A further important function served by the leisure-time structure of interrelations is its use by the members to exchange and ventilate their reactions to the group life they are enjoying or enduring in their respective official groups for work and housing.

"I'm forever hunting her up when I'm agonized which I am a lot of times, she wouldn't let on what a big blow-my-top I am either. This living in a house with 29 other people—it confuses me. •Patty tells me in her house things go on in a way so nobody gets feeling fuzzy and not knowing what's up. What they do is, the bunch gets together, the entire house, and discuss different ways to do things, then you understand in advance of doing something and it's fun, the talk and planning and all and you feel more together-like. It's better for the housemother too because after something is decided there isn't this one and that one objecting or raising a fuss that they don't see why it's necessary. At first, I wanted to transfer to Patty's house but the more I thought about how she said every house *could be* like hers, the more I decided I'd influence mine. That's what I'm doing. I don't ever mention how confused I am, I just drop remarks now and then about how nice it would be to talk over all the advantages and disadvantages of whatever seems to be coming up. So far I got about twelve people interested as much as I am and twice the whole bunch met. Things didn't go so smooth but our housemother said it's only that we need practice. And she likes it better, she said, no matter how much we argue. Patty said it's how you put a point, like if you say, 'I think so and so,' somebody's going to say, 'I don't!' And it's better to say, 'Should we discuss what would happen if . . . ?' and then nobody will think to say, 'no.' "

In this setting the individual receives encouragement that life in his official group can be as "happy" as in other groups which he gains information about from his chosen leisure associates. His attention is also drawn to what factors may be interfering with its "happiness," under conditions where he apparently is receptive to what is told him, perhaps because the teller is able to be objectively disinterested in whether his advice is taken or not. That the influence of such exchange of ideas impresses the individual to the extent of his making efforts to re-make his respective groups accordingly provides, of course, a source of difficulty to the "smooth" running of a work or housing regime on a *status quo* basis. With so highly developed a leisure-time structure as the community under study discloses, no official group could long remain unaffected by the exchange of "notions" between its members and the members of other official groups with whom they were, in this sense, communicating confidences, passing judgments, and exchanging ideas and skills for "doing things over."

"It was Joan who told me how things go in her house. In our house it was so different. She said when you get a foreigner in your midst, don't let her stand around like a stick, ask her things and tell her things, then let her know what you think of her experience in life and ask her what she thinks of yours and that way you get to be like an educated person—you don't expect everyone to be like yourself. The idea is catching on in my house more and more."

The free passing-on of "inside-"views of how other people live and work in their groups and the accompanying satisfactions or dissatisfactions attributed by them to the regime of such groups, across the informal choice network from person to person, in an apparent atmosphere of confidence and trust and intimacy, makes the leisure-time structure an avenue for the development of "community" concern, broadly serving the members of the population as a whole. In this sense, a well-developed leisure-time structure would appear an indispensable vehicle for preventing "official" groups from becoming insulated from one another, provincial in their regimes, and resistant to innovation and development by their respective membership.

Leadership and Isolation in Leisure-Choice Structure

The manner in which the informal choice structure is used by the members suggests that its psychological network is a bearer of kinds of influence which are peculiarly important, though different in emphases from the influence carried on the choice structure of official grouping in the community under analysis.

In the inter-personal structure related to the criteria of living-working, the choice-status of the individual appears directly attributable to the capacities he shows *in interaction* with colleagues to lessen or augment the satisfactions of the common group life. In this sense, choice is found to be evoked towards him or withheld from him, more or less in proportion to *how he carries* his role *in relation to* other members' roles, or, to state it more precisely, in proportion to how others perceive him to interact with them for the benefit of their common group regime. Individuals whose behaviors in this context enable other members to have an expanding experience (by the latter's definition) appear to earn a high choice-status. Individuals whose behaviors in this context are considered to retard or be disruptive to the kind of group experience wanted are found to be isolated or near-isolated from the choice of their fellow members.

In this sense, sheer quantity of choice "earned" by the individual on the sociometric criteria of being wanted as a member in the official groups of the community *is* found to be an index of the extent to which the individual has shown or is showing (in the opinion of his fellow members) capacity to carry the group role in question which they want from him with the sort of interaction they consider aids the milieu of the group to become what they want it to be.

In contrast, no such function and no such "judgment" can be discerned in respect to the sheer quantity of choice earned by the individual on the sociometric criterion of leisure-time association.   In the latter, not only is sheer quantity of choice received by the individual *not* an index to his role *in the informal milieu* of which he is a member, but the role which *any* individual appears to play within it has very much in common with the roles other individuals play within it.

No individual aids many others in the leisure-time milieu so far as is evidenced in this study, in the ways characteristic of the living-working groups.   Likewise, no individual wins from a great number of other individuals in the population their choice for him as a leisure-time associate.

Leadership, then, in a similar sense as found in the choice structure underlying the official groups, is not found in the leisure-choice structure.   In fact, the question arises whether "leadership" is an appropriate term for any aspect of the dynamics of interchange in the informal groupings.

In contrast to the exceptionally great "group service" which is implied in the behaviors of those found to be most chosen in the living-working structure of the community, the interaction of even these same individuals in the informal leisure-choice structure may be said to be a highly *mutual* inter-individual expression, emotionally supportive to the individuals as persons rather than as group members and at the same time remarkably reciprocal in its function—rather than reflecting extreme exertion on the part of some members as is found in the official groupings.   (See pp. 215-17.)   It may be premised that in so far as "service" enters, it appears to be a service which renders each individual about equally indebted to the other and not many indebted to the few who show extraordinary effort in their behalf.

Whatever are the factors important to choice behavior in the leisure-time milieu, there is evident much more "evenness" to the effort made by the different individuals involved as compared with the exceptional effort made by certain individuals and the relatively meager exertion of many others in the official settings.   In fact, the word "effort" may be a misnomer for the kind of interaction that occurs in the leisure setting: here what happens between chooser and chosen takes place with an apparently greater degree of spontaneity and seeming lack of forethought and appears primarily based on compatibility of temperament and outlook between them.

The nature of the "supportive" service itself is not widespread: *i.e.*, from one individual to many other individuals. Only occasionally is an individual found to be "helping out others" in the direction he chooses or, indeed, in his behavior in general during his leisure-time.

"She's responsible that there are so many friendships on the campus. She's always doing for somebody what she did for me—she introduced me to more people that I enjoy and that enjoy me.   She just seems to *know* who will hit it off with who else."

However, if the criterion for leadership is the extent of changes brought about in official group regimes by the influence stemming from one individual to others through the leisure-choice network, then many an individual who is not found in a leader-position in his own official groups is found to hold a "hidden" leadership role. Moreover, the influence thus reflected in "raising" the tenor of group life in the respective groups throughout the community may, by inference, be considered also crucial in a different way from the "direct" leadership displayed within a given group: without such spread of cross-fertilization throughout the community, lending variety and innovations and increasing the cosmopolitanism of understanding of different ways of life through "trying them out" rather than simply knowing of them by hearsay, it may be premised that the individual groups within the community (through lack of such vitalizing communication) could very readily become and remain insulated from one another.

But in general it appears indicated that even above and beyond such a function, the leisure-time structure appears to carry the even more important function of inter-personal sustaining of the morale of the members of the population as a whole. In addition, it appears important in enabling many to carry roles enhancing and expanding to inter-personal and inter-group development.

Leisure-Choice Meaning to the Individual

In the relations in leisure-time, there is indicated an interplay and comprehending receptivity between individuals that, more fully than in work relations (or in other official context), takes account of individual differences, whether of background, mood, or patterning of outlooks. In rare instances even, an individual who is much rejected as a work associate appears to find in relations in leisure-time some degree of acceptance and understanding of *the very behaviors* resented elsewhere.

"She is so pathetic, always feeling people are against her. I see a lot of her in my spare hours. She knows *I'm* not against her. I explain to her that way of feeling will stop as she meets more people. Nobody is going to be so mean to her as her own family was when she was little. I understand because some things hurt me too that happened when I was a child."

Moreover, the individual's ways of behaving at one time and later may change in directions not anticipated without his thereby losing his leisure-time choices. By contrast, in work situations even a relatively minor change (as becoming "not as steady as before" in work production) is often given as the reason for a shift of choice.

"I chose her last time too for leisure and recreation times, she was so jolly and good-hearted. Now she's mighty gloomy for three months but anyway I understand her and I like her, she's more in my heart than ever." (In the official groups, the individual seems expected to hide expression of his moods from view of other members; see p. 193 or p. 197.)

While in many respects the common official group for work or for housing in the community under study apparently provides to some degree, more or less, a place of inter-individual security for nearly all members, the distinctions which are implicitly suggested by the subject's motivations for association in such groups compared with those he gives for leisure-time make it appear probable that the sort of security provided does not genuinely replace that intimate exchange apparently longed for by the individual, wherein he can feel himself valued and even precious in the eyes of another.

In this connection it is of interest that the only two subjects who gave no leisure-time choices imply a perception on their own part of a need not yet met.

"I didn't find anybody so far for a friend. Lena's wonderful in our house but for me she's useless as a personal friend—one minute she says she understands you and the next she's telling you you're just awful. What do you make of that? Me—I get sick about it."

"I think nobody wants to be with me in spare time, I'm a good worker and I know that but I don't know someone who likes me just anywhere anytime the way I see other people here. I keep looking."

On the other criteria, there were no subjects who did not choose.

It is obvious that the leisure-choice structure is built for association in a setting made in a fuller sense by the choosers than is the choice-structure for association in the settings of common housing and working. In the latter, neither the activities nor the formal aspects of the setting could be determined by the individuals themselves in so many ways as could mark their use of leisure-time.

On the other hand, it is also obvious that as none of these ties are official the individual in leisure-time can very easily depart from the company of his selected associates, which is not the case in a work group, and, moreover, he would not lose "face" in the process. It is, in the test-community, as in other communities, very much a matter of the individual's "own business" whom he does or does not care "to be friends with." But the important fact is, as was noted earlier (see p. 236), that such choices appear to be within the conscious control of the individual much less than do work choices. The greater flexibility that he shows in warming up to changes in the ways of behavior on the part of his choice-partners would seem to lend further confirmation to such an interpretation. In work situations, for example, he apparently to a greater extent, "learns" to get along; he shows no such "improvement" in the area of leisure-time association over the same long period of time (eight months).

The leisure grouping, of course, *can* change much more readily in values, codes and expectations of members in accommodating their roles to one another's, because how one member behaves does not affect a great many others so obviously and so directly as it does in a work group or a living-together group. In the test-community, just as in any community, the latter groups built reputations and traditions and customs which they thought of generally as worth carrying on and in whose perpetuation they were interested.

Nevertheless such logical considerations by an observer can certainly afford but a partial, though plausible explanation, of the phenomena found. The greater spontaneity and inferrable intensity of feeling may possibly be a more crucial factor.

It is as if the picture of self which has been considered as carried within the individual he seeks to find "received" by another very much as he sees it himself. Then, apparently, he can take roles *in addition to* his "self" one, in a more impersonal, so-called "self-less" manner (see p. 204) as though he has had or is having enough "self-" satisfaction somewhere in his life context. At any rate, those individuals who appear to find this in abundance in some of the leisure choices received are able to carry roles that interplay, in a highly sustaining and constructive manner, with those of others and result in the projection of many choices to them for work and living situations.

Or, to put it conversely, those individuals who, for whatever reason, in the community under study, do not find a "flesh-and-blood" mirror of themselves in another's interaction with them (or so perceive themselves as finding) do not apparently carry their group roles with the kind of behaviors which bring them either choices on a group-role basis or on an informal person-to-person basis to any appreciable extent.[5]

The leisure-choice structure appears in this community to be a bedrock for its morale and mental hygiene. It is within it that the individual seeks and finds an all-inclusive sort of acceptance of himself, confidence in his own "worthiness," opportunity to work out his problems at a rate more compatible with his stage of development, without the responsibilities, cares, and awarenesses which come with participation in work relationships or common living relationships wherein the same individual may be urged to "improve," "raise the standards," and, in general, may feel threatened with guilt the cause of which he is often at a loss to discern.

The foundations of leisure-choice apparently to a greater extent than the choice for work or living together appear based more exclusively in warmth and good feeling, as ends in themselves. The work and housing groups have goals of a more "distant" sort which the individual appears unable to keep out of his awareness and which he seems persistently to recognize and acknowledge by the direction of his choice behavior. The motivations he gives for leisure association show a simplicity of response that seems to defy or make unnecessary a critical analysis by the chooser of the chosen.

[5] This is also of interest in connection with the studies in recessivism in research in schizophrenia, sponsored by the National Committee for Mental Hygiene (Canada) and the Supreme Council of the Scottish Rite Masons, which report that a child "without a friend" is not accepted by his classmates. See Mary L. Northway, Esther B. Frankel, and Reva Potashin, *Personality and Sociometric Status*, p. 51, 1947. Also see related findings in an important intensive study of boys, age ten to twelve years old, Ruth Edith Hartley, *Sociality in Preadolescent Boys*, 1946. See also the thorough study by Adolph A. Sandin, *Social and Emotional Adjustments of Regularly Promoted and Non-Promoted Pupils*, 1944, which indicates the catastrophic effects upon the child of severing him from his relationships.

It is obvious that in both kinds of choice-structure, the informal, less institutionalized, leisure-time association network and the more formal, more institutionalized, work or living collective's network, there are to be found operating codes, value systems, diversified roles, methods of getting conformity, and in various degrees purposes and objectives. In the one case, however, the individual finds larger "personal" expression, in the other, the group-situation, perhaps as much as its individual members, "tells" him what he can express to a much greater extent. The pervading difference is rather in the *kinds* of codes operating and in the *kinds* of roles the individual can acceptably display and in the *kinds* of conformity expected, sought, or demanded, and last, not least, in the kinds of growth afforded. It appears not a question of *which* kind of choice-structure, that underpinned with person-to-person spontaneity of rapport or that centered to a greater extent in inherited or passed-along "codes for behavior," but of *how* these two structures *appear interdependent* in the individual's life and the life of the community as a whole.

CHAPTER XIII

Structural Differences in Groups: the Psychegroup and the Sociogroup

Choice behavior, as sociometrically surveyed in this study, shows the individual to maintain a consistency in his choice projections (whether positive or negative) which typifies him as a person. At the same time, the group-choice-structure he thus creates with others is distinguished by his projective capacity in inter-personal relations. This capacity is apparently not hit-or-miss in its expression. On the contrary, it produces different "forms" of psychological structure according to the nature of the situation into which the individual carries his emotional expansiveness. It is in these forms *as distinguishably different structures* that a psychological astuteness or what may be called the "intelligence" of the choice process can be said to be made visible.

First, around the given individual it is noted that that portion of his relations marked by greatest mutuality is an area which might be called highly personal—those other individuals with whom he need not share any formalized obligations or experience in a common group setting with others. This area, despite its high mutuality, is much smaller in total volume than another area—the area of relations which are "public," held in common officially with others in a group, and whose maintenance or loss are also easily known since they are carried on in a collective setting of work or common living (in the community of this study, common housing unit or vocational unit).

These two areas are not wholly separate. Some relationships (between the *same* individuals) appear in both areas. Between the two areas, then, are some relations which overlap, existing in both the more personal and more public area. Scarcely any individual has completely separated relations, in this sense.

By study of the contrasting structural features of the two inter-personal areas and, particularly, by following such study into the kind of sociometric position the individual is likely to have in one when he shows a certain position in the other, the hypothesis is suggested that the crucial distinctions in structure come about by the nature of the pressures upon the choice process in the one case compared with the relative lack of pressures upon it in the other, as an important factor accounting for the differences.

The two structures, wherein among many differences between them, there appears in one, by comparison with the other, higher mutuality, a much smaller choice expenditure meeting with a greater amount of reciprocal expression, and a relatively far more even distribution of choice (both by the individual and towards him), suggest: (1) it is not the individual's low ability to attract others which marks the kind of structure he builds in his collective, official groupings; (2) it is not that he is selecting from a different field of others when he shows a remarkably keener and more telling sense for finding reciprocal response in application of the choice process; (3) it is not that the individual does not wish to exercise choice as knowingly in both settings of his existence, formal and informal, personal and official group—it is rather that between him and his use of the choice process potential within him (and provoked by those who are in the same community with him) there intervenes a factor to which he feels he must, as best he can, attune, adapt, re-direct this potential, namely, to fit the expectations he finds facing him when common group membership and the kind of life he and others will have within it are at stake.

These "commonnesses," it may be hypothesized, tend to drive into the background of his feeling processes (in respect to others) that which is truly his most "essential" self—essential, in the sense of that which he would most want to express and share and enjoy with others who would view it with understanding and cherish it *just as it is.*

In brief, within *this* group, he finds society facing him, telling him he is a group member, in a situation which is not for him alone to mold (with persons only whom he would choose). This collective, more or less formalized setting, where concerns must be shared and obligations held in common, as distinguished from that more fluid, informal, relatively un-institutionalized setting, where concerns and obligations and life itself are so much more, in a total sense, at the command of the individual's wants and wishes, might appropriately be called, in the one case, *the sociogroup,* and in the second case, *the psychegroup.*

The term *tele* has been given by Moreno[1] to the factor operating to produce group organization (as reflected in sociometric structure) and the term *tele process* (or *tele factor*) to the process which in a broad sense results in the formation of inter-personal relationships growing out of person-to-person contacts from birth on. Tele, thus, is an inter-personal product and not the product (affect) of a single individual. The tele process is the operation of the double foci in a relationship between two persons which makes one inter-personal relation, dependent upon both individuals and not a sub-

[1] J. L. Moreno, *Who Shall Survive?* pp. 158-164, 1st ed., 1934; and J. L. Moreno and H. H. Jennings, "Statistics of Social Configurations," *Sociometry,* I:342-374, Jan.-April, 1938, pp. 363 ff.

jective, independent product of either person. Tele is, by definition, "positive" when it acts to draw individuals into relationship with each other; it is "negative" when it acts to separate individuals, causing them to reject a relationship. Tele may be positive and active (or negative and active) from one side of a structure and the individual who is the focus of positive tele may be unaware of the other individual's attraction to him. In this case it is in an infra-stage of development from the standpoint of the non-aware recipient. Nevertheless it cannot be considered a one-sided process as the direction it takes is not random but depends upon the second individual. The total tele immediately concentrated upon an individual or expended by the individual towards others makes up an emotionally toned inter-personal structure which is termed the "social atom." It is the smallest total structure or nucleus of relations which can be lifted from the whole psychological organization of the group and still retain every part of the structure which is in contact with the individual or with which the individual is in contact.

The significant fact is that a relationship exists between two individuals such that they are not indifferent to association with each other. In this simple fact is the basis of the intricate larger choice-structure which sociometry has shown to exist and to operate and, indeed, to comprise the skeleton of society itself.

It is to be understood that while, from a sociometric viewpoint, a given relationship appears positively toned from both individuals, or again, negatively toned, it is likely in either case to have components of both positive and negative feeling; the significant "metric" aspect enters in that one complex of feelings outweighs the other to such extent that a choice action is taken by the individual, sociometrically, to retain or discard the relationship. This does not imply it has been experienced as *purely* positive or *purely* negative, respectively, to the participants. Sociometric choice may thus be seen *as a rough index of tele;* it discloses whether the individuals are positively attracted or negatively repulsed at the prospects of association together in specific contexts which are opened for their decision.

Upon the empirical findings of the present research, a theoretical framework may be outlined for the consideration of the sociogroup and the psychegroup.

Sociogroups are groups characterized by a sociometric structure which is based on a criterion which is *collective* in nature; such a *socio-criterion* is working in a *common work unit* (as a shop or office); the tele between the persons *in respect to collaborating with one another* in such sociogroups may be called *sociotele,* since it is founded upon response towards remaining with or wishing to depart from such association in the specific common situation. Sociotele has, in this sense, a *largely impersonalized* base. (I, a man holding membership in this union, feel towards you, as a fellow-worker also holding membership in this union, thus and so . . . , or, I, as a psychologist, feel towards you, as a psychologist and co-working with me *in this research situation,* thus and so . . .)

Psychegroups are groups characterized by a sociometric structure which is based on a *private* criterion which is totally *personal* in nature; such a *psyche-criterion* is *associating in the time the individual has at his voluntary disposal* (as in leisure-time); the tele between the persons *in respect to associating with one another of their own accord* in such psychegroups may be called *psychetele,* since it is founded upon response towards associating or not associating with others as a purely personal matter. Psychetele has, in this sense, a *largely personalized* base. (I, Sally Lynd, feel towards you, Paul Casey, thus and so . . .)

Thus, while it is evident that "private" personality does not and cannot remain totally outside sociogroup life, as "collective performance" (that demanded of the individual by the group as a whole) must come first, the personality of the individual (his role as a person) is of less interest and only a minimum allowance is made for it. Obviously, "private" personality is itself "non-private" in the sense that its expression is an inter-personal phenomenon (see pp. 212-14), but relative to the scope of expression it is permitted in the two groups, it is least restricted in the psychegroup.

As individuals who are members of sociogroups are, of course, persons as well, there is bound to be a residuum of psychegroup structure within the structure that develops in the sociogroup; similarly, individuals tend as psychegroup members to a greater or lesser degree to import into its context ways of behaving which they are currently holding to in sociogroup life. (*E.g.*, they may impose upon one another the expectation of punctuality, highly important in work programs, for their leisure-time dates.) It is the difference in emphases taken by the individual in his exercise of choice and rejection in the two instances which suggests how fundamentally different in meaning for him are the two kinds of groups.

Such a way of thinking about the findings of the present research, makes it possible to obtain a clearer view of how and why the choice process structures the community in the manner disclosed. As used in the present research, a clear-cut delineation between a sociogroup and a psychegroup (both theoretically and empirically) clarifies the study of leadership and isolation as well as interrelationship patterns generally.

With such a theoretical base in mind, a number of the findings may be drawn together for the general view which is thereby provided of the tele process as it is expressed in the psychegroup and the sociogroup.

The finding that in leisure, compared to living-working situations, many more of the choices expended are reciprocated (see pp. 239 ff) may represent choice expression by the individual which is more effective because it is less calculating and more fully an intuitive and impulsive act, reflecting more of the total "self" than goes into choice expression for sociogroups. In the latter, the individual's socio-role tendencies may go in one direction and his personal-role tendencies in another, and thus many individuals may just miss converging with the respective tendencies of others in these two directions. Also the choices in the sociogroup must acknowledge the pressures of the group situation. Thus in any group which has a socio-like focus, the individual is less apt to base his choice so completely upon his reactions as a total organism.

The finding that the individual's choice-status (in terms of the number choosing him) in the sociogroup is highly linked to the amount of mutuality he finds in his psychegroup as well as to his choice-status in sheer number of individuals choosing him for leisure (see p. 251), and particularly the finding that there is *still higher* correlation between the extent to which he is reciprocated in leisure and the extent to which he is reciprocated in sociogroup relations (see p. 252) suggest that capacity to carry sociogroup roles with exceptional inter-personal success depends upon the individual's finding some degree of mutuality in his psychegroup.

Finding one's own self-perception reflected in another's view of oneself may induce a frame of mind favorable to playing the part of a group member in a collective situation, whether of work or of living in common quarters with many others, in a manner which is inter-personally constructive. It is as if before the individual can give himself to the group's objectives, which involves his holding back whatever the group may not need from him while he cooperates by giving whatever it does need from him, he requires a modicum of approved self-perception from others by whom he is wanted in a setting where privately- or personally-oriented exchange is operative; having the latter, he appears better able to face and more willingly to meet the pressures of his other associational contexts.

The finding that the sociogroup makes it possible for *more* individuals to find some degree of choice from others as associates within its context who do not find choice reception outside it (see p. 241) may be the reflection of a "third factor" in it which may serve to mediate the effort of individuals to get into rapport with one another. Since the person-to-person relating exemplified in leisure choice structure has no such "third factor" (as any work or other officially collective group has in the form of more or less definite group objectives around which a group-role develops *via which* the individual can show his interest and make an effort to contribute), the individual is provided with no specific door into its "belongingness." He is obliged much more in such a setting to reveal himself. If one envisions the situation of an individual who does not "accept himself," it would follow that *he cannot let himself* be fully seen and known through the perceptions of others; he must accordingly hold back from leisure association, perhaps even from those he would like to know, since to achieve the latter apparently requires a willingness to interact in a highly self-revelatory or personalized area of associational exchange. Moreover, in the psychegroup, what an individual really thinks and feels *must* be known to others before they can give acceptance. Should the individual be holding self-concepts which are far from what is implied in his daily behavior, he may foresee a wisdom in keeping others at a distance.

In the sociogroup, it may be premised, the group-role is an *insulating factor* between the individuals. On the other hand, the *very lack of insulation* in the psychegroup may cause a speeding up of interaction which evokes more facets of the personality and therefore demands and gets greater mutuality per choice expended. In simple person-to-person relating, the individual faces on his own, as it were, the other individual. He may conceivably experience the person-to-person situation, in some instances, more fearfully than one in which a group role is required of him. He is, so to speak, "psychologically more naked" in the area where there is least cultural protection in the form of the group-role standing between him and others. With increasing intimacy of exchange, the individual shows himself to be increasingly selective in the sense of welcoming fewer into relationships with him. (See pp. 238-39 for comparison of amount of investment of choices.)

The group-role may provide in the sociogroup an easier avenue for choice reception since the individual does not have to interact so nearly as a totality and can legitimately initiate and maintain relationships in a more impersonalized manner. When left in a situation of completely free interchange such as leisure-time may represent, those individuals who are dependent upon official controls and organizational restrictions may feel at a loss, tend to withdraw, and many even express this feeling by not choosing at all. In a work group, as one example of a sociogroup, the same individuals may know, or think they can find out, what is needed in performance. In the indefiniteness of the informal setting, however, they may feel no such assurance since it may demand much more in terms of spontaneity in meeting the unexpected.

At the same time, it may be that the kinds of pressures resulting from standards and competition related to the group-role-factor may act upon the individual in such a manner that he feels he must hide from view whatever his work associates might not approve or might consider inadequacies on his part; this kind of behavior, if it becomes established in the individual's tendencies in his sociogroups, may carry over into his person-to-person relationships in informal settings. Then, instead of communicating whatever he can on a personal level, the individual may deliberately attempt to communicate as little as possible.

It may be hypothesized that this would be especially true for the individual who has a personal history of having been treated in childhood by the adults in his home setting on a highly impersonal basis. Such experience may create in him psychological deficiencies for enjoying relationships of intimacy and friendship. It may oblige him to build a system of values which places greatest merit on being efficient in some concrete skills via which one becomes "worthy" and result in the individual's becoming emotionally out of reach and stylizing his methods of communication instead of expressing thought-and-feeling freely.

Every face-to-face or "primary" group is, of course, not necessarily a psychegroup, nor is it necessarily what is called an autonomous group. Such groups may or may not become either in part or totally what is designated empirically here as a psychegroup, wherein the uniqueness of the individual as a personality is appreciated and "allowed for" with varying degrees of spontaneous indulgence and affection of the kind he seeks and wherein he can count "altogether" as a person.

The psychegroup is operationally definable and it should not be confused with groupings defined at a phenomenological, descriptive level. An example of the latter type of term is "friendship," which is not a scientific word, holding the same meaning wherever it is used; thus sociometric choices cannot be said to measure "friendship."

While at times a psychegroup may be a "friendship" cluster, it is not necessarily identical with it or even tantamount to it. Each of us defines friendship differently and will "put up with" or "not put up with" particular behaviors shown by our friends according to our own system of values or notions about the role of a friend. We are conscious, in turn, of many behaviors we might show (or confidences we might entrust) but which we do not disclose because we think these may run counter to *their* ideas of how we should behave. With some of our friends, however, we feel no such restrictions: *these may be said to be part of our psychegroup.* Further, there are for each of us still other individuals whom we might not feel as free to call upon for a particular favor (as loaning us money) and who are not considered as friends in this sense, yet who give us an intangible sense that we are valued by them for what we are and for these there is a place in our psychegroup. Thus, it may be hypothesized that for any given individual his friendship group will be larger than his psychegroup but show some overlap in membership. Moreover, enjoyable as friendship may be, the psychegroup appears to meet needs deeper than friendship, as ordinarily conceived, can or does.

It is as if being chosen within the milieu of the psyche-group provides the individual with the feeling he is considered by the other as totally *his kind*—without reservations of any consequential sort—thus as being approved, as it were, by *a surrogate for all others*, standing (in the individual's mind) as a counterpart for mankind as a whole. By comparison, the individual's finding of choice in his sociogroup may be conceived as his finding "society's" approval—society which after all is relative to one's life time and the setting in which it is experienced, thus perhaps less important because of its transiency in time and place. It would be conceivably possible for any individual to say to himself, regarding his situation in his sociogroup, "In a different society (different sociogroup), I would likely find many choices as a co-worker"; it would be conceivably harder to face the fact of not finding choice towards one's self as a person, harder to rationalize or to endure.

This is not to imply that all the choices which went to build the leisure-time structure in the test-community consciously carried such implications in the chooser's mind. Some of them may have been "prestige" choices, more or less consciously aimed to raise the chooser's "standing"; yet such choice behavior nevertheless reflects the picture of self the individual carries or "aspires to."

By and large, the directions taken by the choice expression for leisure association point to the individual's use of such choice to fulfill deeply personal needs between himself and others, in answering his own questions or doubts on his concept of himself, as compared with the manner in which he directs his choice expression for sociogroup life.

Moreover, this is also not meant to imply that every choice by the individual for leisure association has equal value in offering to him a psychological mirror of himself; on the contrary, particularly in the case of very complex personalities (in terms of how many roles they see themselves as able to carry, and the intricate relations among these roles in their mind), one of the individual's choices may meet, as it were, but one aspect of his own view of himself, another choice, another partial aspect, and so on, so that, in this sense, the individual appears to need his total psychegroup in a way that he does not need his total sociogroup.   Thus the psychegroup of a particular individual may be said to comprise *that part of* his social atom of most private and personal concern to his own emotional equilibrium.   (Similarly, a psychegroup would comprise comparable sections from the social atoms of all the other individuals who are so interrelated.)

This implication is apparent even when a clearly contrasting psychological pattern appears to underlie the individual's behavior with others in the two settings.

"She's what I like in a friend—she decides everything, she's my initiative, she'll call me up and say 'come on over, I'm going to tell you about how to handle that jam you're in.'   I like the other person to decide in friendship this and that, I guess I'm different, so people tell me anyway; it seems a lot want just suggestions, then do as they please.   Not me, I want a friend to say, 'you do it this way,' —then I'll do it and feel O.K. about it."

(Interviewer: "But you said for your choices for work that they, 'don't take over and run down my ideas, they even help me express them better and get everybody to try them—not brush me off when I don't know how to say something clear.'")

"Yes, I know, but don't you see, that is *work*, what I'm talking about now is friendship: I'm not going to stand for any bossing around any place I work, in friendship it's out of generosity from the heart, and you get what *you* want, their advice, see?   I *want*, it's more than that, I guess I want to do everything a friend says."

Nevertheless, such contrasts appear to present no inconsistency to the individual showing them; he apparently seeks out for each setting that association which will permit him to retain his own individuality of inconsistency, as it were,—one which fits the pattern of behavior which he evidently thinks desirable or feels in need of at the moment.

Thus the role picture of self, as it is seen through the choice process, does not apparently mean a necessarily fully "permissive" picture, in the sense that the individual is "treated well" in psychegroup relations, from some observer's (the investigator's) standpoint. It indicates rather that his choice pattern carries whatever internalized institutionalizations of roles he has acquired through previous interaction with others, which fit in with whatever psychological patterns he may think "ought to be." This may mean quite something else to him than it does to an observer. Furthermore, as in the example, a remarkable lack of awareness of inconsistencies often seems present.

It becomes obvious that we never deal with the individual *per se* but with *the individual in relationships* and, similarly, that we never deal with culture *per se* but with *culture as expressed in relationships in an inter-personal and inter-group context*. These premises become articulate through sociometric analysis.

When dealing with sociometric data, it is often not apparent why simple "amounts" of choice are not a sufficient index of group structure. (See pp. 266-67, 305-308.)

A quantitative treatment of choice, of a purely additive sort, sets aside certain factors which cannot be disregarded in a study of positive and negative choice in general. In the actualities of living it would be fallacious to assume that the difference between no choices and one choice, or between one and two choices, or between two and four, or four and eight, is a difference in arithmetic distance from a given zero point. The difference between being unchosen and chosen by one person is a distance not as yet measurable by any quantitative scale; it involves the difference between being able to evoke positive reaction and being unable to do so. The individual who is shown to be wanted by two persons is not necessarily wanted half as much as one who is chosen by four persons. Both have crossed the gap between the status of being disregarded or unregarded for positive choice by those who surround them in the given community; both have shown capacity to win from others regard for themselves to the extent of their being positive choices for participating along some avenue of exchange.

Moreover, for every choice one individual exercises towards another, rejection of others is involved by the mere fact that selection in one direction is selection over other directions that the choice might have taken; the individual chooses by "rejecting." Thus those we do not choose are rejected by the simple result of their not being chosen. In this sense, there can be no choosing without rejecting; rejecting is tied fast to the action of choice, to the issue of who shall be selected.

Yet tacit rejection as non-attraction, defined by the lack of expression of positive choice for the individual, should not be confused with *active* rejection, defined by the overt expression of negative choice for the individual as an associate. In the latter case, the persons rejecting the individual *select* him for exclusion from association with them; he thus may be considered *actively not wanted* by those who reject him as a fellow member.

It would seem indicated that any additive consideration of data on choice behavior must be seen against a framework of many factors and their interplay.

It cannot, of course, be assumed that a greater amount of expansiveness shown towards a given individual (in terms of the number of choices directed to him) as compared with another individual is an indication that the first individual is a "better adjusted" person. The definition of his "social adjustment" must be thought of in relation to what he has to offer and what others have to offer *in the common interaction: i.e.* in terms of the *most appropriate* pattern in the case of any particular individual as a member of the total group. It can therefore be defined only by comparison with what other individuals are present and express together in the interplay of responsiveness among them.

In sociogroups, this is surely a major consideration in any assessment of "goodness" and "poorness" in inter-personal patterns. For example, in a vocational work group a better adjustment pattern may be shown by the individual whose interaction pattern reflects willingness to take a role supplemental to the more prominent roles assumed by other persons *when this is fitting to the situation as a whole* and who shows this by choosing in a direction which will mean such growth for him, rather than his aiming to outdo another in getting a central role for which he knows he is not as well qualified.

It is obvious, too, that in such an ideal psychegroup as the family occasionally presents, it would reflect quite other than a "good" inter-personal pattern for one parent to capture all of the choices of the children to the exclusion of the other adult partner. The beginnings of such a tendency might indicate the down-fall of this very psychegroup.

In any event, it cannot be premised from the present research that greater desirability *per se* attaches to a high choice-status as contrasted with a low choice-status in any sociogroup without reference to its milieu and functioning. As Loomis and Pepinsky [2] point out, such an evaluation may be "read into" sociometric findings which omit treatment of structural aspects and their relation to behaviors.

In view of the interlocking dependence of one sociometric situation upon another in the structure of a sociogroup, for example, *no leader-position* is "better" or "worse" than another—each is simply different—and none should be assessed certainly in a quantitative hierarchy of amounts of choices received. This would similarly hold for intermediary and unchosen positions alike. It is obvious that intermediary positions are indispensable in the functioning of the sociogroup structure as a whole; it is also obvious that every link in a network is a phenomenon which if it had not developed would cut off into dead-ends the communication possibilities at a given point in question (or cause re-routing in other directions). But even if it is assumed that a given link were severed towards the end of a network, it is as yet impossible to assess whether the resulting loss would correlate in some manner with the simple number of individuals left without linkage to the main body of the structure. What is thrown into the network below a given point and what receptivity is given it (as compared with what is thrown in above a given point and its reception) in a chain of relationships may possibly affect the life of the sociogroup all out of proportion to the "technically measured" importance of the part of the structure in which the individuals are who are severed out towards the lower end of a network.

[2] Charles P. Loomis and Harold B. Pepinsky, "Sociometry, 1937-1947: Theory and Methods," *Sociometry*, XI:3:262-283, Aug., 1948, p. 263.

It is less obvious what importance unchosen (and sometimes highly rejected) positions can have within the total structure of a sociogroup. The difference between particular unchosen positions, however, is indicated by the directions of their sociotele relationships to persons in other positions in the structure. In the test-community, the "lesser" people, sociometrically speaking, in terms of choice-status, do not tend to conglomerate together; they break up into diverse directions in seeking relationships and look to various over-chosen. The implications of these choice behaviors in the psychology of the choice process is the important fact for understanding the behavior of persons in leadership-positions in the sociogroups. Through the fact of the unchosen looking to them, through the "flattery" and "charity" and "understanding" and "getting a hearing" which they optimistically expect to receive from the individuals in leadership-positions, the behaviors of the latter are to a considerable extent affected and determined; moreover, these *in turn* affect the behaviors of the average-chosen towards the unchosen. For example, scapegoating in the test-community appears dependent upon the behavior of the persons in leadership-positions; the stands they take towards such conduct reflect the expectations put upon them by those scapegoated who apparently look to them to act as mediators holding off, as it were, the "average" citizens from exercising such behaviors.

Thus the ideas which the unchosen have, as well as the ideas of the over-chosen, are important in the sociogroup life, affecting what ideas in turn the over-chosen will consider fitting in interaction, and, again, in turn, are pre-eminently important for what behaviors the average-chosen—the great "sociometric middle-class"—will display. If the unchosen in the sociogroups did not look up to the over-chosen, the latter obviously might not feel the "tele-pull" from them to such an extent as to act in their behalf.

For a population to find outlets for fulfillment, a widely ramified psychological structure, sociometrically speaking, appears a necessity. Without a minimum publicity being spread to others by those who know and approve the individual's way of leading, no individual can have a leadership-position beyond his immediate interrelationships. It is here that the power of networks enters. In the test-community, knowledge of fellow members' ideas and actions could be widespread as the psychological inter-individual structure was so well developed. Hence, sociometric choosing did not have to be "in the dark." Similarly, elections of one or another sort did not have to be based on wild guesses. (See p. 119, fn. 2.)

Obviously, it cannot be expected that in every community a high correlation will be found between such phenomena as election returns and sociometric findings. To produce a high correlation between choice-status in sociogroups and election-status for positions to represent such sociogroups, there must be a sufficiently well-developed network in the given community for communication to function.

Even in a population so small as four to five hundred, as in the case of the test-community, one individual cannot know all others. But he can be in authentic communication with the trends of thought and action of the more influential members via relationships with immediate persons who may have network connections with them and whose opinions he trusts. It is here that the crucial importance of the psyche-groups appears.

Unless the community has an actively functioning structure of psychegroup life, interrelations between sociogroups cannot well develop and consequently no authentically based community life can emerge. A "community" without such a structure may be likened to the population of a hotel, no basic communication happening throughout its "membership." Obviously, for effective sociometric community structure to grow in a full sense, some aspects of living in the community must be carried on by the population in common under conditions where the manner of their being carried on *makes a difference.*

Of the many implications of the findings, one deserves especial emphasis in order that its importance may not be overlooked on account of its apparent obviousness: People should not be expected to be alike in their emotional and social expansiveness towards others. Different patterns of inter-personal relations may apparently even carry the *same* import for the individuals showing them. For example, in the informal setting, the individual may "move" about very little in a quantitative sense, exchanging choices with few others and initiating social contacts with many fewer than average, yet this may be *all he needs,* as judged by his choice-position in his sociogroups, compared with that of a second individual who in the informal setting exhibits quantitatively a much larger volume of choice behavior and social-contact-range. Similarly, a very small amount of mutuality may be tantamount to a large amount of mutuality when compared for its significance to the individuals in question.

The functional meaning of a given structure, occurring in different contexts, may, of course, differ in many ways. An example is a structure showing total lack of coordination between directions of choice by and towards the individual.

In the psychegroup, such a structure may represent the individual's fear of coordinating psychically on a reality basis with those who choose him (preferring not to be "known") and he may accordingly continually turn away when reciprocation seems likely, seeking new contacts. Or, it may be that he is an individual who appeals at a distance and is "dropped" by those who come to know him intimately, so that whatever reciprocation occurs is so fleeting it does not last long enough to be caught by the sociometric test. Again, it may, in part, be a reflection of a pronounced neurotic tendency to "mischoose," the individual aiming "without sense" towards those who have no genuine interest in him. All of these apparent factors appear indicated in some of the patterns that are found for the population under study. On the other hand, in the sociogroups, such a structure may simply represent a lack of coordination between the individual's estimate of his abilities and his actually demonstrated performance. Thus, in the one case, the structure may be indicative of a serious personality disorder in inter-personal relations; in the other, a simpler matter of vocational misconceptions.

The two kinds of sociogroups, living and working with, differ in structure, in volume of choice expended, and in other sociometric respects. (See Chapter XI.) While high correlation appears between the extent to which the individual is chosen in one situation, as living together, and the extent to which he is chosen in the other, as working together, the housing situation is productive of a relatively greater volume of choice.

Nevertheless the two kinds of sociogroups show more in common as sociometric characteristics than either of these collectives show in common with the psychegroups.

At the same time, it was noted (see p. 244), that the situation of living together in housing units of 20 to 28 is found to be more conducive to the building of psychegroup relationships than is that of working together, even though the latter units are in general smaller in size, usually not over 12 to 15 persons.   It would thus appear that differences in the respective atmosphere of the two kinds of sociogroups may be affecting the use of the choice process by the individual.   Such a difference may be found perhaps in how wide is the range for different kinds of behaviors within the given context, or, to put it conversely, how restricting is the field for interaction qualitatively as well as quantitatively in the two instances.   It may be that living together is a mixture of the atmospheres found in leisure-time and in working together, and represent a "cross" regime, stimulating to the individuals who like its "informal-formality," *i.e.*, a sort of psyche-sociogroup "compromise."

When Moreno [3] suggests the necessity not to conceive of these two *relatively* distinct inter-personal structures as *absolutely* distinct, he is drawing attention to the very point which requires emphasis: society is not sharply divided into these two kinds of grouping, there is overlap between them, and to think of them in the abstract will not aid research.   Therefore the greatest care must be taken to discern when we are dealing with relatively more or relatively less of one or the other sort.   In the first study, under military auspices, to analyze choice data for psychetele and sociotele components, Maucorps [4] finds a "general factor" which appears to operate

---

[3] J. L. Moreno, "Progress and Pitfalls in Sociometric Theory," *Sociometry*, X: 268-272, Aug., 1947, pp. 271-272.

[4] Paul H. Maucorps, "A Sociometric Inquiry in the French Army," *Sociometry*, XII: 46-80, Feb., 1949. It is of interest that the sociometric data of the United States Office of Strategic Services resulted from applying both bases of criteria and hence could be given a similar analysis; also note that, as in the present study,

throughout the choice expression but least in the data resulting from a psychetelic criterion; he calls this general factor
"efficiency" in collective work situations and notes that "this
distinction between subjective attraction and objective efficiency" is, of course, not absolute and "must not be drawn
too far."

The fact that the sociometric test has shown itself to be an
instrument fine enough to disclose structurally different kinds
of grouping within the same community among the same population (and through two occasions of testing eight months
apart) indicates that further use of sociometric methods can
enable us to learn more and more about how grouping is actually underpinned by characteristic inter-relational efforts
made by the individual in specific settings.

There are, of course, factors having a psyche- and a socio-
base in every inter-personal pattern. Every psychegroup
must reflect such socio-emphases. The point is that the
psychegroup does not focus upon serving the socio-roles of
the overall society; it puts these into the background of its
activities and functions; the sociogroup places them into the
foreground of its emphases. Obviously, even in the most
inviting psychegroup an individual may have, no millennium
exists psychologically; but relative to his other inter-individual alignments, its milieu apparently aims to fit individual
propensities. By contrast, in any particular sociogroup, only
certain aspects of personality are appreciated by other members or allowed by them to come into the interaction approved in the situation as facilitating the tasks and goals

individual differences in expansiveness on different criteria could be compared as no
limit was placed on the number of choices permitted; see *Assessment of Men*, p. 184,
1948. Note in Maucorps' report, p. 48, the new principle of Gurvitch's scission test.

considered important to the specific sociogroup and related to its mores, inherited, cherished, or worked towards.[5]

In the sociogroups for work, many aspects of interaction seem to have a bearing on the individual's choice-patterns. There appears, for example, along with increasing competence in work as such, a tendency on the part of a few individuals seemingly to come to value others on a technical skill basis almost exclusively, disregarding the manner in which the latter might be affecting adversely the group life of the co-workers. Such individuals often themselves show exceptional technical capacity of the sort needed, and in this respect their positive reaction to similar talent seems understandable. But it is, in addition, notable that such individuals avoided exchange on a personal level, even the fun-by-play that was observable to some extent in every sociogroup

[5] Among white and Negro children in classrooms, Criswell's findings indicate that the other racial group is chosen more on a sociogroup basis than on a psychegroup basis. "Another indication of race preference in younger children is contributed by majority-colored classes in which both younger and older subjects consider personal relationships to a greater extent in making choices of their own race. Their feeling toward classmates of the other race is more objective, based more on a consideration of the other race's school ability. But in younger classes intimacy is not so important a factor and this probably accounts in part for the lack of race discrimination exercised in choosing." (Or, the younger the child, the less may intimacy be realizable.)

"Part of the growth of interest in intimacy is a lessening emphasis on prestige. The minority, for instance, shows an age-increase of interest in individuals who will reciprocate their attachments. Young minorities tend to be most interested in a popular but relatively inaccessible majority-member, while older minority groups prefer less popular but more friendly members of the majority." Joan Henning Criswell, "A Sociometric Study of Race Cleavage in the Classroom," *Arch. Psychol.*, p. 70 and p. 77, 1939, No. 235. (Or, with increase in age, they "catch on" and withdraw.)

In this connection also, see William S. M. Banks, "The Rank Order of Sensitivity to Discrimination of Negroes in Columbus, Ohio," doctoral dissertation, Ohio State University, 1949. He finds the order of sphere of interest of the Negro in equal opportunity to function with the white majority is: political, legal, economic, access to public property, and, last or least, sex relations, intermarriage, and social courtesies— confirming in general the trends suggested by Gunnar Myrdal in his *An American Dilemma*, 1944. Thus, psychegroup relations can to a greater extent be satisfied within the Negro minority and the main areas of "hurt" are felt to be blocks to sociogroup roles.

For meanings related to intimacy and non-intimacy between chooser and chosen, see Reva Potashin, "A Sociometric Study of Children's Friendships," *Sociometry*, IX: 48-70, Feb., 1946.

of the community. Such individuals tend at the same time to have a psychegroup structure of the sort showing total lack of coordination in inter-personal relations, although they are chosen mutually to some degree in their sociogroups.

It may be conjectured that unless the individual establishes a minimum of affectionate person-to-person association during his performance as a sociogroup member, the others as well as he will not feel the kind of relaxation which enables them to give fullest application to whatever are the demands of the sociogroup. Perhaps as persons we feel hurt if we sense we are not received as persons in some degree by any individual in any context and are apt to resent reception merely as a sociogroup member, feeling thereby "reduced." In any case, no individual in the test-community was found to have a high choice-status who did not at the same time show a warm responsiveness towards other people. (See Case Studies, pp. 185-205.)

Yet the aspect of our social existence which sociogroups represent must more and more become recognized as requiring the including as well of those few individuals who are generally misfits in the "personal" milieus but who manage, under the protection of the kind of inter-personal distance allowed in the sociogroup, to perform almost like machines. Instead, such individuals are often blocked from contributing to interaction just where they are most able, namely within the more highly non-personalized regimes.

By and large, however, it may be suggested that this skepticism towards the possible worth of an individual who is walled in as a person, establishing no warm relationships in his sociogroups and choosing others for appropriate skills to the situation only, appears well based. Without a minimum of responsiveness which might be termed *personal* within the context of the sociogroup itself, he is apt (whether consciously or not) to thwart the communication efforts of others with him, and thus form a fence against group processes which would otherwise tie members together in common effort and understanding. Especially if he is located near the top of an administrative ladder, his effect may be inordinately felt. What such individuals have actually achieved might be described as an externalization of social skills, through intellectual comprehension (or figuring out) of *how* to behave and *when* and *where*, so that they have an almost complete control over their so-called "social" behavior. They have this control because they are not emotionally committed to the very behavior they are so skillfully exhibiting. Thus the matter becomes one of including them *in such locations* that their emotional deficiencies will not enable them to distort the entire life and development of the sociogroup.

It is fairly comprehensible why the curve of choice in-take (or reception) in the case of official groups should depart so far in favoring the few. (See Fig. 3.) In any official group regime the number of individuals who can, more or less, consistently throughout their life in the given group, identify with other members via the medium of group roles and accommodate their own inclinations to group ends, while at the same time in interaction bringing group objectives more nearly in line with the desires of the members, will perhaps be necessarily few. And, conversely, there may be necessarily those who, through their lack of interest in the regime of a given group, as well as other factors, may not be carried along on whatever interrelation-structure develops among the membership. However, in any basic consideration of any kind of official group, it would seem that the extent of lack of integration of members into an inter-personal structure is a measure of the distance between chances for its membership as a whole to relate to the group purposes and activities in such a manner that their spontaneity towards one another as individuals can find expression.

It may be premised also that a sociogroup will tend to show such an asymmetrical curve of choice distribution in-take since, within it, the relationships, from the standpoint of the individual's "personal" involvement, would be less deep, less intense, and less lasting than would be true in a psychegroup; the individual could therefore afford to select according to ends perceived by him as called for in its situation, especially when he knows the exertion is temporary and the demand is made of all others also.

In turn, it may be premised that the degree to which the curve of choice distribution in-take departs from such a curve will be a measure of how "home-like" the sociogroup life has become; that is, *how little the socio-pressure is experienced as such,* or, to put it positively, how much choice expression in person to person interaction in a full sense has been evoked and spread throughout the membership in spite of the members' job-role interactions with one another.   In such an instance, it might be said, the individuals had mastered their job-relationships to such an extent that they could afford person-to-person relationships.

On the other hand, it is far less clear why the curve of choice distribution in-take in the case of leisure-time should resemble at all that found for official groups.   (See Fig. 3.) It will be noted that while it is in general more evened out and less extended in the fewer and fewer who get more and more, it is still sharper in the rise of the unchosen.

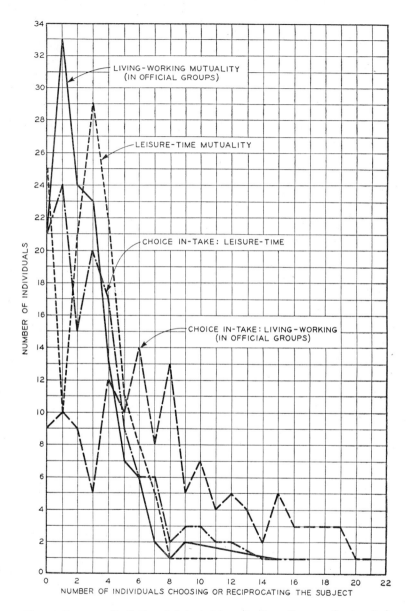

Fig. 3. Frequency distribution of choice in-take and reciprocation according to **criteria** of official grouping compared with criterion of leisure-time. Test I. Population size, 443; subjects, 133.

It is possible to raise the hypothesis that this kind of curve of choice in-take, skewed to the right with relatively many receiving nothing in choice in-take and a very few having a relatively great amount, itself mirrors to a large extent the culture in which it is produced.

Any cultural conditions which, by inference, produce so little appreciation of individual differences *as to* result in the exclusion from the spontaneous positive response of their fellows any considerable proportion of the population—whether for the collective official groupings required of them or within the person-to-person non-official groupings they may desire—can scarcely be said to represent a state of affairs in which inter-personal spontaneity and rapport in groups have really gained a central place in the system of values of that society; its culture might be said to give but secondary consideration to the very social-psychological structure which is basic to its further development.

Nor, it can be hypothesized, need such a curve be considered inevitable, either for psychegroups or for sociogroups. Into the choice process, it was noted, go all the prejudices for this or that kind of interaction which pressures have dictated. As these pressures are lifted or lessened by inter-personal and inter-group development of a society broader in its concepts of what is or is not of worth in inter-individual exchange, it is foreseeable that a truly "more humane" choice-structure would develop—one which reflects on the part of the members of the population a deeper and more widespread appreciation of their interlocked capacities, however different from one another's these might be. And, at the same time, a greater sense of freedom towards interacting, whether as co-workers or simply as people.

CHAPTER XIV

New Directions

For the varied expression of which the individual appears capable in inter-personal relations, various kinds of grouping are distinguishable. The individual appears to seek to form a psychegroup around himself for the kind of participation it offers on a "private" rather than a "collective" plane. He apparently views his social space within it as giving primacy to "personal" satisfactions and, at the same time, views his social space within his sociogroups as appropriately granting primacy to a milieu benefiting all members, each in a socio-role (*e.g.*, fellow-worker) and as functioning towards the attainment of goals which are being continually redefined by socio-interaction for group advance. Also at the same time, he appears to be critical of systems in his sociogroups (such as its social controls, routines, rules) which seem to defeat the individual as a personality while claiming to meet "collective" needs. He seems to try to check his experience in sociogroup life against his experience in his psychegroup life, as if the latter were a sort of final arbiter.

While the sociogroup appears to enforce upon the individual relative anonymity, varying degrees and kinds of regimentation through its collectiveness of functioning, it also provides him with opportunity to use abilities and skills and to gain kinds of group experience he otherwise could not have; the psychegroup, on the other hand, appears to invite expression of his capacities at whatever stage they may be and whether or not these are developed sufficiently or in such manner as to be useful in sociogroup life.

The differentiation within the choice process, shown by the variations in sociometric pattern of grouping, afford one direction of study which merits further exploration. The present research has touched upon but few of the conditions of group life in the community under survey. Discovering the relations between the conditions of life and their reflection in sociometric structure is one major necessity for our increased knowledge of the dynamics of the choice process.

Doubtless also further research must take on as one of its tasks the determining not only what factors throughout a group's history may affect how readily it can be brought to an optimally satisfying group life, but what conditions are so pernicious to human development as group members that the altering of these conditions does not undo the harm which has been done to the individual's spontaneity, only one part of which is his use of the choice process.

For the advance of sociometric research and for the advance of sociometric service to populations, the necessity is not so much for fundamental improvement of the sociometric test itself as for improvement of the sociometric investigator by increasing his sensitivity in regard to what criteria of choice will be most meaningful and motivating to a population.

Not least to be considered in the psychology of choice behavior in the community under study is the accumulative effect of the fact that choice had been allowed to operate for many years. Specifically the population had already been used to choosing for living in the same housing unit, for being in the same vocational situation, and in various ways also within such units [1] had experienced the satisfactions of chosen arrangements. The development of awareness of what can be gained from inter-personal relations, when, as in

[1] H. H. Jennings, "Structure of Leadership," *Sociometry*, I:I:99-143, July, 1937.

the present community, the choices are systematically and democratically carried into operation by the administration, appears to be accompanied by other developments. It apparently also raises the ceiling of what the population comes to expect from the administration (see p. 161). As the members see more and more potentialities in one another, they insist that barriers to their development be reduced and take it upon themselves to locate what such barriers may be.

Moreover, the fact that the individual could freely develop psychegroups within which he might renew his strength, consolidate his ego-gains, and generally recuperate from the strains and criticisms which might be undermining his picture of self in sociogroup life, meant in turn that he was encouraged to import his ideas, with the fresh impetus attached to them in the intimate setting, back into his sociogroups. (*E.g.*, "They told me I was right and I shouldn't let people talk me out of what I think I should be allowed to do.")

The extent to which choice is respected, *i.e.*, the extent to which its execution into practice is thoroughly carried out, may possibly affect the extent to which the members of the population are willing to give an optimum choice expression, authentically representing their feelings, when invited to do so.

In another community without this background of experience in the use of choice, sociometric findings might not show so clear a picture of choice behavior differentiating between criteria which tap such varied aspects of group life as work relations and intimate, personal relations. In particular, the expression of what associations are wanted in leisure-time might not be so readily given. It may be premised that the test-population had gradually developed a sociometric readiness to expand in choice expression to the more intimate area of leisure-time.

In consequence of a lack of readiness to choose on the part of subjects or even their suspicion of the intent of an investigator not to carry out choices in re-constructing grouping promptly and in an "uncensured" manner, it may happen that results are a fusion of many elements. This may lead to confusion as to the meaning of the findings.[2] Such is often the case in sociometric testing of children in school. In interview, the child may respond, "he pays attention in class and wants to pass like I do." Should he be asked, "And has your first choice done other things you admire?" the deeper significance of the choice may be disclosed, as, for example: "He's had troubles like mine and he cheered my mother up for me when my father went off at the beginning of the term. He says you can get along *pretty good* without a father. He does, and that I admire about him something tremendous. He fixed hamburgers and got my mother eating and laughing, saying he's going to be the best cook in the world and didn't she think so and stuff like that. He's a great guy." As in the instance just cited, children's choices appear to take a direction to aid growth towards maturity and suggest that the picture of self is much more "in the making" than in the case of adults in general.

Obviously, too, the degree to which people disclose their motivations (even to such extent as they are able or consciously aware of them) will depend, among other things, upon confidence, freedom, and rapport with the sociometric situation.

Thus, if in a particular community under a sociometric anal-

[2] H. H. Jennings, "Sociometric Grouping in Relaiton to Child Development," in Caroline Tryon (ed.), *Fostering Mental Health in Our Schools*. 1950.

ysis, many of the phenomena found in the present research
to be characteristic of the choice process did not appear, it
would not necessarily mean that the members of the test-
populations in the two instances were "different" as people.
Before such a conclusion could be drawn, it is obvious that a
second investigation would have to be made comparing conditions of group life for the two populations, as the conditions
under which any subject enjoys or endures his group life is
found to determine in very large measure in what manner he
will direct his expression of the choice process.[3]   Moreover,
of course, such a comparison would have to be made before
one study could be considered valid and the other invalid, for
their respective findings on the choice process.   It might turn
out that *both* studies were valid for choice behavior *under
the given conditions.*

It is this representativeness of the field of choice which is
required to arrive at essential representativeness of trends in
the choice process.   Representativeness of subjects only is
evidently not enough: the sampling must be extended from
the subjects to the objects.   In sociometric study, this means
not only how *numerically* extensive is the field for choice but
how available for choice is this number felt or experienced to
be by the subject: how "all right" is it to choose anyone.

In settings where one factor or another may influence the
subject's autonomy in use of choice, such as an official leader
who imposes his selections of under what circumstances who
shall associate with whom, the finding on the subjects'
choice behavior are *not invalid for that particular setting.*

[3] Studies of children's sociometric patterns at different age and grade levels throughout the United States indicate that while, in general, typical patterns are found
according to the age level of the group members from 1st grade on, even these
developmentally characteristic sociometric patterns are susceptible to altering depending upon factors in the group life in the given classroom. See H. H. Jennings, *et
al, Sociometry in Group Relations,* pp. 73-81, 1948.

But, on the other hand, the findings cannot tell anything about what is characteristic for human beings when they *can* exercise their spontaneity in inter-personal choice freely.

Similarly, simply using a field of about 450 individuals "technically available" for the subject to choose into, would obviously not necessarily constitute the subject's experiencing this number as available for choice; the community life might, for example, have been so regimented that he might know hardly more than 30 out of the 450; moreover, he might also be unconvinced that by taking choice action, a re-arranging of grouping would actually follow, so that his motivation for such expression might be undermined.

The importance of the study of the choice process appears at this time more apparent than it did even a few years ago. Much group psychotherapy, for example, has had unfavorable outcomes not because the therapist has been unable but because it was not yet known within what range of others, even in a simple quantitative sense, the average individual can successfully and continuously relate himself to others. The fact that the individual develops what for him is a characteristic repertoire in emotional expansiveness towards others is an important fact.   That he selects according to his needs as well as capacity is another important fact.

If, instead, it were found that the individual could relate to any number of others concurrently, size of group would not be important in psychotherapy.   Moreover, if the individual did not channel emotional choice towards specific other individuals, it would also not matter with *what* other individuals he was placed.   But the individual *is* typified by selectivity in choice and this selectivity is demonstrated to fall within a limited quantitative range, called in this research, his *emotional repertoire* (see pp. 58, 68, 70, 89, and 90), and therefore it may be presumed to matter where and how he is grouped for any purpose.

The findings of Deutschberger [4] in a study of several neighborhoods in two cities confirm the present results regarding the individual's repertoire when he is living in a stable community but show, further, that he tends not to maintain his full repertoire and to "drop" others who are unlike himself in religion and race when the community in which he is living undergoes rapid population changes. Thus in a very broad sense, the nature of the social setting of the individual is shown to affect his expansiveness.

It will be recalled that the average repertoire of positive expansiveness, as measured by the number of other individuals the individual includes in his life situation by positive choice for associating with them, is found to be about eight,[5] when common situations are explored (housing and working), and that this number is increased to about four [6] more when the setting of leisure-time is explored; but, as about one third of the latter overlaps with the former, the average

[4] Paul Deutschberger, "Interaction Patterns in Changing Neighborhoods: New York and Pittsburgh," *Sociometry*, IX:303-315, Nov., 1946.

[5] William B. Baker's findings on Canadian men of a mean age of 21 years show, for like criteria, an average of 8.8 choices of other individuals. His study at the School of Agriculture, University of Saskatchewan, will make it possible to compare the choice behavior of men from rural areas with the test-population of this study and with Deutschberger's urban populations.

[6] This compares with Paul Deutschberger's finding of an average of 3.08 choices made by the individual for free-time associates in his study of 326 adolescents of both sexes, mean age, 17 years, who were mainly in attendance at a teen-age canteen in Pittsburgh (total choices 1006); see his "The Tele-Factor: Horizon and Awareness," *Sociometry*, X:242-249, Aug., 1947. His report also discloses to how great an extent such choices of the individual are invested by him in the direction of bringing return and suggests that such choices may be much more a matter of apperception than direct perception. (For the only comparable study which gives figures on number of choices received, see Harold F. Kaufman, "Prestige Classes in a New York Rural Community," p. 12, *Cornell Univ. Agr. Exp. Sta. Memoir* 260, 1944. Kaufman studied intimate association patterns, based on names of persons visited with most when away from work; he found mean number of choices received was 4.2, which would compare with 3.92 on Test II of the present study.) See also p. 14, fn. 21.

size of repertoire is somewhat less in number than twelve other individuals.

The fact that in a group psychotherapy situation the patients have a *common* situation in which how each behaves can affect how the others behave and ultimately what is attained in therapy for all would suggest the number eight as being closer to optimal than the number twelve for membership size in such a group.

The findings would appear to have a direct relationship to outcomes in group psychotherapy. Wilson,[7] for example, reports that choice for being with particular other patients in group therapy is very significant to what progress the group will make and even to whether it will hang together as a group without members dropping out of therapy. Moreover, that a group below five or above twelve in size of membership tends to divide. If there are twelve members, nine are usually active in participation and three withdrawn. Thus the mental patients in the series studied would seem to differ little from other individuals in the range of their spontaneous interaction. Further, the use of free choice by patients for forming their therapy group, Wilson reports, also results in the membership being composed of patients having different types of syndromes and who, in consequence, "don't have the same blind spots."

Any group psychotherapy faces the question of what constitutes a group. Since it is obvious that no "group" is a group in any basic sense which develops little or no positive relationships among its members, it would follow that group therapy [8] must start out with whatever grouping can be ar-

[7] A. T. M. Wilson of Tavistock Institute of Human Relations, London, in lectures at University of Chicago, summer, 1948.

[8] To this end, psychodramatic and sociometric technique must comprise *one* therapeutic procedure. See J. L. Moreno, *Psychodrama*, 1946; *The Theatre of Spontaneity*, 1947; numerous articles in *Sociatry, Sociometry*, and *Group Psychotherapy*, 1945.

ranged which maximizes within each group a sociometric structure which reflects the capacity of the patients to warm up to one another. Sociometric experiments, it is to be hoped, will gradually clarify what patterns of interrelations are minimal requirements to therapeutic results under different procedures of therapy.

In another area, that of group work, the present findings hold further implications. They indicate the need, for example, of a reversal of some of the present practices. Instead of the group worker setting up "formed" or "fabricated" groups whose membership is recruited around an interest, as art, music, dancing and so on, and then attempting to transform such groups into psychegroups in which each individual through his relationships with other individuals will be able to work out his psyche problems, the group worker would at the very start recognize and respect and allow to operate the individual's tele projections in choices and use these as a guide in any group arrangements in which he was to participate. It is not only a matter of which method is the more economical in expenditure of the time and energy of the professional worker and the participants. It is a matter of recognizing that any group life which is not based to some extent on positive inter-personal response probably places a strain upon its members, as Coyle has illustrated.[9]

Moreover, a group deliberately focussed around an interest first of all (hence a sociogroup minus the fact that it has not yet developed a psychological network among its members) will apparently develop certain characteristic patterns of relationships typical for this kind of group, and, therefore, the group as a whole will tend to be resistant to shifting its

[9] Pioneers in group work have systematically recognized the importance of inter-personal feeling to therapy; see Grace Coyle, *Group Work with American Youth*, 1948; also Gertrude Wilson and Gladys Ryland, *Social Group Work Practice*, 1949.

orientation to the group work emphasis which is this very production of inter-personal response on an intimate personal plane (and not such an emphasis as efficiency in art, music, or whatever).

Nor need the professional group worker be hesitant on the ground that the individuals will through free choice not "benefit" from ensuing interaction: psychegroups tend to form as appears needed for the mental health of their members in a manner that seems aimed at "selves-realization," the very objective of group work.

This of course does not mean that the professional group worker can arrange groups so that each member in them shows sociometric choice for every other member. Obviously no sociometric arrangement can possibly achieve this, and it is doubtful if it would be universally desirable to achieve it since it would mean no new inter-personal soil for the individual's tele production. The aim of sociometric arrangement is to provide a maximum of inter-personal security for each individual compatible with like security in placement of every individual while at the same time placing the individual in such a sociometric setting as can offer him maximum growth opportunity. This will naturally vary according to specific needs. In one case it may mean exposing the individual, while he is in as secure an inter-personal situation as possible, to persons who represent new dimensions of social experience to his own in their backgrounds, value systems, temperamental depths, ways of thinking, and so on, in general potentially enriching his inter-individual "worldliness" through a first-hand chance for contact with "new" others. It does mean, thus, that no individual will be assigned to any group in which he does not choose some other members or where he in turn is not the recipient of some choice.

Similarly, the practice of assigning into one segregated group, euphemistically called a "protected" group, of those individuals who present a "special" problem, as if it were expected that the problems would become a vehicle for meshing the individuals into communication with one another, would be contraindicated.

Under all such implications also, it is understood, goes an authentic eliciting of choice expression from the subjects of the given group, and not instead, a guessing of what their choices may be by some observer, whoever he may be.

In wider areas still, other implications related to the findings reported in 1943 have been confirmed by work on leadership by military personnel of the American, Australian, British and French forces.[10]   J. G. Jenkins' work showed the deep significance of the choice-structure for diagnosis and prediction of group behavior on combat missions of the Air Force and the group-role aspects of choice behavior, "the team player who could be counted on" being most chosen as a colleague.   The findings of numerous workers have settled any question of whether sociometric choices are "popularity" polls or represent leadership criteria.   Work has now progressed to other levels of analysis, including the locating

[10] See, for example, Cecil A. Gibb, "Principles and Traits of Leadership," *J. Abn. and Social Psychol.*, 42:267-284, July, 1947.   See the use of the nomination criterion, "Validation of Officer Selection Tests by Means of Combat Proficiency Ratings," *Medical Field Research Laboratory Report No. 1*, Jan. 18, 1946 *and No. 2*, May 16, 1946, Camp Le Jeune, N. C.; Donald E. Baier, "Note on 'A Review of Leadership Studies with Particular Reference to Military Problems,'" *Psychol. Bull.*, 44:466-467, Sept., 1947; Jenkins, John G. "The Nominating Technique as a Method of Evaluating Air Group Morale," *J. of Aviation Medicine*, XIX:12-19, Feb., 1948. *Assessment of Men*, Office of Strategic Services Assessment Staff, 1948; Robert J. Wherry and Douglas H. Fryer, "Buddy Ratings: Popularity Contest or Leadership Criteria?" *Personnel Psychology*, II:147-159, Summer, 1949.   Paul H. Maucorps, "A Sociometric Inquiry in the French Army," *Sociometry*, XII:46-80, Feb., 1949.   See J. R. Rees, p. 335.

of factors affecting the manner in which groups choose and what re-assignments between and within groups can heighten morale. Further, this work has been shown by Maucorps to be bound up with aspects of choice in which psychetele and sociotele need to be distinguished even though they are found to "act simultaneously"; he reports "the sociometric positions of the overchosen are more fluctuating and more dependent on the specificity of the different criteria ... (which) brings out clearly the fluidity and specificity of the notion of leadership."

Moreover, in civilian life, the recognition of inter-personal networks throughout a community as the psychological media appropriate and necessary to programs affecting members of the given population has been implemented by such sections of our own government as the Agricultural Adjustment Administration.[11] In such work, it has been found that people by and large do a better job of selecting leaders from among themselves than when experts are appointed and, further, that the criteria of their selection includes more factors crucial to inter-personal performance in executing and expanding such programs.

The contribution of Gurvitch in cross-interpretation of sociometric theory with that of microsociology sets a wide base for further development—as do also his new designs for experimental research. His work and that of Zazzo to identify complimentary factors and divergent lacks show that fertilization in this sense is greatly needed for conceptual growth, not only of sociometry but of all the interrelated sciences. The integration Znaniecki early saw essential has been restressed by von Wiese, Loomis, Beegle and Lundberg.

[11] See, for example, Ray E. Wakeley, "Selecting Leaders for Agricultural Programs," *Sociometry*, X:384-395, Nov., 1947, and Charles P. Loomis, "Demonstration in Rural Sociology and Anthropology, A Case Report," *Applied Anthropology*, VI: 10-25, Winter, 1947. For use of block leaders, see I. T. Sanders, p. 336.

It became apparent from examination of the first socio-metric data that advances in statistical methods would be necessary to their analysis because of the structural aspects of inter-personal organization. The advances led by Lazars-feld and Criswell have been furthered by Northway, Forsyth, Katz, Festinger, Beum, and Zeleny, but here again a wide avenue is open for needed exploration. It is to be hoped, however, that research workers will not apply adequate sta-tistical procedures to inadequate data, namely data which are not socio*metric* (as Festinger, in making a genuine statistical contribution has done; *e. g.*, Who are your best friends? Whom do you like most? Dislike most?) as no frame of reference has been provided for the "choosing." (See pp. 276, 284, and 324.)

It is certain that we are on a threshold of understanding much more about how we are affected by our group life and what sort of inter-personal patterns will become possible as we alter the conditions in our society responsible for those patterns which now characterize our relations with one an-other. In particular, the studies of Loomis,[12] Beegle, Long-more, and Bonney show how basic sociometric investigation is to an understanding of inter-personal and inter-group phenomena. Stewart's [13] development of the sociometric-type survey has made it possible for members of a com-munity to cooperate in determining what networks exist and what members represent foci for leadership along specific

[12] Charles P. Loomis, "Political and Occupational Cleavages in a Hanoverian Village, Germany," *Sociometry*, IX:316-333, Nov., 1946. Esp., see C. P. Loomis, J. A. Beegle and T. W. Longmore, "Critique of Class as Related to Social Stratifica-tion," *Sociometry Monog.* No. 19, 1948; C. P. Loomis and J. A. Beegle, *Rural Social Systems*, 1950; and T. W. Longmore, "A Matrix Approach to the Analysis of Rank and Status in a Community in Peru," *Sociometry*, XI:192-206, Aug., 1948. At childhood level, see Merl E. Bonney, p. 325.

[13] Frank A. Stewart, "Sociometric Testing at the Adult Level," *Sociometry*, IX: 147-148, May-Aug., 1946, and "A Sociometric Study of Influence in Southtown," *Sociometry*, X:11-31, 273-286, Feb. and Aug., 1947. See Sanford Winston, p. 338.

lines needed in specific situations. Such work, with that of Infield and Sanders,[14] represents a trend to recognize members of a population as necessarily indispensable collaborators in the discovery of the dynamics of community life.

The use of sociometric method to determine how and where our society is actually stratified into class and caste *in behavioral aspects* and what conditions accompany particular situations has scarcely begun, although Loomis has developed and demonstrated sociometric technique and analysis in many communities. The criterion *visiting* as used in his work may be closely analogous in meaning for certain of his populations to the criterion of *leisure* for the present test-population as both criteria tapped unrestricted contacting between people who are not "forced" to associate in any imposed manner. In consequence, choice action, when taken, may involve a demand to be "treated as an equal" and in any case probably is highly ego-involved, making it appropriate for ascertaining the extent to which cleavage in the sense of "class" exists. As Loomis has stressed, it is always important to know what the criterion for choice means in the specific setting; in certain of his studies other criteria than visiting carry more nearly the import suggested above. In this regard, the discovering of different criteria which are equivalents in different communities would appear basic for the advance of anthropological work, before choice-structures can be compared.

A further extension of sociometric method and analysis is appearing in administrative-sociometric studies of communication and leadership in progress under Shartle,[15] Stogdill and

---

[14] Henrik F. Infield, "A Veterans' Cooperative Land Settlement and its Sociometric Structure," *Sociometry*, X:50-70, Feb., 1947. Irwin T. Sanders, *op. cit.*, p. 314n.

[15] Carroll L. Shartle, "Leadership and Executive Performance," *Personnel*, 25: 370-380, March, 1949, and, Ralph M. Stogdill, "The Sociometry of Working Relationships in Formal Organizations," *Sociometry*, XII:276-300, Nov., 1949.

others. This research is especially important because it examines the work pattern (or role) of the individual in the organization against his sociometric pattern, and thus can throw light on the characteristics of sociometric structure produced when given role patterns prevail.

We do not need any more sociometric research to re-confirm again and again what has been found to be typical for group structure and the individual generally in our society. We do need many studies to ascertain what conditions and processes enable the individual to *so change himself* that the direction of his choices will not be restricted to those who are like himself in attitudes and outlooks, hence in how they see their role. Or, to put it another way, we need to know what experiences can aid the individual spontaneously to enlarge his attitudes towards others so that he is drawn to establish relationships of choice with those whose viewpoints may be very different from his own. We already have some familiarity with what conditions are conducive to a *qualitatively* very narrow range of choice behavior.[16]

It now appears possible, through the advances in technique, to do more than diagnose and evaluate group structure. Hence it is easy to predict that the greatest contributions in the future will come through the use of the sociometric method to facilitate the individual's cultivation of his social space—towards the evolution of a world society knit throughout by inter-personal networks. In this effort, service to populations will go hand in hand with research and enhance the validity of both. Such an example is the work

---

[16] Bernice L. Neugarten, "Social Class and Friendship Among School Children," *Amer. J. of Sociol.*, LI:305-313, Jan., 1946; Else Frenkel-Brunswik and R. Nevitt Stanford, "Some Personality Factors in Anti-Semitism," *J. of Psychol.*, XX:271-291, 1945; E. Frenkel-Brunswik, "Studies of Social Discrimination in Children," *Amer. Psychol.*, 1946, I:456; Mortimer Feinberg, "Background Factors and Sociometric Status," *forthcoming*, in *Sociometry*.

of Northway, with Potashin and Frankel, in Canada, to aid the interrelating of children throughout their school life, in a positive mental hygiene program.

In the United States, numerous sociometric studies in many cities indicate that the atmosphere in children's groups can be so repressive to inter-personal responsiveness that, regardless of the individuals' home settings, the group structure the children of a given age level develop may be typical for a much younger group. On the other hand, the group atmosphere may be so encouraging to interrelating that the children, again regardless of their home settings, build a structure that resembles the sociometric pattern characteristic of older children.[17]   Thus there appears no evidence to indicate that it would be sufficient (even if possible) for every child to have a home situation favorable to his development, that then his relationships to other people would automatically develop.   It suggests, on the contrary, that family relationships do not carry the *exclusively* powerful import that is so often attributed to them; further, it suggests that, in the case of the growing child at least, the overall culture need not leave its mark alike on every individual, but that *the immediate conditions of living* in a particular group affects to a very great degree whether or not the individual will react in a manner typical for people within the same overall culture.   Thus, locating what conditions promote broad interrelationships and aiding such conditions to obtain would appear one of the great possible directions of sociometry from now on.

Another direction of sociometric exploration which would be useful to social science the world over may be suggested in the need to distinguish between what is true for socio-

[17] Jennings, *et. al.*, *op. cit.*, pp. 73-81, fn. 3.

metric structure in a given cultural context and what is true for sociometric structure regardless of cultural conditions.

While it is obvious that any sociometric structure reflects the culture within which it is found and must be interpreted within such a framework, and while it is obvious, too, that the more studies are made in contrasting cultures, as M. Mead [18] suggests, the more insight we can have into how our own patterns directly reflect what is operative in our culture, certain sociometric findings appear to be independent of the cultural contexts in which they are found very much in the same way as the existence of sex attraction is independent of a specific cultural setting.

An example of such a sociometric finding, it may be hypothesized, is the individual's emotional repertoire for expanding in choice towards others, found in the present research and in other studies. This characteristic of the individual, his maintenance of a range of response consistent and typical for him, will, no doubt, be found to be larger or smaller for the individual in different cultures, depending upon what is allowed or encouraged in the way of emotionally relating to others; but, aside from variation in the size of its range, the phenomenon of the repertoire, it would appear, will be found in any setting, since it may be inferred to represent an expression of emotional stability in the individual, which, in turn, is basic to the very existence of society whatever the cultural patterns may be. It may be premised, for example, that no people could form groups which would hold together over any period of time sufficient to develop a culture if each individual were wholly without consistency in his emotional reactions to other individuals.

18 Margaret Mead, "Some Relations between Cultural Anthropology and Sociometry," *Sociometry*, X:312-318, Nov., 1947.

In any case, sociometric method, as Richardson and Danielsson have used it, has shown itself to be a tool which can aid in discovering what are artifacts of culture and what are some of the factors which appear to be basic in the individual's interpersonal expression in varying cultural circumstances.

Another example would be the determining at what age points in childhood the range of the repertoire becomes established within given quantitative limits; we know now only that upon approaching adulthood, it is already stabilized. Such knowledge would enable us to go on to ascertain which period in childhood is most crucial for the child's developing his fullest potential-range for relating to others, and, in turn, to undertake study of what kinds of group experience would protect his spontaneity in this regard to the fullest.

It is conceivable that a culture which would place the importance upon person-to-person responsiveness which such responsiveness evidently has and merits for human development, *i.e.* which would be oriented to respect and foster spontaneity of interaction between individuals, *as well as group-member-to-group-member* responsiveness, would go far to preserve from drying up those wellsprings within the individual which apparently enable him to gain the deepest satisfactions and concomitantly to give such satisfactions to others.

It may be conjectured that when, early in life, the child does not find among those he endows with having emotional importance to him the reflection of his emotions which he seeks, such spontaneity may be greatly reduced and perhaps even shut off in an irrevocable fashion, not only in the area of his own usefulness and enjoyment of himself but as a group member by other group members.

It is here where educational techniques of a passive sort which have long characterized the training methods from pre-school years on up must eventually give place to methods which will bring full personality involvement directly into the classroom, recognizing the individual as an interacting force inseparable from his interpersonal alignments.[19]

Whatever is retarding to spontaneity of rapport in person-to-person relations in the psychegroup context apparently *affects also* the role of the individual in his sociogroups. Thus if we wish to further the productivity of people in their official group roles, we must aid those agencies in our communities which foster and increase opportunities for people to meet and mingle freely with one another on an informal

[19] In this connection, see H. H. Jennings, "Sociodrama as Educative Process," and "Sociometric Grouping in Relation to Child Development," both in C. Tryon (ed.), *Fostering Mental Health in Our Schools*. 1950. In the latter, discussion is given to the psychological staircase phenomenon found to characterize children's choice behavior, namely, choosing in an "upwardly," graduated manner others who are somewhat more mature than the chooser himself. The child appears, in the directions his choices take, to be building himself as a person; through his use of the choice process, the concept of self can be seen, so to speak, *in the making*. The absence of the staircase phenomenon may indicate the child is at an emotionally arrested stage: he may need to seek only acceptance from others, not acceptance plus sympathetically offered challenge towards change in a direction to enlarge or to sharpen his concept of self.

It may be hypothesized that the reason there appear developmental levels in the sociometric structure of groups, according to children's age levels (see pp. 11-12), can be attributed to children's relationships' being comprised primarily of psychetele components. That is to say, as the maturation process proceeds, children "feel out" one another in order to form such alliances as will be supportive to the process of psychological and other growth in which they are involved. (See related "stair-step" phenomena of adult visiting behavior in Longmore, *op. cit.*, p. 206, fn. 12.)

Experimental studies to be reported by McGuire indicate that the pattern of relationships shown at certain age points in adolescence is predictive of the social pattern the individuals later show and maintain in adulthood. See, Carson McGuire, "Sociometry of Adolescences," *forthcoming*, in *Sociometry*. Also see Grace Coyle, "The Critical Period in Social Relations," *forthcoming*, in *Sociometry*.

Thus it would appear that, as adolescence presents a time when a sort of stabilization, into "what is to be typical" for the individual's social pattern, takes place, opportunities to adventure in relating to others must be provided long before then—if the individual is later to enjoy a pattern which adequately represents his particular potentialities.

For a study of first importance for its clinical and research implications, see Hugh Murray's report on 11-year-old boys, *forthcoming*, in *Sociometry*, and p. 334.

basis.   We must recognize that such informal, fun-producing activity as they may carry on is serving a larger purpose than its "wasting of time" would seem to imply.[20]

This appears to be not a simple matter of making conditions such that the individual is exposed to many other individuals through which exposure it is to be assumed he will develop some relationships; it apparently is a matter of providing the *kinds of conditions,* during the exposure, which will set an atmosphere favorable to his developing with others the quality of relationships needed.

It does not appear to be a question of sheer quantity of relationships but a question of what *kind and quality* of relationships the individual becomes able to enter into and retain.

Although the psychegroup confronts its members with no "third" factor, in the sense of interests extrinsic to those evolved by the members themselves, and in this respect contrasts with the sociogroup, it creates its own pressures of a different sort—pressures which are more willingly met, or which might even be described as *sought*—for its pressures are apparently generated by the individual's need, as an organism, to find expression in relationships dictated by its own spontaneity rather than in directions "made to order" by the cultural setting in which it happens to be.

Person-to-person expansiveness in psychegroup life appears as the basic undergirding for sociogroup roles.   In either setting we are dealing with a part system which manifests interdependence with, and interpenetrates, the other

---

[20] "A surprising number of individuals have few, if any, close friends. . . Not only does it indicate a mentally unhealthy state, but . . . eliminates one of the strongest factors of support to mental health, namely, the rewards of friendship." "It is an unfortunate fact (also) that so many people do not recognize that some form of play is essential to the best mental health.   Instead they stupidly brag that they do not know how to play or that they cannot take time to play."   William C. Menninger, *Psychiatry in a Troubled World,* 1948, p. 355 and p. 359.

group structure. As the personal self is enjoyed and sustained by other persons, our capacities apparently become "freed" for the demands of sociogroup life. The sociogroup structure in turn affects the content and level of the psychegroup experience and the inter-personal structures it builds. Thus, isolation and leadership represent end points on a continuum which must be viewed within the framework of psychegroup and sociogroup participation.

"Movements such as sociometry and group work tend, in fact, to reinforce the conception that a new system of disciplines is coming into existence, dealing neither with the individual as such nor with the social structure as such, but with certain types of interpersonal relations which make the sharp distinction between psychology and sociology rather useless and meaningless. One may study for their own sake certain interactions between persons; not as symbols of social classes or social roles, but as social expressions of concrete individuals in all their literal fullness of selfhood." [21]

"Variations in both social structure and value orientation make for a general over-all variation in the nature of social systems. Many writers have attempted to describe these variations by what may be called 'sponge' types . . . (whose) practical utility has been questioned. . . . When (concepts describing social systems) are of such a nature that they may be defined, their elements specified, and their over-all or Gestalt qualities described in objective terms, they may be instruments of science." [22]

---

[21] Gardner Murphy, *Historical Introduction to Modern Psychology*, p. 416. Revised Edition, 1949.
[22] Charles P. Loomis and J. Allan Beegle, "A Typological Analysis of Social Systems: Demonstration of a Means for Integrating Sociometry, Sociology, and Cultural Anthropology," *Sociometry*, XI:147-191, Aug., 1948, pp. 150-151.

GLOSSARY

choice-status — The psycho-social position of the individual in a community (or larger setting) as measured by the extent of positive and negative choice expression focussed upon him by the members of the population.

criterion — A standard used to provide a common unit for comparing the emotional expression of the individual with that of other individuals; examples are the functions in various common life situations, such as, living, work, leisure, study.

emotional expansiveness — The performance of the individual in positive choice of others for inclusion in situations in his life requiring collaboration with others (*i.e.*, the number of persons for whom the individual expresses positive choice on criteria representing his life situation).

emotional repertoire in expansiveness — The individual's range of positive and negative choice expression, found in this research to be a characteristic of the individual: consistency of choice expression.

rejection — The performance of the individual in negative choice of others for exclusion from situations in his life requiring collaboration with others (*i.e.*, the number of persons whom the individual rejects on criteria representing his life situation).

social atom — The constellation of psycho-social projections in positive choice and rejection by and towards the individual as secured under conditions permitting full expression for or against collaborating with others in common life situations.

social-contact-range — The number of other persons within the individual's field whom he has contacted, either through his own initiative or through continuing, however briefly, contacts initiated with him by other persons, as given in such social inventory.

social expansiveness — The performance of the individual in social initiative as measured by the extent of his social-contact-range.

social space — The psycho-social area around every individual circumscribed by the individual's propensity or need to relate himself to others and by the propensity or need of others to relate themselves to the individual. In this area, social contact is direct and holds personal meaning for the individual.

stimulus-value — The extent of positive and negative choice which is aroused towards a given individual, found in this research to be a characteristic of the individual: consistency of choice expression evoked.

BIBLIOGRAPHY

Allee, W. C. "Social Biology of Subhuman Groups." *Sociometry*, XIII: 21-29, February, 1945.

Allport, Floyd H. "The Group Fallacy in Relation to Social Science." *Journal of Abnormal and Social Psychology*, XIX: 60-73, April-June, 1924.

Allport, Gordon W. *Personality, A Psychological Interpretation.* New York: Henry Holt and Company, 1937.

Assessment of Men. Office of Strategic Services Assessment Staff. New York: Rinehart and Company, 1948.

"Autonomous Groups and Mental Health: A Report to the International Congress on Mental Health." Preparatory Commission on Autonomous Groups and Mental Health, Walter Pettit, Chairman, Maria Rogers, Secretary. 1948.

Baier, Donald E. "Note on 'A Review of Leadership Studies with Particular Reference to Military Problems.'" *Psychological Bulletin*, 44: 466-467, September, 1947.

Bain, Read. "Measurement in Sociology." *American Journal of Sociology*, XL: 481-488, January, 1935.

Baker, William B. "A Sociometric Study of Rural Canadian Men." Forthcoming, University of Saskatchewan.

Banks, William S. M. "Rank Order of Sensitivity to Discrimination of Negroes in Columbus, Ohio." Ohio State University, unpublished doctoral dissertation, 1949.

Barker, Roger G. "The Social Interrelations of Strangers and Acquaintances." *Sociometry*, V: 169-179, May, 1942.

Bartemeier, L. H.; Kubie, L. S.; Romono, J.; and Whitehorn, J. C. "Combat Exhaustion." *Journal of Nervous and Mental Disease*, 104: 358-389, 489-525, 1946.

Bavelas, Alex. "Morale and the Training of Leaders," in Goodwin Watson (ed.), *Civilian Morale.* New York: Houghton Mifflin Company, 1942. Chapter VIII.

Becker, Myron G. and Loomis, Charles P. "Measuring Rural Urban and Farm and Non-Farm Cleavages in a Rural Consolidated School." *Sociometry*, XI: 246-261, August, 1948.

Beum, Corlin O. and Criswell, Joan H. "Application of Machine Tabulation Methods to Sociometric Data." *Sociometry*, X: 227-232, August, 1947.

Biber, Barbara; Murphy, Lois B.; Woodcock, Louise B.; and Black, Irma S. *Child Life in School.* New York: E. P. Dutton and Company, 1942.

Bion, W. R. and Rickman, J. "Intra-Group Tensions in Therapy—Their Study as the Task of the Group." *The Lancet*, II: 678-681, November, 1943.

Bogardus, E. S. "A Social Distance Scale." *Sociology and Social Research*, XVII: 265-271, January—February, 1933.

———. "Measurement of Personal-Group Relations." *Sociometry*, X: 306-311, November, 1947.

Bonney, Merl E. "A Study of the Relation of Intelligence, Family Size, and Sex Differences with Mutual Friendships in the Primary Grades." *Child Development*, XIII: 79-100, June, 1942.

———. "A Study of Social Status on the Second Grade Level." *Journal of Genetic Psychology*, LX: 271-305, June, 1942.

———. "The Relative Stability of Social, Intellectual, and Academic Status in Grades II to IV and the Interrelationships between These Various Forms of Growth." *Journal of Educational Psychology*, 34: 88-102, February, 1943.

———. "Constancy of Sociometric Scores and Their Relationship to Teacher Judgments of Social Success and to Personality Self-Ratings." *Sociometry*, VI: 409-424, November, 1943.

———. "Relationship between Social Success, Family Size, Socio-Economic Home Background, and Intelligence among School Children in Grades III to V." *Sociometry*, VII: 26-39, February, 1944.

———. "A Sociometric Study of the Relationship of Some Factors to Mutual Friendships on the Elementary, Secondary, and College Level." *Sociometry*, IX: 21-47, February, 1946.

———. "A Study of the Sociometric Process Among Sixth-Grade Children." *Journal of Educational Psychology*, 37: 359-372, September, 1946.

———. "Sociometric Study of Agreement between Teacher Judgments and Student Choices." *Sociometry*, X: 133-146, May, 1947.

Bronfenbrenner, Urie. "The Measurement of Sociometric Status, Structure and Development." Sociometry Monographs No. 6, 1945.

Brown, Muriel W. "Some Applications of Sociometric Techniques to Community Organization." *Sociometry*, VI: 94-100, February, 1943.

Burks, Barbara S. "A Review of J. H. Criswell's *A Sociometric Study of Race Cleavage in the Classroom.*" *Sociometry*, III: 105-108, January, 1940.

Chapin, F. Stuart. "Trends in Sociometrics and Critique." *Sociometry*, III: 245-262, July, 1940.

Cologne, Rose. "Experimentation with Sociometric Procedures in a Self-Help Community Center." *Sociometry*, VI: 27-67, February, 1943.

Cook, Lloyd Allen. "An Experimental Sociographic Study of a Stratified 10th Grade Class." *American Sociological Review*, X: 250-261, April, 1945.

Coyle, Grace Longwell. *Group Work with American Youth*. New York: Harper and Brothers, 1948.

Criswell, Joan Henning. "A Sociometric Study of Race Cleavage in the Classroom." *Archives of Psychology*, No. 235, January, 1939.

————. "Social Structure Revealed in a Sociometric Retest." *Sociometry*, II: 69-75, October, 1939.

————. "The Saturation Point as a Sociometric Concept." *Sociometry*, V: 145-150, May, 1942.

————. "Sociometric Methods of Measuring Group Preferences." *Sociometry*, VI: 398-408, November, 1943.

————. "Sociometric Measurement and Chance." *Sociometry*, VII: 415-421, November, 1944.

————. "Foundations of Sociometric Measurement." *Sociometry*, IX: 7-13, February, 1946.

————. "Measurement of Reciprocation under Multiple Criteria of Choice." *Sociometry*, IX: 126-127, May, 1946.

————. "Measurement of Group Integration." *Sociometry*, X: 259-267, August, 1947.

————. "Notes on the Constant Frame of Reference Problem." Forthcoming in *Sociometry*, XIII: No. 2, May, 1950.

————. "Sociometric Concepts in Personnel Administration." *Sociometry*, XII: 287-300, November, 1949.

Danielsson, Bengt. "Some Attraction and Repulsion Patterns among Jibaro Indians." *Sociometry*, XII: 83-105, February, 1949.

Deutschberger, Paul. "Interaction Patterns in Changing Neighborhoods: New York and Pittsburgh." *Sociometry*, IX: 303-315, November, 1946.

————. "The *Tele*-Factor: Horizon and Awareness." *Sociometry*, X: 242-249, August, 1947.

————. "Sociometry and Social Work." *Sociometry*, XIII: No. 1, February, 1950.

Dodd, Stuart Carter. "A Systematics for Sociometry and for All Science." *Sociometry*, XI: 11-30, February, 1948.

Dupréel, Eugène. "Variété des Groupes Sociaux." *Cahiers Internationaux de Sociologie*, II: 32-56, 1947.

Eaton, Joseph W. "Experiments in Testing for Leadership." *American Journal of Sociology*, LII: 523-535, May, 1947.

Einstein, Albert and Infeld, Leopold. *The Evolution of Physics.* New York: Simon and Schuster, 1938.

Faunce, Dale and Beegle, J. Allan. "Cleavages in a Relatively Homogeneous Group of Rural Youth." *Sociometry*, XI: 207-216, August, 1948.

Feinberg, Mortimer. "Background Factors and Sociometric Status." In preparation, *forthcoming*, in *Sociometry*.

Festinger, Leon. "The Analysis of Sociograms using Matrix Algebra." *Human Relations*, II: 153-158, 1949.

Fisher, R. A. *Statistical Methods for Research Workers.* Edinburgh: Oliver and Boyd, 4th ed., 1932.

Forsyth, Elaine and Katz, Leo. "A Matrix Approach to the Analysis of Sociometric Data." *Sociometry*, IX: 340-347, November, 1946.

Frenkel-Brunswik, Else. "Dynamic and Cognitive Categories of Qualitative Material." *Journal of Psychology*, 25: 253-279, 1948.

———— and Sanford, R. Nevitt. "Some Personality Factors in Anti-Semitism." *Journal of Psychology*, 20: 271-291, 1945.

Freud, Sigmund. *Three Contributions to the Theory of Sex.* Washington, D. C.: Nervous and Mental Disease Publishing Company, 4th ed., 1930.

Garrett, Henry E. *Statistics in Psychology and Education.* New York: Longmans, Green and Company, 2nd ed., 1937.

Gibb, Cecil A. "Principles and Traits of Leadership." *Journal of Abnormal and Social Psychology*, 42: 267-284, July, 1947.

Gordon, Mary Martha. "Discriminatory Leadership and Its Effect on the Relations between the More and the Less Privileged Subgroups." University of Iowa, unpublished doctoral dissertation, 1940.

Guilford, J. P. *Psychometric Methods.* New York: McGraw-Hill Book Company, 1st ed., 1936.

Gurvitch, Georges. "Microsociologie et Sociométrie." *Cahiers Internationaux de Sociologie*, III: 24-67, 1947.

————. "Microsociology and Sociometry," *Sociometry*, XII: 1-31, February, 1949.

Hartley, Ruth E. *Sociality in Preadolescent Boys.* New York: Bureau of Publications, Teachers College, Columbia University, 1946.

Howell, Charles E. "Measurement of Leadership." *Sociometry*, V: 163-168, May, 1942.

Infield, Henrik F. "A Veterans' Cooperative Land Settlement and its Sociometric Structure." *Sociometry*, X: 50-70, February, 1947.

Inkeles, Alex. "Developments of Sociometry, the War Years 1941-1945." *Sociometry*, IX: 379-382, November, 1946.

Jenkins, John G. "The Nominating Technique as a Method of Evaluating Air Group Morale." *Journal of Aviation Medicine*, XIX: 12-19, February, 1948.

Jenkins, William O. "A Review of Leadership Studies with Particular Reference to Military Problems." *Psychological Bulletin*, 44: 54-79, January, 1947. *See under Baier, Donald E.*

Jennings, Helen H. "Sociometric Studies," a supplement in J. L. Moreno, *Who Shall Survive?* Washington, D. C.: Nervous and Mental Disease Publishing Co., 1934. *See under Moreno, J. L.*

――――. "Control Study of Sociometric Assignment." *Sociometric Review*, 54-57, July, 1936; only one issue appeared; the *Review* was superseded by *Sociometry*. Sociometry Monographs No. 7.

――――. "Structure of Leadership — Development and Sphere of Influence." *Sociometry*, I: 99-143, July-October, 1937.

――――. "Quantitative Aspects of Tele Relationships in a Community." *Sociometry*, II: 93-100, October, 1939.

――――. "Individual Differences in the Social Atom." *Sociometry*, IV: 269-277, August, 1941.

――――. "Sociometry and Social Theory." *American Sociological Review*, VI: 512-522, August, 1941.

――――. "Experimental Evidence on the Social Atom at Two Time Points." *Sociometry*, V: 135-145, May, 1942.

――――. "Sociometric Measurement of Personality." *Psychological Bulletin*, 39: 457-458, July, 1942.

――――. "A Sociometric Study of Emotional and Social Expansiveness," in R. G. Barker, J. S. Kounin, and H. F. Wright (edrs.), *Child Behavior and Development*. New York: McGraw-Hill Book Company, 1943.

――――. "Sociometry and Democracy Unlimited." *Sociometry*, VI: 293-298, August, 1943.

――――. "Leadership—A Dynamic Redefinition." *Journal of Educational Sociology*, XVII: 431-433, March, 1944.

――――. "A Graduate Seminar in Psychodrama (with sociometric tests),

Stanford University, Fall, 1945." *Sociometry*, IX: 162-165, May, 1946.

Jennings, Helen H. "Note sur quelques Concepts Sociométriques." *Cahiers Internationaux de Sociologie*, II: 102-107, 1947.

———. "Sociometric Differentiation of the Psychegroup and the Sociogroup." *Sociometry*, X: 71-79, February, 1947.

———. "Leadership and Sociometric Choice," in T. M. Newcomb and E. L. Hartley (edrs.), *Readings in Social Psychology*. New York: Henry Holt and Company, 1947.

———. "Sociometry in Action." *Survey Midmonthy*, LXXXIV: 41-63, February, 1948.

——— in Association with the Staff of Intergroup Education in Cooperating Schools, Hilda Taba, Director. *Sociometry in Group Relations*. Washington, D. C.: American Council on Education, 1948.

———. "Military Use of Sociometric and Situation Tests in Great Britain, France, Germany and the United States." *Sociometry*, XII: 191-201, February, 1949.

———. "Sociometric Grouping in Relation to Child Development," in Caroline Tryon (ed.), *Fostering Mental Health in Our Schools*. Washington, D. C.: Association for Supervision of Curriculum Development (N.E.A.), 1950.

———. "Sociodrama as Educative Process." For publisher, see next above, in *Fostering Mental Health in Our Schools*.

Jennings, Herbert Spencer. *Behavior of Lower Organisms*. New York: Columbia University Press, 1931.

———. *The Universe and Life*. New Haven: Yale University Press, 1933.

———. "The Beginnings of Social Behavior in Unicellular Organisms." *Science*, 92: 539-546, December, 1940.

———. "The Transition from the Individual to the Social Level." *Science*, 94: 447-453, November, 1941.

Katz, Leo. "On the Matrix Analysis of Sociometric Data." *Sociometry*, X: 233-241, August, 1947. (Also see *Sociometry*, XIII, No. 2, 1950.)

Kaufman, Harold F. "Prestige Classes in a New York Rural Community." *Cornell University Agricultural Experiment Station Memoir 260*, Ithaca, N. Y., 1944.

Kerstetter, Leona. "A Sociometric Structural Graph." In preparation.

Krout, Maurice H. "Personality-Testing in the Light of the Situational Approach." *American Journal of Psychiatry*, X: 839-854, March, 1931.

Krout, Maurice H. *Introduction to Social Psychology*. New York: Harper and Brothers, 1942. (Sociometric discussion, pp. 234-239, 654-657, 686.)

Lazarsfeld, Paul F. and Gaudet, Hazel. "Who Gets a Job?" *Sociometry*, IV: 64-77, February, 1941.

Lewin, Kurt. "Environmental Forces," in Carl Murchison (ed.), *Handbook of Child Psychology*. Worcester: Clark University Press, 2nd ed. rev., 1933.

———. *Principles of Topological Psychology*. New York: McGraw-Hill Book Company, 1936.

———; Lippitt, Ronald; and White, Ralph K. "Patterns of Aggressive Behavior in Experimentally Created 'Social Climates.'" *Journal of Social Psychology*, X: 271-299, May, 1939.

Lippitt, Ronald. "An Experimental Study of Authoritarian and Democratic Group Atmospheres." *University of Iowa Studies*, XVI: 43-195, February, 1940.

———. "The Morale of Youth Groups," in Goodwin Watson (ed.), *Civilian Morale*. New York: Houghton Mifflin Company, 1942.

Lippitt, Rosemary. "Popularity among Preschool Children." *Child Development*, XII: 305-332, December, 1941.

Longmore, T. W. "A Matrix Approach to the Analysis of Rank and Status in a Community in Peru." *Sociometry*, XI: 192-206, August, 1948.

Loomis, Charles P. "Social Relationships and Institutions in Seven New Rural Communities." Social Research Report, No. XVIII, Bureau of Agricultural Economics, Washington, D. C., January, 1940.

———. "Informal Groupings in a Spanish-American Village." *Sociometry*, IV: 36-51, February, 1941.

———. "Ethnic Cleavages in the Southwest as reflected in Two High Schools." *Sociometry*, VI: 7-26, February, 1943.

———. "Political and Occupational Cleavages in a Hanoverian Village, Germany." *Sociometry*, IX: 306-333, November, 1946.

———. "Demonstration in Rural Sociology and Anthropology, A Case Report." *Applied Anthropology*, VI: 10-25, Winter, 1947.

———; Baker, W. B.; and Proctor, C. "The Size of Family as related to Social Success of Children." *Sociometry*, XII: 313-320, 1949.

——— and Beegle, J. A. "A Typological Analysis of Social Systems." *Sociometry*, XI: 147-191, August, 1948.

——— and Beegle, J. A. *Rural Social Systems*. New York: Prentice-Hall, 1950.

Loomis, Charles P. and Davidson, Dwight M. Jr. "Sociometrics and the Study of New Rural Communities." *Sociometry*, II: 56-76, January; 84-94, April; 24-42, July, 1939.

———— and Pepinsky, Harold B. "Sociometry, 1937-1947." *Sociometry*, XI: 262-286, August, 1948.

———— and Powell, Reed M. "Sociometric Analysis of Class Status in Rural Costa Rica." *Sociometry*, XII: 144-157, February, 1949.

————; Beegle, J. A.; and Longmore, T. W. "Critique of Class as Related to Social Stratification." *Sociometry*, X: 319-349, November, 1947. Sociometry Monographs No. 19.

Lundberg, George A. "Social Attraction-Patterns in a Rural Village." *Sociometry*, I: 77-81, July-October, 1937.

————. *Foundations of Sociology*. New York: The Macmillan Company, 1939.

————. *Social Research: A Study of Methods of Gathering Data.* New York: Longmans, Green and Company, 2nd ed. rev., 1942.

————. "Marketing and Social Organization." Parlin Memorial Lecture, 1945.

———— and Steele, Mary. "Social Attraction-Patterns in a Village." *Sociometry*, I: 375-419, January-April, 1938.

———— and Beazley, Virginia. " 'Consciousness of Kind' in a College Population." *Sociometry*, XI: 59-73, February, 1948.

————; Hertzler, Virginia Beazley; and Dickson, Lenore. "Attraction Patterns in a University." *Sociometry*, XII: 158-169, February, 1949.

Maas, Henry. "Non-Verbal Validation of Group Changes in Social Attitude through Sociometric Choice." *Sociometry*, XII: 170-178, February, 1949.

Maller, Julius B. and Morton, Mary. "A Test of Leadership Ability." Read at annual meeting of American Psychological Association, 1949.

Maucorps, Paul H. "A Sociometric Inquiry in the French Army." *Sociometry*, XII: 46-80, February, 1949.

McCandless, Boyd Rowden. "Changing Relationships between Dominance and Social Acceptability during Group Democratization." *American Journal of Orthopsychiatry*, XII: 529-535, July, 1942.

McGuire, Carson. "Sociometry of Adolescence." *Sociometry*, forthcoming.

Mead, George Herbert. *Mind, Self, and Society*. Chicago: University of Chicago Press, 1934.

Mead, Margaret. "Some Relations between Cultural Anthropology and Sociometry." *Sociometry*, X: 312-318, November, 1947.

Medical Field Research Laboratory Report No. 1, January 18, 1946 *and No. 2*, May 16, 1946. Camp Le Jeune, N. C. "Validation of Officer Selection Tests by Means of Combat Proficiency Ratings." (M. & S. Research Project No. X-620.)

Menninger, William C. *Psychiatry in a Troubled World*. New York: The Macmillan Company, 1948.

Moreno, Florence B. "Sociometric Status of Children in a Nursery School Group." *Sociometry*, V: 395-411, November, 1942.

———. "Combining Role and Sociometric Testing." *Sociometry*, IX: 155-161, May, 1946. *See under Moreno, J. L.*

Moreno, J. L. *Who Shall Survive? A New Approach to the Problem of Human Interrelations*. Collaborator: H. H. Jennings. Washington, D. C.: Nervous and Mental Disease Publishing Company, 1934.

———. *Das Stegreiftheater*. Berlin: Gustav Kiepenhauer, 1923. (Translation in *Sociometry*, IV: 205-226, May, 1941.) Also published as *The Theatre of Spontaneity*. New York: Beacon House, 1947.

———. "Organization of the Social Atom." *Sociometric Review*, 11-16, July, 1936. Also in *Sociometry*, X: 287-293, August, 1947.

———. "Inter-Personal Therapy and the Psychopathology of Inter-Personal Relations." *Sociometry*, I: 9-76, July-October, 1937.

———. "Sociometry in Relation to Other Social Sciences." *Sociometry*, I: 206-219, July-October, 1937.

———. "Foundations of Sociometry." *Sociometry*, IV: 15-35, February, 1941.

———. "The Advantages of the Sociometric Approach to Problems of National Defense." *Sociometry*, IV: 384-391, November, 1941.

——— and Jennings, H. H. "Advances in Sociometric Technique." *Sociometric Review*, 26-40, July, 1936. Sociometry Monographs No. 7.

——— and Jennings, H. H. "Statistics of Social Configurations." *Sociometry*, I: 342-374, January-April, 1938.

———, Jennings, H. H.; and Sargent, Joseph. "Time as a Quantitative Index of Inter-Personal Relations." *Sociometry*, III: 62-80, January, 1940.

——— in collaboration with Whitin, E. Stagg. *Plan and Technique of Developing a Prison into a Socialized Community*. New York: National Committee on Prisons and Prison Labor, 1932.

Moreno, J. L. in collaboration with Whitin, E. Stagg. *Application of the Group Method to Classification.* New York: National Committee on Prisons and Prison Labor, 1932.

——. "Sociometry and the Cultural Order." *Sociometry*, VI: 299-344, August, 1943.

——. "Scientific Foundations of Group Psychotherapy." *Sociometry*, VIII: 315-322, August, 1945. Or see *Group Psychotherapy: A Symposium*, pp. 77-84. New York: Beacon House, 1945.

——. *Psychodrama.* New York: Beacon House, 1946.

——. "La Methode Sociometrique en Sociologie." *Cahiers Internationaux de Sociologie*, II: 88-101, 1947.

——. "Contributions of Sociometry to Research Methodology in Sociology." *American Sociological Review*, XII: 287-292, June, 1947.

——. "The Social Atom and Death." *Sociometry*, X: 80-84, February, 1947.

——. "Progress and Pitfalls in Sociometric Theory." *Sociometry*, X: 268-272, November, 1947.

——. "Experimental Sociometry and the Experimental Method in Science," in Wayne Dennis (ed.), *Current Trends in Social Psychology.* Pittsburgh: University of Pittsburgh Press, 1948.

——. "Origins and Foundations of Inter-Personal Theory, Sociometry and Microsociology." *Sociometry*, XII: 235-254, February, 1949.

——. "Sociometry and Marxism." *Sociometry*, XII: 106-143, February, 1949.

—— and Moreno, Florence B. "Spontaneity Theory of Child Development." *Sociometry*, VII: 89-128, May, 1944.

Murphy, Gardner. "Personality and Social Adjustments." *Social Forces*, XV: 472-476, May, 1937.

——. "The Research Task of Social Psychology." *Journal of Social Psychology*, X: 107-120, February, 1939.

——. *Historical Introduction to Modern Psychology.* Revised edition. New York: Harcourt, Brace and Company, 1949.

——; Murphy, Lois B.; and Newcomb, T. M. *Experimental Social Psychology.* New York: Harper and Brothers, 2nd ed. rev., 1937.

Murphy, Lois Barcley. *Social Behavior and Child Personality.* New York: Columbia University Press, 1937.

Murray, Henry A., and others. *Explorations in Personality.* New York: Oxford University Press, 1938.

Murray, Hugh. "An Investigation into the Stability of Personal Relations Among Educationally Sub-normal Children Living in an Institution." On file: Sheffield, England: Sheffield University, 1949.

Myrdal, Gunnar. *An American Dilemma.* New York: Harper and Brothers, 1944.

Neugarten, Bernice L. "Social Class and Friendship among School Children." *American Journal of Sociology,* LI: 305-313, January, 1946.

Newcomb, Theodore M. "Community Roles in Attitude Formation." *American Sociological Review,* VII: 621-630, October, 1942.

———. *Personality and Social Change.* New York: Dryden Press, 1943.

———. *Social Psychology.* New York: Dryden Press, 1950.

Newstetter, W. I.; Feldstein, M. J.; and Newcomb, T. M. *Group Adjustment.* Cleveland: Western Reserve University, 1938.

———. "The Social Inter-group Work Process." School of Social Work, University of Pittsburgh. 1948.

Northway, Mary L. "Children's Social Development." *Bulletin Canadian Psychological Association.* III: 3-5, 1943.

———. "A Method for Depicting Social Relations Obtained by Sociometric Testing." *Sociometry,* III: 144-150, April, 1940.

———. "Social Acceptability Test." *Sociometry,* V: 180-184, May, 1942.

———. "Outsiders." *Sociometry,* VII: 10-25, February, 1944.

——— and Quarrington, Bruce. "Depicting Inter-Cultural Relations." *Sociometry,* IX: 334-339, November, 1946.

——— and Wigdor, Blossom T. "Rorschach Patterns related to the Sociometric Status of School Children. *Sociometry,* X: 186-199, May, 1947.

———; Frankel, Esther B.; and Potashin, Reva. "Personality and Sociometric Status." Sociometry Monographs No. 11, 1947.

Partridge, E. De Alton. *Leadership among Adolescent Boys.* New York: Bureau of Publications, Teachers College, Columbia University, 1934.

Potashin, Reva. "A Sociometric Study of Children's Friendships." *Sociometry,* IX: 48-70, February, 1946.

Price, Louise. *Creative Group Work on the Campus.* New York: Bureau of Publications, Teachers College, Columbia University, 1941.

Redmon, Edward J. "Social Processes Motivating Employee Behavior in the Factory Workshop." *Sociometry,* IX: 372-378, November, 1946.

Rees, J. R. "Mental Health and World Citizenship." *Survey Graphic,* XXXVII: 213-215, April, 1948.

Richardson, F. L. W. Jr. and Sheldon, R. C. "Community Resettlement in a Depressed Coal Region III." *Applied Anthropology*, VII: 1-27, Fall, 1948.

Richmond, Winifred. "Sociometric Tests in a Training School for Nurses." *Sociometric Review*, 41-49, July, 1936.

Roethlisberger, F. J. and Dickson, W. J. *Management and the Worker*. Cambridge: Harvard University Press, 1939.

Rogers, Maria. "Human Problems of Industry." *Sociometry*, IX: 350-376, November, 1946.

————. "Analysis of Role of Autonomous Groups." *Autonomous Groups Bulletin*, I-IV, Editor, 22 E. 47th Street, New York 17.

Sanders, Irwin T. "Sociometric Work with a Bulgarian Woodcutting Group." *Sociometry*, II: 58-68, October, 1939.

————. "The Use of Block Leaders in Effective Community Mobilization." *Sociometry*, XII: 265-275, November, 1949.

Sandin, Adolph A. *Social and Emotional Adjustments of Regularly Promoted and Non-Promoted Pupils*. New York: Bureau of Publications, Teachers College, Columbia University, 1944.

Schutzenberger, M. P. "Etude Statistique d'un problème de sociométrie" in *Gallica Biologica Acta*, Paris, 1948.

Scott, J. P. "Group Formation Determined by Social Behavior: a Comparative Study of Two Mammalian Societies." *Sociometry*, VIII: 42-52, February, 1945.

Shartle, Carroll L. "Leadership and Executive Performance." *Personnel*, 25: 370-380, March, 1949.

Shoobs, Nahum E. "Sociometry in the Class Room." *Sociometry*, X: 154-164, May, 1947.

Smith, Mapheus. "Some Factors in Friendship Selections of High School Students." *Sociometry*, VII: 303-310, August, 1944.

Smucker, Orden. "Prestige Status Stratification on a College Campus." *Applied Anthropology*, VI: 20-27, Summer, 1947.

————. "Near-Sociometric Analysis as a Basis for Guidance." *Sociometry*, XII: 326-340, 1949.

Sociometry in France and the United States. Comprises *Sociometry*, Nos. 1-3, 1949, in book form. New York: Beacon House, 1949.

Solby, Bruno. "Group Psychotherapy and the Psychodramatic Method." *Sociometry*, VIII: 288-291, August, 1945.

Sorokin, Pitirim. *Society, Culture, and Personality: Their Structure and Dynamics*. New York: Harper and Brothers, 1947.

Sower, Christopher. "Social Stratification in Suburban Communities." *Sociometry*, XI: 235-243, August, 1948.

Stewart, Frank A. "Sociometric Testing at the Adult Level." *Sociometry*, IX: 147-148, May, 1946.

———. "A Sociometric Study of Influence in Southtown." *Sociometry*, X: 11-31, 273-286, February and August, 1947.

———. "Some Sampling Problems in Sociometric Surveys." *Sociometry*, XI: 301-307, November, 1948.

Stewart, Isabel A. "An Interviewer's Report on Adult Sociometric Study." *Sociometry*, XI: 308-319, November, 1948.

Stogdill, Ralph M. "Personal Factors Associated with Leadership: A Survey of the Literature." *Journal of Psychology*, 25: 35-72, 1948.

———. "The Sociometry of Working Relationships in Formal Organizations." *Sociometry*, XII: 276-286, November, 1949.

Strang, Ruth. *Group Activities in College and Secondary School.* New York: Harper and Brothers, 1941.

Sutherland, J. D. and Fitzpatrick, G. A. "Some Approaches to Group Problems in the British Army." *Sociometry*, VIII: 443-455, August, 1945.

Sweetser, Frank Loel. *Neighborhood Acquaintance and Association.* New York: 1941. Privately printed.

Vaughn, C. L. "The nominating technique," in G. A. Kelly (ed.), *New Methods in Applied Psychology.* College Park: University of Maryland Bookstore, 1947.

Vaughn, K. W. (ed.) "National Projects in Educational Measurement." Volume XI, Series I, No. 28, August, 1947. In relation to this treatment, see Paul Lazarsfeld, "Some Notes on the Use of Indices in Social Research," unpublished, and, R. Duncan Luce and Albert D. Perry, "A Method of Matrix Analysis of a Group Structure," *Psychometrika*, XIV: 95-116, 1949. See last item under Criswell in connection with Bronfenbrenner; also re D. S. Edwards, "The Constant Frame of Reference Problem in Sociometry," *Sociometry*, XI: 372-379, November, 1948.

Vreeland, Francis McLennan. "Social Relations in the College Fraternity." *Sociometry*, V: 151-162, May, 1942.

Wakeley, Ray E. "Selecting Leaders for Agricultural Programs." *Sociometry*, X: 384-395, November, 1947.

Weiss, Paul. *Principles of Development.* New York: Henry Holt and Company, 1939.

Wherry, Robert J. and Fryer, Douglas H. "Buddy Ratings: Popularity Contest or Leadership Criteria?" *Sociometry*, XII: 179-190, February, 1949. Also in *Personnel Psychology*, II: 147-159, Summer, 1949.

Whitehead, Alfred North. *Process and Reality*. New York: The Macmillan Company, 1930.

Whitehead, Thomas North. *Leadership in a Free Society*. Cambridge: Harvard University Press, 1936.

Wiese, von, Leopold. "Sociometry." *Sociometry*, XII: 202-214, February, 1949.

Williams, S. B. and Leavitt, H. J. "Group Opinion as a Predictor of Military Leadership." *Journal of Consulting Psychology*, XI: 283-292, 1947.

Wilson, Gertrude and Ryland, Gladys. *Social Group Work Practice*. Boston: Houghton Mifflin Company, 1949.

Winston, Sanford. "Leadership in War and Peace." North Carolina Agricultural Experiment Station Special Publication 1. Raleigh, 1946.

Wolman, Shepard. "Sociometric Planning of a New Community." *Sociometry*, I: 220-254, July-October, 1937.

Zazzo, René. "Psychology and Sociometry." *Sociometry*, XII: 32-45, February, 1949.

Zeleny, Leslie Day. "Sociometry of Morale." *American Sociological Review*, IV: 799-808, December, 1939.

――――. "Leadership," article in *Encyclopedia of Educational Research* (Paul Munroe, ed.), 1941.

――――. "Objective Selection of Group Leaders." *Sociology and Social Research*, XXIV: 326-336, March-April, 1940.

――――. "Selection of Compatible Flying Partners." *American Journal of Sociology*, LII: 424-431, March, 1947.

――――. "Selection of the Unprejudiced." *Sociometry*, X: 396-401, November, 1947.

Znaniecki, Florian. *The Method of Sociology*. New York: Farrar and Rinehart, 1934.

――――. "Sociometry and Sociology." *Sociometry*, VII: 225-233, August, 1943.

INDEX

A

Acceptability, 222n

Acquaintanceship, 17

Acquaintance volume, 43

Activities, group, behavior affecting, 152, 164

Adjustments, interrelation, 79, 102-103, satisfactory, 126, leaders' notion of, 200-201, criteria of, 289-290, 293-294

Affection, need of, 159, minimum needed in relationships, 297-299

Age, chronological,
choice-status and, 132-134, 141-142, 211-212
emotional expansiveness and, 132-133
isolated-position and, 136-138
leader-position and, 136-138, 141-142

Aggression, 200

Agricultural Adjustment Administration, 314

Allee, W. C., 325

Allport, Floyd H., 325

Allport, Gordon W., 24, 325

Aloofness, psychological, 202

Anxieties, reactions to, 165

Assignment, sociometric, 28, 28n, 230, 304-308

Assessment of Men, 295, 296, 313, 325

Atmosphere, affecting choice behavior, 248-251

Attention, absorbing leader's, 200

Attitude changes, social relationships and, 15

Attitude(s), social,
component in inter-personal relationships, 15, 273
impersonal, 158-159

Attraction, choice and, 165

Authority, attitude towards, 155-159

Autonomous group, 324

Average-chosen, behavior of, 151-163, 199-201

B

Baier, Donald E., xi, 313

Baker, William B., xi, 309n, 325, 331

Bain, Read, 325

Banks, William S. M., 297, 325

Barker, Roger G., 17, 33, 224, 325, 329

Bavelas, Alex, 325

"bawling out," by leader, 201

Beazley, Virginia, 332

Becker, Myron G., 325

Beegle, J. A., 314, 315, 323, 328, 331

Behavior (characteristics)
differentiating Under- Average- and Over-chosen, 151-159, 161-163
aggressive, 152, 163
attention, requiring no special, 154
avoidance, causing, of individual, 152
changing conduct of others, 154
circumventive, 153
complaining about peers, 161
constructively relating people, 155
cooperative, 153
criticalness of, 157
dominant, 152, 163
evenness of disposition, 154
getting-even, 153
gratefulness in, 157
initiatory, 152-153, 161, regarding distrust of, 157
insight, evidencing, 161-162
interrupting group activities, 152
intolerance, resenting, 158
irritable, 151
minor roles, willingness to accept, 154
morale, pernicious to, 152
nagging, 152
nervous, 152
opportunities, making most of, 154
organization and planning in, 154

LEADERSHIP
AND
ISOLATION

*A Study of Personality in
Inter-Personal Relations*

By HELEN HALL JENNINGS

Second Edition

DR. JENNINGS' book is the first socio-metric work based on direct qualita-tive and quantitative data of the social choice process. Here are pre-sented the results of a study of four hundred and fifty individuals, cor-relating their mutual approvals and rejections with the personality traits of all the participants — the first behavioral data available on the dif-ferences between the under-chosen, the average, and the over-chosen. In addition, the choice process is carefully analyzed and new meth-odologies are utilized. The book contributes to the related fields of sociology, social psychology, person-nel psychology, mental hygiene, general psychiatry, and social case work.